Ana's Land

Ana's Land

Sisterhood in
Eastern Europe

edited by
Tanya Renne

WestviewPress
A Division of HarperCollinsPublishers

Copyright © 1997 by Westview Press, A Division of HarperCollins Publishers, Inc.

Published in 1997 in the United States of America by Westview Press, 5500 Central Avenue, Boulder, Colorado 80301-2877, and in the United Kingdom by Westview Press, 12 Hid's Copse Road, Cumnor Hill, Oxford OX2 9JJ

Library of Congress Cataloging-in-Publication Data
Ana's Land : sisterhood in Eastern Europe / edited by Tanya Renne.
    p. cm.
  ISBN 0-8133-2831-4. — ISBN 0-8133-2832-2 (pbk.)
  1. Feminism—Europe, Eastern. 2. Women in politics—Europe,
Eastern. 3. Europe, Eastern—Social policy. 4. Europe, Eastern—
Social Conditions—1989– I. Renne, Tanya.
HQ1590.7.A78 1996
305.42′0947—dc20   96-33535
                                                            CIP

The paper used in this publication meets the requirements of the American National Standard for Permanence of Paper for Printed Library Materials Z39.48-1984.

10   9   8   7   6   5   4   3   2   1

*To the women in
Bosnia and Herzegovina
past and present*

Contents

Acknowledgments

Preparing this book has been a grassroots endeavor in and of itself. There are many dozens of women to thank for their support, encouragement, and insistence on its completion. First, I wish to sincerely thank each of the women who contributed essays to the book for sharing their lives with me, opening their homes and hearts to me, sharing their frustrations, allowing me the privilege of encouraging them in their fundamentally important work with women, and, not so incidentally, for putting up with changing deadlines and vague requests. A warm and tender thank-you to all the women, contributors and noncontributors alike, for opening their homes and kitchens so readily when I arrived, often with short notice, in their respective cities.

In particular, my deepest thanks and warmest affection go to Lepa Mladjenovic, my roommate and mentor in Belgrade and a dynamic, if exhausted, activist, feminist, and lesbian who embraces each and every element of her identity with strength and passion; she is a model for us all. Nela Pamukovic, Martina Belic, Michaela Rosa, Neva Tolle, and the rest of the women of the Center for Women War Victims (Zagreb); Autonomous Women's House, Zagreb; and Zagreb Women's Lobby gave me a home in winter when I most needed one.

Special thanks also go to Suzanna Walters, who laid the egg of the idea in my head over iced coffee on a hot day long ago and far away. To Margi Duncombe, Carol Neel, and Louise LaFond I attribute much of my confidence and ambition to complete this anthology.

I thank Joscelyn Gay and her unquestioned belief in who I am and what the women of Eastern and Central Europe mean to me. And lastly and most deeply, I offer gratitude to Judit Hatfaludi for her encouragement and support in sharing herself and her life with me.

Tanya Renne

Disparaging Digressions

Sisterhood in East-Central Europe

TANYA RENNE

Movement? What movement? We don't have
anything we could call a movement.
— **Bulgarian feminist**

Although the transition to multiparty elections came quickly to all nations in Eastern Europe following the "revolutions" of 1989 and 1990, in many cases only right-wing conservative and/or religion-affiliated groups had enough structure, history, or influence to put forth a campaign and run for election.[1] Decades of mono-ideology had left the people without a structure to create or deal with choice. "Options" as a concept had disappeared from social memory, to be replaced by complacency and ambivalence toward anything as "dirty" as politics. People were unprepared to be citizens, lacking, as they did, political consciousness, awareness, and motivation.

Neoconservatives and the momentum generated by the demise of communism in Eastern and Central Europe brought the people of these countries a reinvigorated sense of purpose, hope, excitement, and national pride, thereby inspiring renewed nationalism. National customs and traditions were embraced with a rediscovered enthusiasm, and religion began to occupy a primary place in many people's lives. With these new pleasures and responsibilities, most countries harkened back to former "free" periods, periods before World War II, Nazi occupation, and Soviet "liberation." New conservative politicians sought to bring their countries back to "true," untainted-by-communism, identities.

For Poland, that meant a state increasingly religious in character and the consequent dismantling of any communist law or policy that contradicted Catholicism. In Slovakia and the Czech Republic, it meant a suspicion toward anything political and a preoccupation with the practical affairs of everyday life. In Romanian society, it meant the rejection of all laws and policy enforced by the brutal Ceausescu regime, not the least of which was the political advancement of women. In Croatia, it meant the renewed embrace of Catholicism and all its trappings, heretofore subdued under Marshal Tito's Yugoslavia. For Slovenia, a republic that had undergone reforms since the mid-1980s and in which alternative social movements had been growing, the reaction against socialist policies was the least radical in East-Central Europe but nonetheless threatening to certain social policies, which were renegotiated or sacrificed under a new democratic government.

For feminism, the fall of communism has meant categorical rejection. It is seen either as an imported Western ideology to be rejected out of hand or as an old communist principle to be proudly refused. People of the region are painfully familiar with the use of the women of the Communist Party to spread the propaganda of their governments. Until 1989 the women's movement was under the guidance of the party, and as a result few people can see the difference between that women's movement and the independent strains emerging today. In many places it is assumed that women's groups are the Communist Party in disguise: new name, old policy. Although independent feminism is relatively new to Eastern Europe, it is clearly unwelcome; many in these changing nations see it as a threat.

This rejection of any concept resembling that of socialist policy has sent women back in time. Ironically, it puts them in a similar position to Western women facing abortion restrictions in the wake of the sweeping victory of Christian Democrats across Europe. The issues and destinations are similar, but their origins and means are different.

The experiences of East-Central European women under communism have shaped the present group of feminists and women helping women in the region. As Nanette Funk remarked in her introduction to *Gender Politics and Post-Communism,* context and concepts must be understood in relation to the experiences of an individual culture. In Eastern Europe today, individual or small-group political activism and influence are unknown. The legacy of communism's consistent and constant oppression is a passive population hesitant to change what has made life difficult, in spite of promises of a rich and prosperous future.

The legal structures in specific countries make the existence of independent groups difficult. In Bulgaria and Romania, unofficial groups have no means of getting recognized as some do in, for example, Slovenia. Eastern Europeans think of political influence as something exercised by groups and organizations (often the larger, the better) while at the same time associating such structures with the obligations imposed by communism. In response, Eastern Europeans avoid groups, except when the church is concerned. In Romania, a women's group has grown out of the offices of

UNESCO, and uses foreign support and influence to establish a meeting place. Other groups have no place of their own, however; they must conduct business in cafes, restaurants, and kitchens. Some groups are losing space they acquired during earlier stages of transition; such space is being sold or rented out from under them to foreign investors or private firms. Still fewer are acquiring space to conduct their work with the aid of foreign women's groups invested in the progress of their sisters to the east.

Feminists and other activists in each and every country persevere against negative public opinion and difficult, if not impossible, conditions. They have their own way of maneuvering without compromising. The totalitarian context of restrictions and historical ways of dealing with the system pays off when women simply get around these restrictions. In Romania, philosopher Mihaela Miroiu put on a radio show about feminism together with her husband, also a philosopher. He presented the first few programs to encourage legitimacy in the anti–woman leader atmosphere of post-Ceausescu Romania; after his introduction she went on to finish the programs. In Hungary, the Feminist Network waged a campaign against abortion restrictions under the banner "Campaign for a Free Choice," deciding not to use the term *feminist* lest it hinder the cause with negative public opinion. In Romania, Bulgaria, and the Czech Republic, gender studies programs or the seeds thereof have been planted using the academic, marginally accepted term *gender relations*, rather than the "dirty word *feminism*," which would have incited argument around a term instead of provoking discussion about issues and problems facing women. Women in Serbia have dared to call their courses *feminist studies* but do so and conduct their courses away from university and institutional support and acceptance.

For example, in Poland a women's hotline has been established. But it has not been set up to deal with rape trauma or the effects of other kinds of violence against women, as we might assume. Rather, the purpose of the hotline is to address the profound and torturous lack of access to all kinds of information experienced by women in each and every country considered here; giving information to women in this case is truly revolutionary. Nevertheless, consciousness about violence against women, as well as the rise in violence itself, has prompted telephone hotlines for women in Slovenia, Croatia, Serbia, Hungary, and the Czech Republic. The groups that run them are becoming increasingly demanding of their governments, which are looking for European Union approval.

The ways in which the women in each Eastern European country negotiate their politics and projects reveal the flavor of feminism and its acceptance in their societies. The situation of women in each country appears similar, yet the situation of feminism and feminist–friendly concepts varies greatly. There is a clear spectrum in the region of feminism and progress in putting forward women's concerns.

In Poland, the history of some kind of women's movement is long and arduous. Women's groups are plentiful relative to other countries, and the movement has both academic and grassroots activist groups. The two kinds of groups had not mixed much until the recent successful attack on abortion rendered it all but illegal and brought forces from all over Polish society together to fight back. For example, in Wroclaw the Women's Solidarity Commission was disbanded in response to Lech Walesa's support of abortion restrictions; now Kristina Politacha runs the affairs of the "unofficial" group out of her office, where she works for the Department of Transportation. She is lucky enough to have a sympathetic supervisor who lets her use the phone and fax to organize women around the referendum for abortion. Although estimates show that the vast majority of a very-Catholic Poland are against abortion restrictions, the government has refused the public plea for a referendum to let the people decide, claiming it is "too important a decision to leave it in the hands of the irresponsible Polish public."

This push for a referendum has formed a space for all different aspects of social and political interests to join forces. In every large city in Poland, there is a committee made up of old communists, new liberals, new leftists, and women's organizations collecting signatures and putting pressure on the political functionaries in their region. Even though abortion has stolen the floor from other women's concerns, it has created in Poland a new sense of political involvement by individuals and a need to react as citizens. The women of Poland are beginning to question the wisdom of being sent back to the home, even though they still view politics as an area out of their reach and beyond their concerns.

Feminism in the Czech Republic shares the characteristic calm of that nation, concentrating on the academic aspect of the movement while supporting some activist groups. Nevertheless, the two parts of the movement are still separate and largely unaffiliated. The influx of a large number of Western tourists into the republic can perhaps be held partly responsible for inciting the acute vocal frustration with Western feminists heard more often from Czech feminists than others. Because Prague is currently the "place to be," women there have achieved instant fame and have therefore hurried the movement along faster than the position of women has changed, making it difficult for them to navigate so many uncharted waters. The living conditions in the Czech Republic and Slovakia, as well as in most other countries in the region, yield a harsh daily life, one filled with practical concerns, too full for organizing and consciousness-raising. Intellectuals and young women have more time to think about and discuss issues "brought from the West," as well as "old Marxist principles," and therefore the women's movement centers on universities and young groups of activists. Environmental concerns have also motivated mothers and other women to action. Although these women fight for the concerns of all, especially health concerns, their voices are becoming increasingly insistent as the structures for maintenance and control shift and crumble and reinstate themselves.

In Bulgaria and Romania, thinking and writing about gender, although threatened categories of scholarship, exist and on some levels, especially and perhaps solely on the university level, enjoy marginal acceptance among scholars. Feminism in these two countries is still largely academic; it has not yet taken account of everyday women's concerns and certainly has not reached a grassroots level of activism in most cases. One of the biggest problems faced by feminism in Romania is the legacy of Elena Ceausescu, who is seen as spectacularly cruel and perhaps more responsible for suffering and dictatorial rule than Nicolae Ceausescu himself. In response, Romanian women have sworn off political involvement and any kind of progress toward women in government for fear of being equated with the villainous first lady. In both Romania and Bulgaria, academic feminism is allowed, but progress is slow going—for a female academic proving herself is difficult enough, let alone reaching out to raise consciousness as well as combating the infrastructure of the university.

Hungary may be the most patriarchal country in the region in its attitudes toward women. The women's movement there is a young one, but it is a movement all the same. Both activists and scholars are forming groups and are loosely connected through student-aged interested women. The establishment of the Magyar Orszag Nok Alampogar (Hungarian Women's Foundation, or MONA) has forged a common link and information base for all women's groups in Hungary (feminist and nonfeminist alike). The first feminist group in Budapest, the Feminist Network, has already branched out to include an SOS hotline, NANE! (Nok a Nokert az Eroszak Ellen), for which staffers are trained by Serbian and Croatian women. Other grassroots groups include a feminist group in Szeged and a women's club in Sopron. An ombudswoman project has been initiated in Budapest as well, which includes a women's center in its future goals.

Although the history of Yugoslavian feminism resembles that of other movements in the region, Yugoslavia's status as a nonaligned country and the charismatic rule of Tito under communism gave Yugoslavs the benefit of travel, information, literature, and culture without the presence of the Soviet Army. For this reason, the feminist movement in Yugoslavia has a longer "modern" history and a greater connection to ideas and understandings first stated in the West. The passionate personality of the women in Serbia and Croatia and the presence of a war make the groups of today particularly active and demanding of change. In this way the scholarship and academic nature of women's studies are combined with grassroots activism.

Slovenia is perhaps at the far end of the spectrum of women's movements in Eastern and Central Europe. Academic and intellectual, the Slovenian women's movement has become more passive now that conditions for women seem more stable and progressive. Slovenia's optimism stems from the possibilities that arise with new nationhood, a high standard of living, a growing percentage of women in parliament (as opposed to the opposite phenomenon in other countries), and an intelligent and well-planned government effort to do anything that will enhance the country's chance of being admitted into the European Union. Fortunately for women, government actions include some funding (although meager), legislative measures, and attention to the concerns of minorities to better the position of women.

Although all women's issues are given a public airing to some extent in the region, there are some central issues that receive more time and effort. The most important of these is abortion. Poland represents the extreme case of absolute restriction, and Slovenia occupies the other end of the continuum, with the right to abortion successfully protected in the new constitution. Hungary has narrowly escaped a similar fate as Poland, getting away with relatively minor restrictions in comparison. The Czech Republic faces effective limitations in financial terms (as of spring 1993 the average price for an abortion was equal to one month's salary). Slovakia is waiting out threats from a Catholic conservative force to put restrictions on the abortion rights of Slovakia's women, and in Serbia, where restrictions are unofficial, abortion is strongly discouraged so that women can produce more "soldiers." Women in every country in the region have expressed concern over abortion rights. This is even the case in Romania, where abortion was free on demand as of winter 1993—a response to the ousted and executed regime, which had restricted abortions to women who had already borne four offspring and then made abortions available only by council and, of course, for "good reason."

Other issues that demand a great deal of attention, and will do so increasingly in the future, include violence against women, unemployment, information and women's studies programs, women in government, sexuality, and war, as it is the dominant occupation of women in Croatia and Serbia. Hotlines and awareness about violence against women are spreading throughout the region, albeit slowly, by way of squatted flats, rented rooms, women's living rooms, and newly acquired spaces. Small groups of volunteers are taking on the burden of supporting women over the phone, negotiating with police and court officials, and relocating women and children to safer places in cases of domestic violence.

Unemployment is on the rise as redundant positions are eliminated and new technology is imported.[2] This development, together with the existence of a conservative majority, means that women's place is now increasingly in the home, a means for taking the pressure off the job market. Some women go willingly, grateful to get out of the "forced" labor that they took on out of economic necessity, not for "liberation" through financial independence, as many of their Western sisters did. Others are forced home and are beginning to question the viability of traditional demands.

Women's studies programs are seen by feminists as imperative for consciousness-raising about women's concerns, ideas, and issues. In every country there are small established groups meeting to talk about literature, history, and politics in a women's studies context. The women's group that meets in the rooms of UNESCO in Bucharest (consisting of scholars, intellectuals, and students) hopes to form a women's information center where there will be translations and courses on women's studies. The Gender Studies Center in Prague operates out of its founder's living room. Similar projects are under way in Slovakia, Bulgaria, and Slovenia, and Women's Infoteka (Women's Information and Documentation Center) in Zagreb has been functioning since spring of 1994. Many of the projects for women's information and centers also support the initiatives of publications such as *Zene za Zene* (Women for Women, Belgrade), *Kruh i Ruze* (Bread and Roses, Zagreb), and *Aspekt* (Bratislava). These publications consist of poetry, essays, and art by women of their respective areas.

Issues of women in government are addressed in most places but usually by women who are already there or are in affiliated fields. A women's parliamentary commission and a corresponding office for women in the government have been established in Slovenia. Throughout the region, political parties have had the wisdom to form commissions for women's concerns, but few of these parties have women in ranking positions or in positions in which they represent the party when women's concerns intersect with concerns of the "larger public." Attention to strictly political concerns and to the placement of women in government seem more and more like long-term projects—outside immediate, more relevant concerns such as abortion rights and consciousness-raising.

Lesbianism is becoming increasingly visible and, in some places, accepted. The gay and lesbian population is mixed in its organization; few gays and lesbians associate themselves with feminism at this point. In every country there is a gay magazine that allows a few of its inner pages to be devoted to lesbians. In every case the situation is the same: too few pages and too many men for women to feel comfortable buying it. In the Czech Republic, a group of lesbians and gays presented themselves as "sexual deviants" in need of a support group and thereby got permission to form an alliance before the revolution. In recent years the group has split into two groups, with the women forming the L-Klub. Croatia's lesbians align themselves with gay men and also with the Transradical Party. The most progressive country in terms of lesbian organizing is, again, Slovenia, with a new "feminist and lesbian" group Kasandra operating a sometime-cafe and information center.

War is the central issue for Croatian and Serbian women, as is evident in the writings provided here. But the issue affects women in other countries in the region, whether it be through solidarity (as is the case with the spreading of the movement Women in Black), work with refugees, or the threat that nationalist tendencies might bring to a woman's own back door.

All in all, the progress that Eastern European women have made in securing their rights depends directly on the security of their respective country's economic affairs and on political openness as much as on the presence and influence of a strong religious faction. It will come as no surprise that these fledgling democracies are putting women's concerns far behind economics and national security and thus do not encourage, or support, those exceptional women who are demanding change. For anyone interested in the situation of women in Eastern Europe, it is no secret that information is scarce, if not nonexistent. With the changes that the region is undergoing, there is more and more information about Eastern and Central Europe available in English, although, sadly, for feminists and other women interested in the advancement of women, little of it is about women's concerns. Texts by and about women are few and far between. A handful of anthologies targeted at different audiences and interests have come to the market recently. Chris Corrin's *Superwoman and the Double Burden* is an encyclopedic presentation of available facts about women and their lives in Eastern Europe and the former Soviet Union. Nanette Funk and Magda Mueller have compiled a Western-targeted theoretical reader of women's concerns entitled *Gender Politics and Post-Communism*. Both of these volumes supplement the present text well, Corrin with data and Funk and Mueller with extended concepts. Information about women before the changes of 1989 can be found in Sharon Wolchik and Alfred G. Meyer, *Women, State, and Party in Eastern Europe*. All of these sources are valuable and diverse but certainly not reflective of all the information and changes about women's lives in Eastern and Central Europe.

The text at hand is meant to be a snapshot, not a comprehensive or definitive examination, of what women are doing for each other amid these changes, an attempt to capture an explosive movement so that women in Eastern Europe will have something to refer to in the future. Not only does this anthology intend to redress the grievance of insufficient research by and about women in the region, but it also helps to show how feminism has shaped and grown, transformed and evolved in Eastern Europe. It was my goal to include writing by women fighting for similar causes in similar and different ways so that other women in the region can see the commonalities, as well as the differences, that may inspire. Perhaps the loss of abortion as a right in Poland will make the women of Croatia more weary of the resurgence of the Catholic Church and the reappearance of rich conservative ex-patriots; perhaps the inclusion of such a right in the new Slovenian constitution will inspire us all to such success.

Eastern European women know more about Western women and their movements and demands than they know about each other. Common occupation (with the exception of Yugoslavia) held them oddly isolated from each other. Now as women and women's groups tackle the problems of unemployment, the loss of heretofore assumed rights, violence, and forced domesticity, they find themselves in the same sinking ship with their neighbors. The rights they were allowed by contract and creed—not so incidentally often unrealized or unbalanced—have gone with the winds of change and reform. Western women have fought for as many decades as Eastern women "enjoyed" such privileges as equal work and equal pay, often unsuccessfully or only to lose those same rights to amendments and revisions to laws and constitutions.

Although the charge that some Western feminists try to colonize their Eastern sisters may be partially accurate, it is my experience that such an act is impossible. When faced with a concept—from any part of the world—the women of Eastern and Central Europe seize it, change it, make it their own, and render it absolutely specific to their lives. Not surprisingly, the social factors that discourage women's progress do not necessarily discourage these powerful women. "What movement?" is invariably the response of such women, out of touch with their own importance, overwhelmed by the monstrous work that clearly lies ahead.

A central purpose of this book is to demonstrate that sisterhood and common struggle do exist in the region and that there is a movement demanding change, making moves, and addressing oppressive conditions. As a contribution to the framework of solidarity in Eastern Europe, this book is an attempt to introduce the women of Bulgaria to the women of Serbia and the women of Hungary to the women of Poland.

In "Is Sisterhood Really Global?" Laura Busheikin introduces the writings that follow, and she discusses the frustrations, tensions, anxieties, and successes that Western feminists and Eastern European feminism have encountered together. This essay is intended to provide Western readers with a context for reading the rest of the book, whereas for Eastern readers it simply addresses their fears and frustrations in a written form.

The essays are arranged by country and reflect the interests of the contributors. Some of the women whose writing appears here have published before and may be known for their more theoretical work; other women are publishing here for the first time. I asked all contributors to avoid theory as much as possible and to keep the language accessible so the greatest number of women would have access to the book in its final form. All but a few of the texts were written originally in English. At first I left it to contributors to write about what interested them, although I did request historical documents and personal testimonies. As the book began to take shape, I amended my requests to include basic histories, histories of groups, and essays on specific topics.

The resulting body of work is in some ways fragmented and in other ways redundant. Both characteristics are important because they reflect the nature of the movement country by country. For example, nearly every essay in Part 1, which is about Poland, concerns some aspect of abortion, which simply reflects how vital the issue is to women's concerns.

Part 2, which looks at Slovakia and the Czech Republic, is, regrettably, primarily about the Czech Republic since contributors from Slovakia were difficult, if not impossible, to reach. I allowed the Czech pieces to include information on Slovakia as the historical information comes from the former Czechoslovakia. The concerns here revolve largely around consciousness of women's issues and the appropriateness of applying Western feminist principles to the East.

Part 3, on Hungary, includes historical texts, abortion campaign documents and results, and an essay about the women's movement at the turn of the century. This last piece can be considered representative since all Eastern European countries have histories of a women's movement at the end of the nineteenth century or before—some of the movements have been well documented with the help of contemporary historians, whereas information on others is hidden in the dusty, decaying archives of national libraries. Part 3 also includes an essay about a Gypsy activist. Gypsies are the largest minority in Europe but have so little voice as to be unknown and unheard in nearly every circle.

Part 4, which looks at Romania, has only three essays, although they are rich in their offerings to women. This part contains a discussion of the namesake of the book, "Ana"; an interview with five high school women, feminists, philosophers; and an interview and composite of the director of the Romanian Association of University Women, Maria Antoaneta Ciochirca.

Part 5, on Bulgaria, consists of a short history of the Bulgarian women's movement, Rossica Panova's personal testimony as a woman with a disability, and Kornelia Merdjanska's analysis of sexism in the Bulgarian language. When I visited Bulgaria, I found that Western feminists, with their conferences and offerings, had lured many of the writing feminists away to lands undoubtedly more friendly to feminism.

In Part 6, about the former Yugoslavia, the essays overlap historically but are otherwise separate. The Serbian and Croatian essays deal exclusively with war and the consequences of it, including nationalism and peace. Slovenia is represented here with a joint theoretical essay by Mirjana Ule and Tanja Rener, an introduction from the Office for Women's Politics, a summary of women's activities involving abortion rights legislation, and a personal experience piece about refugee life in Slovenia.

The question of whether sisterhood is global remains to be answered, but as this book demonstrates, sisterhood, in all its complexities and transparencies, is clearly Eastern European.

Notes

1. Nanette Funk and Magda Mueller, *Gender Politics and Post-Communism: Reflections from Eastern Europe and the Former Soviet Union* (New York: Routledge, 1993), p. 2.

2. For a longer discussion, broken down by country, on how unemployment is affecting women, see Chris Corrin, *Superwoman and the Double Burden* (London: Scarlet Press, 1992).

Is Sisterhood Really Global?

Western Feminism in Eastern Europe

LAURA BUSHEIKIN

When Ann Snitow said to a small audience at her 1993 lecture in Prague, "This is the hardest thing I've ever encountered in twenty-three years of feminist organizing," I felt vindicated. "This" referred to the relationship between Eastern European women and Western feminists, and I figured Snitow ought to know: founding member of the Network of East-West Women, one of the initiators of Prague's two-year-old Gender Studies Center, and a distinguished veteran of the American feminist movement.

I, too, know something about this relationship: I work at the Prague Gender Studies Center—a Canadian feminist among the Eastern Europeans[1]—and I felt vindicated because I, too, find the relationship very, very difficult. One could say that the iron curtains have been replaced by blinds. The pun may be a little too crude, but as it suggests, the space for this relationship is already occupied—by preconceptions, ingrained habits of thought on both sides, and a panoply of various myths. And even when the myths are banished, there's no relief—the resulting clarity illuminates the deeper obstacles that make talking together, let alone acting together, so fraught with tension.

We already have a wealth of lucid and insightful writing explaining the historical, cultural, and political differences between Western and Eastern European women.[2] These huge differences go a long way—but not all the way—toward explaining the tensions that run through the East-West relationship. There is something in the structure of the relationship, in its context rather than its content, that seems to put the participants (and observers) on edge. To truly understand—and thus cope with—the tensions, it is necessary to look past the myths to the shape of the relationship, which means naming the power dynamics. These are much more ambiguous and complicated than they may at first seem.

Myth #1: The International Feminist Brigade

This topic, at the moment, is covered (in both meanings of the word: "dealt with" and "hidden") by the dominant mythology: the messianic Western feminist trying to brainwash hapless Eastern European women into our wicked feminist ways. One woman, in an article published in the English-language weekly the *Prague Post,* dubbed us the International Feminist Brigade, come to Eastern Europe to "bang the drums of feminism. . . . It's just like the Kremlin!" On a less paranoid note, my coworker Jana Hradilkova wrote, "We can label the Western (approach to East-West dialogue) as offensive and the Czech one as defensive."

But it is not so simple. We Western feminists are on the defense, too. I've seen it, and I've felt it. We have quite a few reasons to find ourselves in a defensive position. Although we can laugh at the notions of an international feminist brigade, the allegation of insensitivity and cultural imperialism always lurks in our own minds, and we're continually called upon to defend ourselves by those who accuse us of "having our own agenda" or "not listening." Furthermore, our self-assurance takes a beating if we openly identify ourselves as feminist. To call oneself a feminist in the Czech Republic is to invite abuse and ridicule. The media seem to take pleasure (or perhaps it is simply a matter of selling newspapers) in ridiculing feminists. Of course, we can try to ignore it, but that's already a defensive position. And few of us have the elephant-thick skin needed to stay untouched. I remember talking with a young, very pretty British journalist. She had just interviewed a well-known Czech woman songwriter who had trashed feminism with apparent glee. "Show me one young, pretty feminist who is able to attract a man, and I might change my mind," she had said smugly. The journalist was too nonplussed to respond, but afterward she raved to me: "What about me? I was sitting right in front of her!" Some antifeminist offensives are more, well, offensive—for instance, a cartoon in the monthly magazine *Mlady Svet* showing a man killing a chicken while his whole family looked on silently: "She was beginning to squawk like a feminist," he explained in the caption. Just a joke, right, but still enough to make the average feminist take pause (didn't Marc Lepine say more or less the same thing before he shot fourteen women engineering students in Montreal several years ago in one of Canada's most gruesome cases of random violence?). And then there was the Prague art exhibit dedicated to antifeminist art. Of course, if we object to this, we are told that we have no sense of humor. It is all quite demoralizing.

Myth #2: Our Backward Eastern Sisters

If the notion of the crusading Western feminist doesn't reflect reality, the picture of her "victim," the bewildered Eastern European woman in danger of indoctrination, is absurd. The literature coming from feminists in Eastern Europe makes quite plain that, rather than accepting Western frameworks and terminology, the writers are challenging both and adapting them to the situation. In reading over recent work by Czech women to put together a small anthology of women's writings in the Czech Republic, we found a great many articles questioning the relevance of Western feminism for Eastern Europe, and we found writers able to very clearly explain, "Here is where Western feminism can be useful for us, and how, here is where it can't, and why, and here is where is seems, in light of our experience, simply wrong."

After forty years of resisting communist social engineering and Soviet control, Eastern Europeans certainly aren't going to let anyone tell them what to think, let alone what to do. Rather, there's a tradition of refusal that is already part of the Eastern European psyche—refusal of propaganda, ideology, political messianism, big liberatory ideas.

Also, because Eastern Europeans are well aware that the West didn't have much accurate information about Eastern Europe during the Cold War, they are acutely conscious of how hard it is for any outsider to grasp the social and psychological effects of living under the previous regime and therefore are skeptical of any Western analysis of their social structures. Even if the alleged drumbeats of the International Feminist Brigade get beyond this thick wall of resistance, we still have to take into account the individual intelligence of women and the fact that inevitably they will compare what they hear to their own situation (which is generally beyond the ken—in other words, outside of the descriptive and theoretical frameworks—of Western feminism). Eastern Europe simply isn't a promising place for feminist brainwashing.

Reality: What's at Stake

Rather than a simple, polarized relationship (Western aggressor/Eastern victim or Westerners bringing light/Easterners emerging out of the dark), we have a much more complex situation. Certainly, the Western partners tend to be "offensive" (in both senses of the word, alas), but Eastern women respond with an offense of their own, and often both partners feel and behave offensively and defensively all at once. For instance, American Nanette Funk sent Croatian writer and feminist Slavenka Drakulic an invitation to contribute an essay for an anthology on postcommunist gender politics. Several months later Funk read Drakulic's contemptuous account of the invitation in her book *How We Survived Communism and Even Laughed,* which presented Funk as an ignorant American pushing Western feminist frameworks on Eastern European women. Funk's account of this episode, which she included in the anthology, conveyed hurt feelings, puzzlement, and resentment. Here we have plenty of offensiveness and defensiveness on both sides.

Offense-defense/defense-offense: There is territorial behavior on both sides, there is mutual fear, and some sort of power is being contested. I realize that this sounds more like a description of international state politics than international feminism, and of course the situation is not *that* bad. There is a relationship going on, often a very positive one, but it runs parallel with various tensions. Or perhaps "runs parallel" is the wrong expression: It implies separation. Rather, the tension, fear, and power issues are inherent in the relationship and help shape it even at its best. So it makes sense to look at what's at stake for the various partners in this dialogue.

One thing is indisputable: The Western partners do have more power. We grew up with free speech and freedom of movement, with practice in speaking to other cultures, and we know that the rest of the world knows all about us. Furthermore, by being "Westerners," we are on the winning team in global politics, economy, and culture, and many of us come from countries that have or had imperialistic tendencies. Even if we dissent, and even if we are from the underprivileged class (but few poor, nonwhite, non-university-educated Western women are involved), we carry this power with us, with its very concrete privileges. The East-West debate tends to take place in spaces created by Western wealth and influence: conferences in the East that are funded by Western money and attended by Western women who have access to enough funds to fly halfway around the globe, conferences in the West attended by Eastern European women who have received money from Western women for the trip, in books and magazines published in the West, with articles either written by Western women or by Eastern women at the request of (and often according to the requirements of) Western women, at Western universities that have funded an Eastern student, at Eastern universities that have got Western funding to bring a Western expert to teach, at Eastern European gender studies centers, like ours, that are funded by Western money. Western scholars climb their career ladders by these activities, whereas in Eastern Europe the space for a career based on feminism, women's studies, or gender studies barely exists. Of course, all these activities take place in English, which is a great advantage for those who speak it as a native language or grew up studying it.

I don't want to imply that all this is bad—in fact, in general it is very welcome—but I do think we must recognize the flavor it gives to the relationship. Perhaps the self-assurance that this English language/Western domi-nance gives a Western woman (a self-assurance that feels deserved, feels like a triumph of feminism, feels like something we have worked so hard to achieve) is in this case a liability.

That's not the only type of power that clings to Westerners—we also have the huge leverage of our feminist tradition. When it comes to explorations of gender issues, we know the lay of the land—in fact, we've already made a map, and we've brought it with us. When East and West sit and talk about our experiences as women, Westerners have a whole feminist framework they bring to the discussion. We can pull names, theories, histories, facts, analyses, out of our heads with a breezy "of course."

On a basic level, this treating of complex issues with such "of courses" is annoying and a bit of an assault to the self-esteem of any woman who doesn't share this tradition. On a deeper level, it threatens loss of identity. (I remember once talking to a psychologist about ways in which psychology can harm. "The worst thing," she said, "is to have someone analyze you and tell you who you apparently are without your full trust, consent, and participation. It's a way of stealing your soul." I believe the same holds with any type of analysis.) On an intellectual level, reductionism can be destructive, blocking the potential development of new and different frameworks. Under totalitarianism, Eastern Europeans didn't have a healthy environment in which to pose questions about gender. Gender was already being used in very specific ways by the regimes *and* as part of people's resistance. Not surprisingly, there has been and is a half-consciousness resistance to starting the discussion before both individuals and society are ready. The debate around the term *feminism,* which can be so frustrating, may be seen as a way of biding time, keeping the waters stirring but avoiding the big waves.

Now, this very factor—that Western women situate themselves within a feminist tradition—marks the place at which the tables are turned and East poses a threat to West. Eastern European women have the power of *the other*—the power to reduce all our theories, traditions, and convictions to rubble. In Eastern Europe, we have a situation we can barely understand—it seems to be, and perhaps it is, outside of the descriptive and theoretical frameworks of feminism. As Eastern European women begin to theorize about their experiences and positions, they challenge feminist *basics,* such as patriarchal oppression. Also, basic feminist practices are often irrelevant here. How many times have I seen a young Western woman, sitting in the Gender Studies Center, say something like, "We should organize a take-back-the-night march," only to meet reactions of incomprehension or even anger and ridicule (I've done it myself—both the proposing and, lately, the rejecting).

This making of Western-based suggestions to "uncomprehending" Eastern European women is made worse by the fact that feminism has often

placed itself politically somewhere on the left, frequently avowedly socialist. Postcommunist Eastern Europe calls into question the validity of all socialist ideas, which makes being a feminist here even more difficult. Speaking with the people who actually lived under socialism can make a
Westerner feel pretty stupid—or worse—for supporting it. This sheepish
feeling presages a huge intellectual task: disentangling feminism from socialist analysis and ideas, sorting through the pieces, and putting them back
together.[3]

Even feminists who never allied themselves with the socialism of the Left
are reminded how much their ideas, goals, and language resemble those of
the oppressive communist system, which also spoke of an oppressed group
and promised liberation. We can protest that we mean such words in a different sense, but we have to explain what we do mean—to a very skeptical
audience. So we are afraid: What if we've been wrong? What if feminism
flounders on the borders of Eastern Europe? What if the ground on which
we stand doesn't hold? *And what if sisterhood isn't global after all?*

Well, maybe it's not. But we're talking, working together—the relationship is progressing and, in spite of all the intersecting lines of tension, is
bringing concrete results as well as insight, pleasure, and hope for many individuals. There are goodwill and desire—mutual desire—to speak and to
listen.

Push-Me-Pull-Me

So how does the relationship work? Sometimes the relationship reminds me
of Dr. Doolittle's "push-me-pull-me," an animal with no hind end but
rather two front ends, with heads facing opposite ways.[4] How can it move?
When one end wants to move forward, the other feels it's moving backward, and vice versa. The only way it can travel anywhere is for each end
to realize it is connected to the other and temporarily let go of its own point
of view about which way is forward. This may feel horrible, but it makes
for a fascinating journey. After all, forward may not always be the direction
in which we are facing. And perhaps we have more than just two choices of
which way to move. With the push-me-pull-me, everything gets muddled,
confused, complicated—the whole binary notion of forward/backward is
destroyed.

So it is with this East-West feminist debate: back to the kitchen? or forward toward free choice? forward into feminism? or backward into yet another ideology? Yes and no and no and yes. . . . The East-West relationship
takes the form of an experimental push-pull that makes use, by necessity, of
the very tensions that threaten it. Take the case of Drakulic and Funk:
Drakulic did write a piece for Funk's book, and despite her quite acerbic

writing about Western feminists' approaches to Eastern European women, she was one of the founding members of the Network of East-West Women, which suggests that she is committed to the relationship. Funk, also a member of the Network, used the episode as the jumping-off point for an article that affirms, in spite of tensions and occasional lapses in communication, a common ground for East-West relationships. Perhaps Funk was insensitive in her initial approach, perhaps Drakulic was a tad harsh in her response, but all of this became not only the impetus but also the substance of further dialogue and discovery. Funk started out with a set of standard Western feminist questions, and she ended up with something new. As Jana Hradilkova wrote: "Sometimes we are wondering how misunderstandings and conflicts in communication, or backlashes towards certain ideas, can have educational effects for our own projects, plans and ideas. . . . We are operating with something that is disturbing. . . . [This] can be highly effective for discovering another alternative."

(Of course, it doesn't always work out so nicely. I think with sadness of the case of a Czech woman who was very active with a local women's group, who went to Germany for a couple of years to attend a women's studies program. She came back disenchanted, quit her work with women, and declared that she wanted nothing to do with feminism ever again. End of story.)

The fact is, we Westerners *are* "importing feminism," but it only works when we let this feminism be transformed by the journey. Look at the development of the Prague Gender Studies Center. It was started at the urging of Ann Snitow and Sonia Robbins of the Network of East-West Women: It was their idea; they provided the initial money and books. They waited until they had an interested Eastern partner, Jirina Siklova, but they didn't wait for her to suggest it. However, the center was then left to its own fate. They knew they had started something but weren't about to dictate what that would be. Enter Jana Hradilkova, hired on as a part-time librarian and secretary. She was interested in librarian work, not gender issues, but soon became curious, started organizing discussion groups (East-West and East-East) at the center, attended international conferences, and today is deeply involved in writing, thinking, and speaking about gender issues and encourages others to do so. It's likely that without the Western impulse, Jirina Siklova's living room would still be a living room and the public and private reevaluations of gender that the center has initiated would not exist. But the center is not a replica of a comparable Western center, the women who are involved are developing their own analyses and practices, and rather than encouraging Czech women to imitate Western feminism, the center has provided space for them to choose their own priorities, find their own words, and develop their own methods of working.

And what happens to the Western feminists? Remember the push-me-pull-me. Usually the Western feminist finds herself pulled along in a direction that doesn't resemble anything she's ever imagined as forward. But she can't do anything about it; she can't say, "No, wait, stop, do it how I think it should be done!" What she has to do—what I have had to do—is think hard about what aspects of her feminism she can and should hold onto, what needs to be reconsidered, and what has to be jettisoned. She has to identify, moment by moment, the line between cultural sensitivity and wimpyness, between sticking up for her convictions and sticking her cultural presumptions where they aren't welcome. She has to try to understand a whole different history and culture as well as explain her own. She has to resist the eager quest for similarities, which too often leads to false analogies, and at the same time seek for the commonalities that hold the relationship together.

This is confusing, but it's also fascinating and invaluable. The total reevaluation and reconfiguration of terms, ideas, values, and practices, which the relationship demands, have the power to incite a transformation for both individuals and, perhaps, for feminism itself as a movement/belief/approach.

Contemporary Western feminism is already trying to cope with the challenge posed by *Western* women, primarily women of color and poor women, who feel it doesn't sufficiently address their realities. It took white middle-class feminists a long time to stop talking about power only in terms of patriarchy—to accept that "men oppressing women" is perhaps too simple a formula, that we have to give up celebrating sisterhood and begin celebrating differences, and that it's necessary to move beyond a binary us-and-them mentality. If we begin to listen to Eastern European voices, we are taken even further in this direction, and we find ourselves in entirely new territory. Now it has become fashionable in the West to talk of "race, class, and gender" as intersecting lines of oppression, but this doesn't offer a framework that can fully account for Eastern European women's experience. If we really want a feminism that is about women and not just some women, we need to understand and work with Eastern European women.

Looking for Liberation?

For both of us, East and West, this relationship is a journey into the unknown, fraught with difficulties and fears, but full of promise. Perhaps we are not sure what we are looking for, and perhaps it is something different for each of us. It is clear to me that the East-West relationship cannot simply develop upon the traditional promises of feminism—"equality," "liberation from patriarchal oppression," "emancipation," and so on. These words no longer describe what I am looking for; they seem tired, old, limited, and yet I can see how important they are in an Eastern European context.

I am certainly not the only Western feminist reexamining her goals, language, and frameworks in the context of the East-West relationship. As an example, I quote from a letter to Jana Hradilkova from a New Yorker who has close contacts throughout Eastern Europe:

I think that many of the American feminists got excited about Eastern Europe in the first place because it gave them the sense of mission and vibrancy that they had not felt here since the 60's and 70s. They have the idea that involvement in East and Central Europe will help rekindle the feminist movement in the United States. But I think they already see that with this expectation they might be disappointed. . . .

I am not a feminist-activist in the pure sense. . . . I don't feel like I need to fight for my equality because I know I am equal, never doubted it for a moment. Maybe what I feel is more closely matched by New Humanity (a Prague-based women's group), that we all need healing:

Because the relations between human beings and nature, between men and women, between parents and children, between an individual and the state long deformed by dull subordination as practiced by the military Bolshevik spirit (and, the writer adds, military capitalist spirit)—*because man's and woman's shares on the face of the world are precariously disharmonious, with female influence missing from society and male influence from the family . . .*

I like that. And for this I understood your resistance to the label of feminism. Maybe it's time for something new.

As Jirina Siklova wrote:

Our experience may be interesting for you. I think that on the border where Western feminist experience with oppression from capitalist patriarchy and our experience with oppression from a communist totalitarian system meet, there may be space for the development of a new direction for feminism. . . .

If we proceed from both your and our experiences, from different types of oppression and stress, then something new may arise from it, not only for feminism, but perhaps also for the whole of Europe and the world. I would welcome this.

These are not proclamations of global sisterhood, rather, they imply a disinterest in the whole issue. We—myself, all the women quoted in this article, and many others—are not in search of global sisterhood at all, and it is only when we give up expecting it that we can get anywhere. It is each other's very *otherness* that motivates us, and the things we find in common take on greater meaning within the context of otherness. There is so much to learn by comparing the ways in which we are different, and which the same elements of women's experience are global, and which aren't, and wondering why, and what it means.

Is sisterhood really global? As Slavenka Drakulic wrote in response to Nanette Funk, "Why don't you try asking something else?"

Notes

1. It is with some unease that I use my experience working with women in the Czech Republic as indicative of Eastern Europe in general; I don't mean to dismiss the many differences within Eastern Europe (nor do I want to dismiss the many differences within Western feminism), but through experience, reading, and listening, I have seen that there is undoubtedly *a pattern* of East-West relations, with similar characteristics everywhere.

2. For some examples from the Czech Republic, see Smejkalova, Jana Hradilkova, and Jirine Siklova in *Bodies of Bread and Butter: Reconfiguring Women's Lives in the Czech Republic* (Prague: 1994); and Hana Havelkova in *Gender Studies and Post-Communism,* ed. Nanette Funk and Magda Mueller (New York: Routledge, 1993).

3. *Feminist Review,* no. 39, has some interesting articles by women undergoing this very process, articles "full of question marks," as writer Cynthia Cockburn pointed out in her short piece "In Listening Mode."

4. Dr. Doolittle is a veterinarian hero in a series of children's books.

Part One

Poland

Tradition and Reform

I told my father that I wanted to study political
science. He said, "What will you do when the
system changes?" I said, "You're crazy."

—Feminist archivist, Zagreb

P resent-day Poland is clearly hearkening back to a more traditionally Catholic Poland. The church and its power are largely uncontested. Bills have passed requiring censorship of radio and television according to a prescribed system of "family values"; crosses have appeared in political forums, even where there were none before; and suggestions that divorce be outlawed have been considered. Urszula Nowakowska begins Part 1 with "The New Right and Fundamentalism," a critique of this new conservatism. The church, seen as a protectorate during marshal law, is difficult for most Poles to criticize, and their unwillingness to do so has solidified the power of the New Right and religious fundamentalists. Nowakowska suggests that perhaps this is only a phase on the way to "real" democracy, but she fears the New Right and religious fundamentalism are new forms of manipulative ideology to replace the old communist one. Ewa Gontarczyk-Wesola goes on to argue that, "despite major changes in the roles and rights of women, traditional values and patterns are still prevalent."

In her piece entitled "Women's Situation in the Process of Change in Poland," Ewa Gontarczyk-Wesola details an urgent need to "initiate more effective activities to solve the problems of women and improve their situation." She and her contemporaries throughout the region often cite the assumption "A democratic state cannot be created without the realization of the principles of gender equality" in order to point out the difference between theory and reality. Gontarczyk-Wesola articulates what many women throughout Eastern Europe are feeling: increasingly disappointed with what "democracy" has to offer them as women.

Abortion rights and a severely restrictive abortion law in Poland have easily made reproductive rights the most central and vital issue for both feminists and the general population. Although the vast majority of the people are against restrictions, the governing bodies refuse to allow a referendum for the people to decide. In response to attacks on abortion rights, a new women's foundation, the Federation for Women and Family Planning, was formed. It includes a dozen women's groups and serves to address women's concerns in general and abortion legislation in particular. Wanda Nowicka analyzes the abortion law and its effects on women in her two essays "Ban on Abortion in Poland. Why?" and "Foundations of the Law."

Beata Lesciak presents the "ideal Polish women" as that image is put forth by popular women's magazines and journals. She analyzes the impossibility and contradiction of women's expectations in fashion, career, and personality when juxtaposed with the maintenance of a fundamentally traditional home and set of priorities. Her piece "The Polish Woman of

Today" is an exhaustive look into the mass media's presentation of women, women's images, and aspirations.

Ewa Gontarczyk-Wesola reviews the need for women's studies in Poland in "Opportunities for Feminist Perspectives." She details the growth around the world of interest in research about women and how it has led to greater knowledge in general. She says that the women's liberation movement and women's studies have "effect[ed] great changes in women's condition, gender relations, and society as a whole in terms of progress toward gender equality and equal opportunities for women." But she cautions, "Such great changes have not yet occurred in Poland." In this essay she talks about why these changes haven't occurred and what is keeping Poland from realizing its full potential as a newly "liberated" state.

Lesbian issues are also considered in "Lesbians in the Middle," a short interview with Romana Ciesla, who, with her partner, has organized lesbian meetings for Polish women from all over the region. As members of ILGA (International Lesbian and Gay Association)–Krakow, they are striving to break down isolation between lesbians in small towns and cities across the nation.

Throughout Poland there are a great many women's groups. The Women's Solidarity Commission, which broke with Solidarity when President Walesa supported abortion restrictions, operates "unofficially." Lodz hosted a women's studies conference in January 1993, and there is a yearly women's congress held in Krakow, drawing women from all over the region.

Although the threats to abortion have prompted women and men alike to organize around a dominantly female issue, it remains to be seen whether these groups and commissions will continue to focus on women's issues or stray to other concerns that again leave women behind to tend to the children, waiting for the time when their issues are of relevance again.

❖ The New Right and Fundamentalism

URSZULA NOWAKOWSKA

Discredited as the idea of a national unity front seems to be, it remains alive in Poland. Only the point of reference has changed. Communism has been replaced by Catholic and free-market ideologies. With the collapse of communism, Polish society has started to redefine national values and concentrate more on group interests. The idea of national unity through an enemy has appeared again more sharply. Once it was the bourgeoisie; today communist nomenclature works as a scapegoat for new propagandists. Communists are the ones responsible for all the mistakes on the way to "real" democracy. We have to keep revolutionary vigilance and reunite to defend our young democracy. Communist agents could be anywhere, and it is necessary to purge society of them. In totalitarian policy there are only two possibilities—us and our enemy. Whoever is not with us is against us. To be accused of communist convictions is the worst thing a citizen of the Third Republic of Poland (the postwar period did not get its number in this chronology) can be accused of. One who is not Catholic can hardly be accepted by some fundamentalists as truly Polish. One who dares to criticize the neoliberal economic philosophy of Friedrich Hayek and Milton Friedman is against the free market and is a supporter of the communist system. "Socialist," as well as "feminist," is a discrediting label.

Instead of building a pluralistic society, we have just replaced quasi-religious Marxist ideology with the only one right doctrine, namely, that of the Catholic Church. Architects of the new political system who reject communism as artificial and not "natural" tend to believe that it is possible to create a "natural" social order. Natural means traditional, Catholic, conservative, and national. Poland in the period between the wars is one point of reference. "The restoration of our broken past and the return to our roots" are indeed phenomena of the revolutionary changes in the postcommunist world.

Those who believe in the return to the past try to wipe the last forty-five years from public memory. But the ritual killing of historical memory cannot lead to "normality." The church, because it fought communism, should be a moral guide. (The position of the church in Poland was always special.) It is incontestable that a church that contributed a lot to the defeat of communism is now reaping fruits of this historical victory.[1] It is sad to realize that history repeats itself and that the new winners have just used the same methods as their recent antagonists.

There are a lot of similarities between the implementation of the Marxist ideology fifty years ago and Catholic ideology presently. A good example is the same lack of respect for the law and the less than democratic way it was created. In the 1940s propagandists of the new order appealed to historical rights; ideologists of a new Poland now use the language of natural rights. Natural law is always supposed to have primacy over any existing one. It is often considered patriotic to violate laws on the grounds that they have communist roots. But what is right and what is wrong according to natural law? Only the leading force of the nation knows. The authoritarian language of the instructing society is also used by politicians. Polish society is not mature enough to make its own decisions and has to listen to those who are more familiar with right and wrong.

Intensive Catholic indoctrination in schools and mass media, increasing examples of censorship, intervention, and discrimination based on restriction of "people's conscience"—are these to lead us to a Catholic fundamentalist state? Even some Solidarity politicians accuse the church of trying to introduce theocracy in Poland. A Christian society is not enough for churchmen; they want to have a Catholic state with Catholicism as the officially recognized religion. An episcopate sent an official letter to parliament asking it to withdraw from the new constitution a statement of the principle of the separation of church and state, arguing that it carries negative connotations from the communist past. A very influential political party supported by the church, the Christian-National Union, is also openly appealing for a Christian state. The position and actions of the Polish Catholic Church betray the Second Vatican Council's acknowledgment of the validity of the separation between church and state.

Religious ceremonies are ever-present in Polish political life. Priests act as political advisers; crosses are hung in every public place. It is well known that President Walesa built a chapel in Belweder, the Polish White House, and starts the day with mass. He used to invite ministers and other politicians for breakfast; that way mass became an obligatory ceremony for his guests. The official confessor to Walesa is present at all of his meetings. The first session of parliament was consecrated by one of the bishops. In fact, the consecration of everything is very fashionable these days in Poland. Even the first privatized beach on the Baltic was solemnly sprinkled with holy water. Pilgrimages to Czestochowa are also official rituals for those who want to be considered important in the political life of contemporary Poland.

One can argue that part of the Catholic hierarchy supports the idea of a national conscience based on Catholicism. Events in the former Yugoslavia show us how dangerous this mixture can be. The church and our Prime Gemp were very much involved in the last parliamentary election on behalf of a coalition of some Christian parties. Many priests campaigned in churches, calling parishioners to vote for church candidates. The church can, of course, cross the border between sacred and profane, but bishops are wise to remember that this limits the church to the role of political force and that one day it can lose that position.

One of the first steps of the Catholic Church's indoctrination was the introduction of religious education in public schools. Theoretically, regulations require that options be available for all children, but in practice only Catholic instruction is available. In theory participation is also voluntary, but in practice the pressure on children and adults makes it compulsory. "We must reject the idea of schools as ideologically neutral," said the former minister of education during mass in Czestochowa.

Where is the Polish Catholic Church going? What was valuable in the Polish church—a spirit of dialogue, an openness to different opinions—has disappeared, even in the most influential Catholic circles. It seems that after the collapse of communism, the church found another "enemy" of Christian values: the secular Western state and its materialism, neutral schools, tolerance of abortion, drugs, but, above all, empty churches.

Can Catholic fundamentalism be realized in the heart of Europe at the end of the twentieth century? I am afraid it can. *Cuius regio, eius religio*—this medieval principle doesn't seem to be a shameful part of history. The extremely strong position of the Catholic Church on the Polish political scene undoubtedly frustrates the process of democratization and emancipation of society. None of the important political forces can jeopardize its reputation with an open disagreement with the church. In Poland even the New Left refers to its Christian background and especially to the theology of the work of Pope John Paul II, our great Pole.

Expectations that a postcommunist Poland will be a modern liberal democracy with an open tolerant society have yet to be fulfilled. Today we know that the way to democracy is not easy and a totalitarian system can't be changed into a democracy overnight. We must only believe that the situation we have now is not just a simple exchange of places between the communist regime and an authoritarian theocracy but a temporary stage in the process of transformation to a new political system. There is a chance that, like the communist system, Catholic fundamentalism and neoliberal fundamentalism are not going to work in Poland either. Poles have never been good at being governed by totalitarian regimes. The loyalty they feel toward the church is still very strong and compensates for frustration over the church's efforts to replace the totalitarian state with a theocracy. There are already signs that the church is losing its popularity. The church used to be first among the most popular institutions in Poland; recently it dropped very cleanly into second place.

It is clear that Catholic fundamentalism and the ideology of a free-market economy constitute the biggest threat to women's rights and their status in society. Women are the most visible victims of the period of transition, and they are going to pay the biggest price for economic and ideological reforms (revolutions). The Catholic Church and closely cooperating right-wing parties have created a very unfavorable political climate for women's rights. They propagate traditional, patriarchal models of the family, with a man as its head. Under communism women were seen as ideologically equal to men. Now it is just the opposite. The ascetic patriarchal church is unable to deal with women as autonomous human beings of equal dignity and status as men. In Catholic ideology women are viewed mainly in terms of their sexual functions. "I want to remind young women that motherhood is the vocation of women. . . . It is women's eternal vocation," said Pope John Paul II in his weekly general audience on January 10, 1979. The church in Poland is strongly promoting women's role as wife and mother as the only morally correct one. Women are supposed to renounce the social activities contradictory to their feminine nature that were imposed by communism. The "new ideology" spreads the opinion that politics is men's prerogative. In the natural order women have primacy in the home and men in public life. Women are viewed by conservative parties and the church as the guardians of traditional morality entrusted with the "sacred duty of bearing children" "for the nation" and rearing them in the spirit of national and Catholic identity. Idealization of the family and women's role within it is intended to help women choose the natural and proper place in life. Unfortunately, women themselves do not yet feel that their rights are in danger and that it is worth fighting to retain them.

Opinion surveys show that the majority of women (more than 60 percent) would like to leave the job market and return home. They don't see this as a defeat but as a relief from a double burden, an option not accessible to them under communism. Furthermore, the church, while pushing its agenda into public life, has established one of the most punishing policies on women in our part of the world. The church's Charter of Family Rights is now a foundation document for our government concerning social policy. Women's rights issues, like any other connected to the communist past, are perceived as politically suspect and, as such, rejected. Women are not considered a social group having specific interests different from those of the society as a whole.

None of the political parties has a policy on women. The case of the most Western European–looking party—the Congress of Liberal Democrats—is a good example of conservative and manipulative attitudes toward women. During the campaign before the last parliamentary elections, the party asked a friend of mine to prepare a statement on women's issues. Although she wrote a very moderate report, the party's leaders refused to put it into the program. In addition to this, it was the only party that did not have a single female candidate. But what can we expect from men while very few politically active women consider problems of equal rights and equal opportunities an autonomous issue of social importance? Women's rights are seriously threatened not only because of the leading Catholic ideology but also because of economic and political pressures. Today, when so many people crave power, sending women home under any pretext is just a practical way to eliminate potential rivals.

It is not surprising that the number of women in political representation is decreasing in this political crisis. Archaic ideas concerning women are quite common among right-wing politicians and even among members of parliament. One of the most "radical" opinions about women's political representation is that of the leader of the conservative liberal party, the Union of Real Politics, a member of parliament. He thinks that women have to be deprived of their right to vote because, as he explains, they vote however their husbands do. Despite this blatant discrimination, there is a growing consciousness among women that formal democracy is not synonymous with real representation of interests.

Women's noninvolvement in politics is also due to a lack of time. Studies have shown that women have much less leisure time than men because of a double burden of housework and work outside the home. Communist emancipation didn't change that; 80 percent of women working full-time are also responsible for domestic labor. According to the dominant ideology, the Polish woman has to be strong and subordinate her own interests for the well-being of the family and the nation. Discussion about women's rights is, at best, of secondary importance, at worst a luxury or simply an unnecessary activity.

A transition toward a market economy is leading to the pauperization of the weakest social groups—women and pensioners are obviously among them. Women's work has always been regarded as secondary and their wage as only a supplement to that of their husbands. Women are the first to be laid off, which everybody considers reasonable. They are already the majority of the unemployed. It is much more difficult for women to find a new job because of the discrepancy in offers for men as opposed to women. Announcements for jobs are usually gender specific, and employment agencies deal with men and women separately. To eliminate unemployment, the church and right-wing parties suggest sending women home to fulfill maternal duties and leaving the higher wages to men. The Solidarity trade union is also supporting this so-called family wage. Women are often denied jobs on the grounds of their sex, and there are no laws against sexual discrimination in hiring. The reasons are often given openly: Women get pregnant, have children, take maternity leave. The difficulties continue: As a result of the withdrawal of the state from social and welfare provision, about 60 percent of child care facilities have already been closed; this problem is likely to grow in the future. Those facilities that still exist are increasingly more expensive such that many women cannot afford them. Yet another way of forcing women back into the home is to point to the dramatic rise in juvenile delinquency, explained by a lack of insufficient maternal care.

A tightening up on divorce laws is supposed to keep the family together, with the subordinated role of women within. A new regulation was conceived and pushed by churchmen; now it is more difficult to obtain a divorce. Instead of going to a local court, petitioners for divorce have to travel to a more distant, district court. Apart from this, divorce has become an expensive luxury.

The prevalent view is that violence against women is a totally private matter and is not sufficient reason to break the holy ties of marriage. There is a proposal to introduce into the civil code the institution of marriage as separate from canonical law and a complete ban on divorce. It is already possible to get married in the church without civil decree. Episcopate recommendations for school curricula advise that schools pay more attention to teaching girls skills more suited to the role of wives and mothers instead of emphasizing intellectual development.

The success of many of the church's proposals is linked with the Polish pope (Poles are very proud of him) and the strong ties that bind him to Walesa. When, for example, Walesa appointed a minister of women's affairs, the bishops appealed for a minister who was Catholic, married, at least forty years old, and with two or more children. They got what they wanted, but they overlooked the fact that Miss Popowicz did not support a ban on abortion.

The direct threat to women's rights is most visible in the area of reproductive freedom. The church has been most persistent in this area. Since 1989, the Episcopate has been agitating for antiabortion legislation, a campaign personally endorsed by the pope. The church started an intense, multifaceted, and even vicious campaign against the law permitting abortion. Catholics were threatened with denial of the sacrament of communion if they refused to sign an antiabortion petition. Church activists were even collecting signatures from children in primary schools. Often after viewing the antiabortion film *The Silent Scream,* children were asked to sign petitions "in defense of their brothers and sisters." "Thank your parents that you weren't killed," intoned a priest to a seven-year-old child.

This so-called social consultation on abortion appears to be scandalous manipulation and blackmail on the side of the church. Pro-choice people are accused of being Stalinists, and abortion is compared to the Holocaust.

While calling for a referendum about the criminalization of abortion, de-fenders of the fetus compared pro-choice Poles to the advocates of the con-centration camps. The Prime Gemp publicly called critics of the church's political line barking dogs (curs). The first step in eliminating reproductive rights was to limit and then ban abortion, then limit and finally ban contra-ception. In April 1990 the church successfully promoted a Ministry of Health regulation requiring a woman seeking an abortion to obtain the ap-proval of two gynecologists, her family doctor, and a psychologist (who is supposed to discourage her). Since the institution of this regulation, at least one woman has reported that she self-induced because she was afraid the psychologist would report her to the parish priest. It is worth noting that a number of doctors pledged not to "murder" innocent, conceived children. Their loyalty to the leading force advanced so far that they were even refus-ing to prescribe contraceptives.

The church and antichoice forces won their biggest victory when the Na-tional Doctors' Guild drafted a new code of ethics that sharply restricted women's access to abortion. According to the code, doctors can perform abortion only in cases of rape or when the life or health of the mother is threatened. The decision as to whether a pregnant women can undergo pre-natal tests for genetic defects rests solely with her doctor; sanctions against doctors include suspension of a doctor's license. This medical ethics code took effect May 3, 1992. Only the government plenipotentiary for women's and family affairs objected to these provisions, which she did in a letter sent to an annual doctors' convention from which a neutral ombudsman had been banned. Soon she was dismissed from her post, and her position is still vacant. The rest of the government remained silent. It is also worth noting that the code states that a doctor should provide the same quality of medical care to any patient regardless of "age, race, nationality, religion, social back-ground, financial status, or political beliefs," but there is no reference to sex. Although the regulations in the ethics code concerning abortion were illegal, they were written into the Constitutional Tribunal and put in practice. In spite of the declaration of the ombudsman that he would defend all doctors performing abortion according to the existing law, doctors were afraid of losing their licenses, and most were not performing abortions. Abortion tours have already begun, most often to the former Soviet republics.

The social and political atmosphere created by Catholic and neoliberal fundamentalists is encouraging discrimination, posing serious threats to freedom of conscience, women's rights and human rights, and freedom at large. I want to believe that the Polish church, like many of us, hasn't yet found its place in the postcommunist world and that this return to past models and values is simply its reaction to the new situation. We just can't go back in history, and one day churchmen must realize that. The church in the beginning of the twenty-first century cannot be the same as it was in the period before World War II—lacking contact with the real world. Today one's opportunities in social and political life depend once again on one's ideological background.

Notes

1. The Catholic Church is widely seen as having protected dissident groups from persecution during marshal law.

Women's Situation in the Process of Change in Poland

EWA GONTARCZYK-WESOLA

This essay is an attempt to briefly present the situation and most recent experiences of Polish women and to consider some aspects of the most recent changes in Poland. I refer only to some aspects of this situation because currently there is not much research on women in Poland and therefore profound description and analysis are impossible. The research shows that, despite major changes in the roles and rights of women, traditional values and patterns are still prevalent. This contradiction is attributed to a variety of factors. It is due largely to the impact of opposite tendencies on social policy and practice. Therefore, there is an urgent need to initiate more effective activities in order to solve the problems of women and improve their situation. A democratic state cannot be created without the realization of gender equality. Although the comments made in the following pages relate specifically to women's situation in Poland, I believe that this situation is not, in fact, a specifically Polish problem.

As the number of cross-cultural studies on women increases, it is becoming clear that there are sex inequalities in all contemporary societies, everywhere the status of women is lower than that of men, and women's issues are subordinate to other priorities in most social, political, and economic changes. In Poland today, there is no doubt that the situation for women is not satisfactory—for women themselves and for society at large.

The statistical data (*Kobieta w Polsce* 1985; *Zatrudnienie w gospodarce narodowej* 1989) show that the majority of women are gainfully employed; women constitute about 46 percent of the labor force. Hence, the great number of women in the labor force is a significant factor in any plan to alter the position of women in Polish society. But they work mainly in low-status jobs and in traditional female occupations such as teaching, medical care, social work, and food and clothing industries. These jobs and occupations are low-paying; on the average women's wages are 33 percent lower than those of men's. These professions do not offer many opportunities for promotion to managerial or decisionmaking positions. Only a minority of women are employed in traditionally male occupations or in high positions in either female or male domains. Thus, there are still not many women who hold better-paying, managerial, professional positions (Adamski 1984, 296).

In considering the situation of women, we might compare the participation of women in the occupational sphere with their participation in education. The data show great progress in women's participation in education; women constitute about 50 percent of all students. But an analysis of the fields of study shows that women are mostly concentrated in the typically feminine fields. At the same time, however, the number of women in typically male fields is increasing (Gontarczyk-Wesola 1986). This means that the preparation of women for occupational roles (as reflected in their relatively high and differentiated professional qualifications) is, to some extent, wasted.

Despite the fact that women's right to work is officially accepted, thereby enabling women to achieve social and political liberation and economic independence, there are many people, both men and women, who do not fully accept this right. Polish research (Adamski 1984, 292–301) confirms this opinion. In this research, the majority of respondents maintained that women's place is at home and that they should take only the role of wife, mother, or homemaker. Women's occupational role is mainly accepted as appropriate for unmarried women or, eventually, for married women without children. The research on women who are not gainfully employed shows somewhat different results. These women more often hold the view that women should be gainfully employed. It is clear that there is a contradiction between official acceptance and social opinions regarding women's occupational role and work.

It is also widely acknowledged that married women work out of economic necessity because husbands are not able to earn enough for the family. In this respect, however, the attitudes of women themselves toward their gainful work are particularly important. Recent research (*Situacja spoleczno-zawodowa kobiet* 1988, 133–144) reveals that the majority of women work because they want first of all to secure the basic means of maintaining the family, raise the family's standard of living, ensure financial independence for themselves, or maintain contact with a wider environment.

They do not attach great importance to achievement or success in their work or to the need for self-development. Nor is the desire to achieve a certain social position or take advantage of their occupational qualification strong. Only women with higher education show greater interest in their work and desire to use their professional skills. This research also shows that some women express reluctance to work. They say that their work does not suit them and that they prefer to take care of their children and home. Among women with higher education, this reluctance is very seldom expressed, but if it is, these women also mention their wish to take care of their children and home.

There are some contradictions, however, in research results concerning highly educated women. In articles published in women's magazines, and in some private conversations, these women often express the desire to give up their jobs. Some say that they feel guilty. Because of their professional work, they neglect their children and home. Sometimes, they admit that only the family is important to them, not the work. The fact that some women express a preference for returning to a very traditional pattern of women's roles is significant. It indicates that some women are not aware of the existence of other ways of solving their problems—ways that probably would be much more advantageous for themselves, their children and family, and society at large.

In an analysis of the situation of Polish women, it is important to take into account women's preference in lifestyle, which may be used as indicators of women's position, attitudes, and choices. The following translation of models of lifestyles shows precisely what kind of models were taken into account and how they were defined in the research on women (*Situacja spoleczno-zawodowa kobiet,* 1988, 80–91); the translation also presents more details of the situation of contemporary Polish women. (The numbers in parentheses show the percentage of women's responses: The first refers to their preferred model—the lifestyle they see as correct; the second, to their realized model—the way they are actually living. In relation to the realized model, 2.3 percent of the women did not respond because they were not married and did not have children.)

1. "Women should most of all take care of the family, even at her own costs, perform most of household duties, and not work professionally" (preferred, 20.9 percent; realized, 25.8 percent).
2. "Women should treat household duties as a kind of a profession that enables the achievement of success, have her own interests, have time for herself, cultivate a partnership in the family, live in a circle of family matters, and not resign from her own needs" (preferred, 22.0 percent; realized, 17.1 percent).
3. "Women should work professionally but quit work to raise children, cultivate a partnership in the division of home duties, prefer a harmonious family life to a professional career" (preferred, 33.5 percent; realized, 28.9 percent).
4. "Women should work professionally, treat the wife's duties as equal to the husband's duties, cultivate success in professional work as well as in a family life" (preferred, 22.9 percent; realized, 22.5 percent).
5. "Women should treat success in professional life as most important, be satisfied with her work even at the cost to the family" (preferred, 0.7 percent; realized, 3.4 percent).

Because of time and space constraints, I do not intend to discuss in detail all aspects of this research. However, I do want to point out that 41.5 percent of the women with higher education preferred the fourth model, but only 20 percent of these women had realized this lifestyle.

It is clear that the majority of women prefer and follow traditional lifestyles; in fact, the formulation of the models itself also reveals the very traditional attitudes of researchers toward women's roles. These results are confirmed in other research on lifestyles in Polish cities (Tarkowska 1988, 245–247). This work shows that wide differences appear in the lifestyles of men and women, especially throughout marriage, which bears important consequences for both sexes, particularly women. Women are much more home-centered. They are expected to concentrate on the present, whereas men concentrate on the future. Moreover, families follow rather traditional patterns in the division of gender roles. Other research (*Situacja spoleczno-zawodowa kobiet* 1988, 15–34) reveals only significant exceptions in this division. In general, women cook, wash dishes, clean, wash clothes, iron, mend clothes, do everyday shopping, help children with homework, and sometimes settle family business, whereas men settle family business and sometimes clean and do everyday shopping.

The research (Tarkowska 1988) also shows that marriage and housekeeping, particularly under the difficult conditions of everyday life in Poland, demand from many women more or less voluntary resignation from career aspirations and interests. Eventually, for the sake of the family, women often reduce their lives to a small private sphere. Even if they have a job, it only adds to their burden. The research indicates that in many cases, this sacrifice for the family is accompanied by feelings of regret, a sense of disappointment, and a conviction that they live only for husband and family matters. The research also shows that active opposition against such situations does not often occur.

The process of changing the traditional roles and attitudes of women and raising the status of women is very slow in Poland. Women are primarily expected to fulfill the roles of wife, mother, and homemaker. Even though the occupational roles of women are accepted officially, most men and many women still consider these roles secondary and subordinate to the domestic roles. In fact, despite almost universal participation of women in both gainful work and performance of the majority of domestic duties, it seems that their contribution to both home and national economy is not as highly acknowledged and valued as men's contribution. Thus, it also seems that there are still many women who are not able to develop their abilities, gifts, and interests; achieve high status; and take advantage of the principle of equality of the sexes guaranteed in the Polish constitution and accepted as official policy.

One should not overlook the many gains women have made in legal rights; the high proportion of women in education and paid work; women's activity in social, political, and cultural life; and social provisions for maternity and child care. However, there is still much to be done, even in these areas. Many changes should be introduced to remove such sex inequalities as sex segregation in the fields of education and occupations; the concentrations of women in low-paying occupations; discrimination in hiring, pay, and promotion; the division of domestic duties and roles; and sex-role stereotypes.

From this brief review of the situation and experience of women, it is clear that, despite major changes in the roles and rights of women, traditional values and patterns of behavior are still prevalent in Poland. There is also evidence of sex inequalities, as well as discrepancies between officially accepted and legally guaranteed equal rights and the real situation of women. These contradictions may be attributed to a variety of interrelated factors.

Partly, they are due to the fact that the role and position of women in contemporary Polish society are still conditioned by traditional patriarchal attitudes toward women. The traditional views on women are based on the assumptions of significant differences between the sexes, the inferiority of women, and the natural or biological determination of their roles. As a result, women's roles are limited to the domestic duties of wives, mothers, and homemakers; these duties are recognized as the primary roles of women. Within this traditional approach, the occupational roles of women are in many cases accepted; this acceptance, however, seems to derive from the economic situation of the majority of Polish families. Moreover, in this context the occupational roles of women are generally restricted to typically feminine domains, which are closely connected with women's domestic duties, and they are recognized as subordinate to women's primary roles.

In contrast to this tendency, a very brief review of the history of women's condition in Poland (Braun 1904; Ihnatowicz 1988) reveals much evidence of activities for the emancipation of women and efforts undertaken to bring about improvements in women's situation. Therefore, the role and the position of Polish women are also conditioned by a long tradition of progressive attitudes toward the fulfillment of women's aspirations and the acceptance of their social equality.

Furthermore, in the last few decades it was generally claimed that the situation of women had been radically altered after World War II in Poland. The need to reconstruct and develop the country, as well as shortages in the labor force, created the possibility and necessity of women's training and employment. At the same time, the principle of sex equality in all spheres of state, political, economic, cultural, and social life was declared and granted in the constitution of the Polish People's Republic in 1952. Moreover, other legislation was adopted to guarantee women's equal rights in education, work, and marriage and family life; to protect women's maternal roles; and to enable women to combine occupational and family roles. This legislation was an extension and a continuation of rights granted to women in the 1920s. It was also claimed that women could attain equality only under socialism and that the full emancipation of Polish women would be only a matter of time. Consequently, the continual improvement of women's condition and efforts to overcome difficulties were universally reported in research (*Kobieta w Polsce* 1986), as well as voiced in the mass media.

In fact, because of the lack of profound research into women's situation, any evaluation of a real impact of these changes seems to be a very controversial issue at the moment. As far as the improvement of women's situation is concerned, there is no doubt that it, too, is a very divisive question. How one looks at this issue depends on one's expectations and concepts of women's roles. If one assumes that women are naturally inclined to fulfill the roles of wife, mother, and homemaker and that these are women's primary roles, then one is satisfied, for instance, with only about 10 to 30 percent female participation in typically male professions, positions, and careers; with 70 or perhaps 90 percent of women toiling in typically female low-paying domains and positions; with the rather simple addition of women's occupational roles to their domestic roles; and with the wishful thinking and hope that some men will be fair enough to help women with their duties. Consequently, those who believe that women's position is getting better may term these instances of aid to women as improvements or sex equality. Nevertheless, after forty years of "the implementation of the principles of sex equality," one might expect more changes in the situation of women, in attitudes toward women's roles, and in the conditions for women's self-actualization as human beings.

The complexity of women's situation, experiences, and needs, as well as sex inequalities and gender relations, was not properly taken into account by the powers that be. In fact, it seems that social policy and practice, as well as an approach to women's and gender issues in research, were greatly influenced by traditional attitudes toward women's roles and the very superficial propaganda of sex equality. The Polish experience also shows that the emphasis on legal equality was based on a very optimistic assumption of the power of legislation to bring about changes in society. It overlooked the limitation of legal reform and the inability of legislation to change attitudes. In general, attitudes have been slow to change, especially when they involve the acceptance of new ideas of women and their place in society.

In fact, only some women have been able to take advantage of the opportunities open to them. Thus, still more encouragement, guidance, and equitable conditions should be provided to the majority of women (as well as men) in order to make them aware of alternative choices in education, professional work, and gender roles in social life.

In Poland at present, one might assume that conditions are more favorable to women since so many changes are occurring in social, economic, and political life. Moreover, much effort is being made to continue these changes, and many assurances are given regarding the creation of a demo-

cratic state. In this context, however, one should not overlook the total neglect of women in reforms and public debates for the improvement of
women's position, as well as the increasing unemployment rates among
women; the decreasing number of women in parliament, government, local
administration, political parties, and trade unions, particularly in leadership positions; proposals to scale down women's education to prepare them
only to fulfill family roles; projects to turn abortion into a crime; and a
questioning of women's right to vote and work as professionals. In fact,
women have lost many of their previous gains. Thus, new women's problems are becoming evident, while old ones have not yet been solved. Opportunities for the achievement of a real sex equality are becoming even
more illusory.

In relation to the aforementioned aspects of women's situation, reforms
concerning women should be a priority. Otherwise, a democratic state
would be created only for men, and the Polish state, instead of being whole,
would be reduced to half (in Plato's words). Would Poland still be a democratic nation or rather not democratic at all? Paradoxically, it seems inevitable in light of current conditions to refer to Plato's concepts (*Sympo-
sium, Republic, Laws*) in order to indicate that, although the idea of
women's advancement and gender equality was articulated such a long time
ago, throughout the centuries there have been so many changes, revolutions, and social and political problems that women's problems have remained unsolved. Despite recent political and economic changes in Poland,
women's situation seems to be static, if not deteriorating.

In this context, an urgent need to reconsider the right to and opportunities for real gender equality, as well as the unrealized potential of women, is
emerging in Poland. In this way, society will get the best value from women
because difference in sex is not, in itself, a proper basis for differentiation
of occupational and social function. Women should appeal, demand, act,
and struggle, as women in the past did and in many countries do, because
the transition of contemporary Polish society toward a democratic one cannot be achieved without the realization of gender equality and without
women as equal citizens. Moreover, it cannot be achieved without the activity of women in their own behalf. Thus, it is important not only to reor-
ganize social structures, relations, and institutional arrangements but also
to bring about changes in personality formation and gender relations. Further efforts toward the spread of a feminist movement and the development
of feminist research seem the most relevant contributions to the creation of
a clear and detailed picture of women's situation and to the raising of
women's consciousness. These activities may also stimulate women to move
toward the improvement of their situation and the achievement of real gender equality.

References

Adamski, F. *Socjologia malzenstwa i rodziny* (The sociology of marriage and the family). Warsaw: PWN, 1984.

Braun, L. *Historia rozwoju ruchu kobiecego* (The history of the women's movement). Warsaw: GiW, 1904.

Gontarczyk-Wesola, E. "Towards the Changing Pattern of Women's Education." In *Women Challenge Technology,* ed. Mona Dahms, Lone Dircknick-Holmfeld, and Anette Kolmos. Alborg, Denmark: University of Alborg, 1986, 3:661–670.

Ihnatowicz, I. et al. *Spoleczenstwo polskie od X do XX wieku* (Polish society from the tenth to the twentieth century). Warsaw: KiW, 1988.

Kobieta w Polsce (Women in Poland). Warsaw: GUS, 1985.

Kobieta w Polsce (Women in Poland). Warsaw: IPiSS, 1986.

Situacja spoleczno-zawodowa kobiet (The social-occupational situation of women). Warsaw: GUS, 1988.

Tarkowska, E. "Pokolenie i plec a Zroznicowania stylow zycia" (Generation and gender versus differentiation of life styles). In *Styles of Life in Polish Cities,* ed. Sicinski. Wroclaw: Ossolineum, 1988.

Zatrudnienie w gospodarce narodowej (Employment in national economy). Warsaw: GUS, 1989.

Ban on Abortion in Poland. Why?

WANDA NOWICKA

On February 15, 1993, President Lech Walesa signed a restrictive antiabortion bill (the Law on Family Planning, Human Embryo Protection, and Conditions of Admittance of Abortion). It went into effect on March 16, 1993. The bill's passage was not unexpected; it followed an antiabortion campaign of more than three years.

This campaign has been associated with the collapse of communism, an event looked forward to by most of our society for so long. This political transformation has brought many necessary positive changes, but, unexpectedly, it has also brought negative changes, especially for the condition of women. These can be observed on at least two levels: economic and legal.

On the economic level, the transformation from a communist economy to free-market economy has caused unemployment, which was unknown under communism. This phenomenon affects women to a greater extent than men: Women constitute 54 percent of the registered unemployed. Employers are not willing to employ a woman unless she can work as a secretary and is under thirty.

On the legal level, changes with respect to women are mainly connected with pressure from the Catholic Church and Christian fundamentalists advocating a complete ban on abortion. Polish Catholicism has always been strong, and it became even stronger under communism. For many, it was a shelter for any political opposition. When communism collapsed, the Catholic Church started a policy aimed at institutionalizing its position. The first step in this direction was the introduction of Catholic instruction into public schools in September 1990. Other examples of this policy are religious symbols and practices in offices, parliament, the Polish Army, and elsewhere. And the Law on Family Planning mandates that Christian values be "respected" by Polish radio and TV. Some fundamentalist forces push for the abolition of the church and state separation that is guaranteed, at this point, by the Polish constitution. A new constitution is being prepared, and an article on separation perceived by some as a remnant of communism is seriously threatened.

Some political groups, very strong in parliament, support the reestablishment of Christian values in all spheres of life. For women, this means that their only proper role is as wife and mother. It is easy to understand how this political aura could produce an antiabortion bill.

History

Abortion was legalized in 1956. For reasons such as lack of sex education in schools, low availability of reliable and safe contraception (especially in rural areas), lack of reliable information, ineffective institutions responsible for spreading information and distributing contraceptives, and a campaign on the part of the Catholic Church against contraception, there is a very low rate of contraceptive use. A survey made in summer 1991 (SGM/KRC Poland–Gazeta Wyborcza, October 16–18, 1992) showed that 40–50 percent of respondents did not use any form of contraceptives (varied according to age group). Only 4 percent used the pill, and 3.8 percent used spermicides. It is not surprising, then, that the abortion rate is high. The actual number varies drastically, however, depending on the source of information (from sixty thousand to three hundred thousand yearly).

In 1990 the Ministry of Health tightened regulations for abortion at publicly funded hospitals (the regulations require a woman to obtain permission from two gynecologists, her local physician, and a psychologist). In November 1990 Professor Waclaw Dec, head of the Obstetrics and Gynecology Department at the medical academy in Lodz, publicized the deaths of three women from self-induced abortions. He attributed these deaths to the new abortion regulations. Dec also revealed that pressure had been put on him by Ministry of Health authorities to change the classification of these three cases. At the present time, doctors have noticed increased numbers of spontaneous abortions (commenced miscarriages). For example, the director of a hospital in Zdunska Wola stated in an interview with *Gazeta Wyborcza* (December 18, 1992) that in 1989 doctors performed seventy-four induced abortions and treated forty-eight spontaneous abortions at her hospital. In 1990 there were only nineteen induced abortions and eighty-five spontaneous abortions.

Serious restrictions on access to abortion were introduced to the Ethical Code of Physicians, which has been enforced since May 3, 1992. According to this code, abortion may be performed only when a mother's life or health is in danger or when pregnancy is the result of a crime. Genetic deformity of the fetus is not a justification for abortion. Prenatal examinations such as amniocentesis are not permitted unless it is guaranteed that the fetus will not be affected. The Ethical Code, though it is not compatible with Polish law, caused public hospitals to stop performing abortions. Conversely, a number of doctors still performed abortion on a private basis for double or triple the price.

This schizophrenic legal situation, neither recognized nor abolished by the Constitutional Tribunal, has already resulted in many tragedies. In Silesia women with a defective pregnancy, such as a brainless fetus, are obliged to take the pregnancy to term. Such cases of deformity are more common in Silesia than in other parts of Poland as a result of pollution caused by outdated heavy industry. (According to the World Health Organization's annual report, issued in Geneva, Poland placed second in the world with respect to male-infant death rate and placed third with respect to female-infant death rate. These numbers are high because of the infant mortality rate in Upper Silesia, where two newborns per one thousand die as a result of disturbance in the genetic code.)

In many cases, a woman's life or health is threatened because doctors in public hospitals are working under pressure and are afraid of performing abortions even if there are serious medical indications. Several such cases were reported by the Polish mass media. In these cases, hospitals either sent women away without a medical examination, referring to their internal hospital regulations, or they demanded numerous certificates. When the twelfth week of pregnancy is over (the abortion deadline according to Polish law), doctors refuse with a "clean conscience." Some women have come close to dying as a result of not having an abortion performed in a timely manner. For example, one woman could not obtain an abortion even though her fetus was dead. Another case was that of a forty-one-year-old blind woman suffering from epilepsy. Her pregnancy was the result of rape. She was refused an abortion. A forty-year-old woman had a tumor in her uterus, hypertension, and allergies to most antibiotics. She was refused an abortion at first. Later, she was finally permitted an abortion under critical conditions resulting from an internal infection.

In November 1992 the Extraordinary Parliamentary Commission accepted a draft of an antiabortion bill that was more restrictive than the Ethical Code of Physicians and a former draft of the bill. According to the later draft, abortion could be obtained only when a mother's life was threatened. Some contraceptives, such as intrauterine devices (IUDs), and some new-generation pills were to be forbidden. Doctors or women self-inducing abortion could be penalized for up to two years in prison.

The draft evoked spontaneous resistance among some parties previously trying to not get involved in the "abortion issue," as well as among ordinary people. Zbigniew Bujak, the member of parliament from the Labor Union Party, urged the committee to create a referendum concerning the penalization of abortion. This idea was enthusiastically embraced by thousands and thousands of citizens, although there is hardly any legal basis for the referendum. However, in the draft of a charter of civil rights proposed by President Walesa, there is an article stipulating that the referendum may be initiated when five hundred thousand signatures have been collected. But such a charter has yet to be passed.

Nobody expected such a civil movement for the referendum. Over twenty local committees were established. People collected signatures at work, in the street, in neighborhoods, or in stores. By January 1, 1993, three hundred thousand signatures had been collected. Society, passive up until now, seemed to be waking up. The more antiabortionists, including church authorities, there were yelling to stop the movement, the better; the people understood that the struggle for legal abortion was a struggle for real democracy.

This movement certainly influenced the parliamentary voting over the antiabortion bill. During the final voting in Sejm (January 7, 1993) and in the Senate (January 29, 1993), this restrictive draft did not pass. According to the bill that passed, abortion would be possible, only in public hospitals, when a mother's life is threatened, when prenatal care proved serious incurable deformity of the fetus, or when pregnancy is the result of rape or incest reported to the police. Doctors will be penalized for up to two years in prison for performing abortions, and women will not be penalized in the case of illegal abortions. Prenatal examinations will be possible but limited only to some cases in which serious suspicions of genetic deformity exist.

In general, lawyers consider the law to be poorly thought out, poorly written (it is filled with vague, quasi-religious terminology), and unclear in its implications. Lawyers interpreting the law are not sure, for instance, whether giving information about abortions abroad is legal. The legislation also poses a serious threat to such contraceptives as the pill and IUDs (which are hardly available, being used by only 5 percent of Polish women). According to the bill, they are "early abortives" and might be forbidden. By contraception, antiabortion fundamentalists understand only "natural methods" (in the new edition of *Medical Home Manual,* a general home reference for women and their health, the chapter on birth control methods was edited to delete any reference to methods other than "natural" ones, a change made in response to pressure of church authorities). There is strong propaganda against the pill and IUDs as being very dangerous for women's health. Although the antiabortion bill obliges education authorities to introduce some elements of sex education into school curricula, the vice-minister of education, Kazimierz Marcinkiewicz, officially stated that the government policymakers did not intend to do this; he explained that "pro-family education is covered in other subject areas, such as literature or biology."

The interpretation of the law and the way in which it will be understood by authorities are very important not only to authorities but also to organizations that intend to help women. In 1992 the Federation for Women and Family Planning was established by five prowomen, nongovernmental organizations. At present, we have nine organizations-members: the Polish Feminist Association, Pro Femina Association, Neutrum Association, the YWCA, the League of Polish Women, the Society for Family Development, the Democratic Union of Women—Section Ewa, the Movement for the Protection of Women's Rights (an affiliated member), and the Polish Sexology Society. This federation intends to fight for safe and legal abortion and aims at assisting women in preventing unwanted pregnancies through sex education and contraception. One of our activities is a hotline. Many women who call feel insecure and confused about the new law. New problems cause new situations.

Another movement struggling for legal abortion is the Movement of Committees for the Referendum, which was so active before the law passed. This movement has not been as strong since the less restrictive bill has passed. The movement has to decide whether to become a formalized, structured organization or keep the status quo.

Several public polls show that the majority of Polish society is in favor of legal abortion, but not on demand. Eighty-one percent are in favor of it if a woman's life is endangered, 80 percent are for legal abortion when the fetus is deformed or suffers from an incurable illness, 74 percent are in favor of abortion when a woman is in a difficult financial or social situation, but only 23 percent accept abortion on demand.

There is one positive side effect of these extremely unfavorable conditions for women. Women have become aware of the need to organize and to be more conscious about their own issues. We were given liberal regulations much earlier and easier than many other women in the world. We took these for granted, and whereas most women in the world had to fight for their rights, the majority of Polish women believed in the appearances of freedom and equality. Many of us did not perceive a danger until recently. But what is given can be easily taken away. Now, it is our turn to struggle for our rights.

▣ Foundations of the Law

WANDA NOWICKA

The antiabortion law takes away women's dignity. It expresses the conviction that women are not able to make moral and responsible decisions and that they therefore must be prevented from "making mistakes." Women's well-being and health are not acknowledged as values; they must yield to other values, such as the "human embryo's protection."

It is sad that when the rest of the civilized world has developed an understanding of reproductive rights as human rights, Poland moves quickly backward. Women's rights were all but absent in the discussion around the abortion issue, not because they were not raised by feminist groups, but because they couldn't be heard publicly as a result of their lack of significant access to mass media. Even very well-known Polish organizations promoting human rights have no entry for "reproductive rights as human rights" in their databases.

Factors Worsening the Situation

Fear paralyzing doctors who face pregnant women with medical problems is a very important factor in the significant worsening of women's reproductive health. Doctors are afraid of issuing prescriptions allowing abortions. They often send women away without an examination, or they direct women to other specialists in order to avoid responsibility for making these decisions. Many doctors treat women with disrespect, using foul language.

This happened to a pregnant blind woman who knew that she would not be able to have another child (her husband was also almost blind, and they had two children). A director of one hospital told her that "she should not go to her husband's bed." Even after many visits to various specialists, this woman could not succeed. Some doctors she visited admitted that she should have an abortion, but they would not venture to issue the necessary prescription. Another woman who had had a mastectomy the year before was also terribly mistreated by many doctors and sent away with nothing. These are some of many such anecdotal experiences women encounter on a regular basis.

47

Not only are women's rights violated by an extremely restrictive abortion law. Also, the legal situation is worsened by the fact that authorities do not fulfill the duties that should accompany the introduction of the abortion law, and the community of doctors, for many reasons, does not help women it could and should.

Reproductive Rights as Human Rights

The Right to Life and Survival

Article 6.1 of the Political Covenant (which is similar to a constitution) provides that "every human being has the inherent right to life. This right shall be protected by law. No one shall be arbitrarily deprived of his right." Although according to the antiabortion legislation known as the Law on Family Planning, Human Embryo Protection, and Conditions of Admittance of Abortion, abortion is legal when the mother's life and health are threatened, in practice this rule is not observed. When doctors are working under pressure, when they are doing everything to avoid "the problem," no woman can be sure that when her survival is in competition with the right to life of the embryo or fetus, the doctor will choose to save her over it. There is *no* law protecting women. Sometimes it may turn out that saving a fetus would be safer for a doctor than saving a woman. Such cases have already happened and have been reported by the Polish media.

The Right to Liberty and Security

Article 9(1) of the Political Covenant states that "everyone has the right to liberty and security of (their) person. . . . No one shall be deprived of his liberty except on such grounds and in accordance with such procedures as are established by law."

In Poland women have no practical access to means of fertility control. Although the state does not officially deny it, the practice shows something opposite. There is no sex education in schools, contraceptives are rarely available outside big cities, and prices for contraceptives are high. These are some of the reasons that only 8 percent of the population effectively uses birth control methods. Under such circumstances, it is difficult to exercise reproductive choice and be free and secure from unwanted pregnancies.

Article 7 of the Political Covenant provides that "no one shall be subjected to torture or punishment." Compelling the blind woman to continue her pregnancy and pressuring her to have a baby in order to give it up later for adoption are cruel and inhumane.

The Right to Private and Family Life

The Political Covenant (Article 17, built on Article 12 of the Universal Declaration, a section of the Political Covenant) provides that "no one shall be subjected to arbitrary or unlawful interference with his privacy, family, home, or correspondence, nor to unlawful attacks on his honor and reputation." Polish law, in contrast to international law, does not recognize a right to privacy as encompassing a woman's right to reproductive freedom. There are few other spheres that should be excluded from the state's interference more readily than reproductive freedom.

Personal data are violated in Poland. It happened to the blind pregnant woman. The hospital where she was seeking help gave her phone number to an organization arranging adoptions. She was harassed several times by phone calls pressuring her to have the baby and give it up for adoption.

Rights Regarding Information

Article 10(1)of the European Convention protects "the right to freedom of expression[, which] includes freedom . . . to receive and impart information and ideas without interference by public authority regardless of frontiers." Newspapers often refuse to accept paid advertisements for foreign clinics performing abortions by hiding behind the internal regulations of the newspaper.

Rights Regarding Education

Article 26 of the Universal Declaration provides that "everyone has the right to education." It may serve the goal of individual and reproductive health. This right is not observed in Poland with respect to sex education. Despite all possible consequences of lack of sex education in schools, especially under the antiabortion law, the Ministry of Education, completely controlled by Catholic Church authorities, does not intend to introduce a separate course.

The Right to Health

Article 12(1) of the Women's Convention provides that "State's Parties shall take all appropriate measures to eliminate discrimination against women in the field of health care in order to ensure, on the basis of the equality of men and women, access to health services, including those related to family planning." This law has been violated in Poland in numerous aspects. Pregnant women can no longer rely on their doctors. Doctors who have pregnant patients take into account not only dangers for their patient's health but also their professional careers. Pregnant women are refused certain services (amniocentesis) on the pretext that it may endanger the fetus. Pregnant women seeking abortions are often not examined in hospitals regardless of whether there are medical indications for abortion. Young girls wanting contraception are often treated with disrespect by the doctors ("You are too young to think about such things"). Doctors often misinform women about birth control methods for ideological reasons.

The Right to the Benefits of Scientific Progress

Article 15(1)(b) of the Economic Covenant recognizes the right of everyone "to enjoy the benefits of scientific progress and its applications." Polish women have no full access to the medical results of scientific advances. The list of the pills of the third generation available in Poland is very short, the medications on the list very expensive. Sterilization is illegal. Abortion in Poland is performed with old methods (no vacuum method), often without anesthetic. Amniocentesis, which used to be a routine test for pregnant women over thirty-five, now is limited to very few cases.

As soon as the Law on Family Planning came into effect (on March 16, 1993), organizations that had joined the Federation for Women and Family Planning undertook efforts to influence three ministries responsible for introducing the law: the Ministries of Health, Education, and Labor. In the Ministry of Health there are certainly people who genuinely understand the importance of sex education and contraception under the present law. The Program for Promotion of Health, including sex education and AIDS prevention, was created by government policymakers. In that program, nongovernmental organizations, including the federation, were to play an important role as organizers and supporters. The program was to consist of two parts. Initially, experienced sex educators were to gather in order to create a unified curriculum. Subsequently, a group of instructors was to be trained, and they would teach at schools or in youth centers. Unfortunately, as a result of pressure from the Catholic Church, the first conference of sex educators, organized by the Ministry of Health in early May, was "invaded" by antichoice activists commanded by several priests. The agenda of this meeting could not be realized. It is unclear if the ministry intends to continue this initiative.

As for the Ministry of Labor, we were informed that there are about seventy houses for single mothers in Poland with about four hundred places. There are only minor projects being considered to improve this situation. The Ministry of Education ordered that civil servants be approved by church authorities and is not interested in cooperative efforts with nongovernmental organizations or with the Ministry of Health in forming interdisciplinary programs, including sex education.

Some Activities of the Federation

The federation started a hotline for women in October 1992. It is focused on reproductive health counseling. The number of phone calls concerning these issues is systematically growing. The hotline plays an important role in collecting information about how the abortion law affects women's lives.

Many negative results can already be observed. One result is sexual psychosis—sexual life begins to be perceived as dangerous. Women call directly after sexual intercourse scared that they could get pregnant. Husbands call to say that their wives are refusing sex as a result of the law. Another result is that abortion in a hospital is impossible to get even when a woman's life and health are threatened. The federation has issued several publications concerning reproductive health, distributed to various nongovernmental organizations, mass media, parliamentarians, schools, and other counseling posts.

Bibliography

Cook, Rebecca J. "International Human Rights and Women's Reproductive Health." *Studies in Family Planning*, no. 24.

_____. "International Protection of Women's Reproductive Rights." *International Law and Politics* 24:645.

Freedman, Lynn P., and Stephen L. Isaacs. "Human Rights and Reproductive Choice." *Studies in Family Planning,* no. 18.

Hernandez, Berta E. "To Bear or Not to Bear: Reproductive Freedom as an International Human Right." *Brooklyn Journal of International Law*, no. 2 (1991).

Toranska, T. Interview with Wiktor Kulerski. "W ktorym miejscu jest bumerang" (In the year of the boomerang). *Rzeczpospolita,* no. 112.

The Polish Woman of Today

Analysis of a Model

BEATA LESCIAK

Each period creates its own models, which change with time and become more or less popular. At all times, male and female models differ from each other irrespective of women's liberation, character traits, norms of behavior, or way of life attributed to women. This is true for both propagated and accomplished models. The present analysis concerns the model of a woman in today's Poland. My focus is the contents of women's journals (highly popular periodicals with a large circulation).

The analysis of periodicals shows not only what a modern Polish woman would like to be but also, to some extent, what she really is, what she wants, and what she aims at. Only journals that emerged between 1989 and 1992 are analyzed; as follows even from perfunctory observation, the systemic changes of 1989 resulted in changes in the social sphere and in the propagation of new values, attitudes, and personal models. This is also apparent in journals. Defining their own range of interests, the editors of such periodicals stress the intention to implant new values in their readers, to propagate "a specific lifestyle, custom, fashion, interpersonal relations[,] ... to bring closer to the reader those we all admire and respect, those who can teach us a thing or two."[1]

What models are propagated in such new journals for modern women? Presented decidedly more often are Polish, not foreign, personages. What they all have in common is the fact that they have succeeded in life, have made their way right to the top. The women interviewed are successful businesswomen, actresses, painters, journalists, politicians, managers, directors, scientists. They are active women who control their own life and career, tough and stubborn go-aheads able to pursue their aims. One such woman says, for example: "I cannot afford it to submit to anybody. ... I don't believe in stars, prophecies, the soothing effect of religion. I believe in myself."[2] These traits have made it possible for those women to succeed and overcome adversities. The heroines of the articles are women who managed to overcome their own weakness, who ventured a radical change of their lifestyle, who took up new professional roles in the changed socioeconomic conditions and scored a success. They are models of enterprise, competence, and professionalism, which helped them achieve more than others.

Propagating this model, the journals not only present successful women but also openly exhort the readers to follow in their footsteps. A woman, these journals argue, should never limit herself to family life, solely the home, the husband, the children. One of the journals appeals to its readers as follows: "Invest in yourself: your looks and your pleasures. You lavish attention and care on others, but what about yourself? Are you really inferior?"[3] The author of another article finds it regrettable that Poland still has so few women of enterprise, although "we have many fine, well-educated and vigorous women who droop as soon as they get married and have children."[4]

This is not to say that being a wife and mother is not contained in the model of a Polish woman of today. Admittedly, there is a belief in these Polish periodicals that women who are not burdened with the duties of wife and mother find it much easier to get to the top and succeed in their job. The heroine of a report states: "Of course, what speaks for me is the fact that being single, I am always at my employer's service."[5] Another woman confesses: "I am not prepared to make this decision: Okay, let's get married, have children, and give up the career. I've worked too hard for it."[6] This attitude is characteristic of young women at the beginning of their professional careers. What the women's journals propagate is a squaring of the duties of a wife and mother with professional ambitions. No journal prompts the women to give up their career and to stay at home, but none suggests that they should do the opposite either. The women presented in the Polish press are usually wives and mothers who did not resign their own professional passions and try to square the two roles. The family matters a great deal to them—but the career matters just as much. An interviewed female politician states, "My family is still my haven: but it has never been an aim in itself."[7] This attitude is shared by many women who tell about their outlook on life in the discussed journals. It is possible to square the home with a career, and intense professional activity does not make them worse wives and mothers, they argue. Nothing but a combination of those two spheres can provide genuine self-fulfillment. This outlook is exemplified by a businesswoman's statement: "The head and moral leader of the family is the woman. The woman's mental and physical condition determines her family's situation. If she lets the hardships defeat her. If she renounces herself, her own ambitions and needs—such an attitude is sure to affect the entire family. . . . One should never use devotion to one's husband and children as an excuse to grow sluggish."[8]

Despite the propagation of the women's professional activity, the values shown as paramount or at least very important still include a happy married life, a good and understanding husband, fine children, a partner's sincere and deep affection. Ambitious women set on professional success often find this rather difficult to achieve: A succession of relationships end with divorce or breakups. A woman disappointed with her marriage explains: "In everyday life, men prefer their wives to be plain and meek"[9] rather than active and above average. The model of a Polish woman of today that follows from the journals under analysis also calls for assertiveness and enterprise in the sphere of relations with the opposite sex. The woman should value affection but prevent it from dominating her; love should not involve docility and submission to a partner. On several occasions the journals instruct their readers, "You should never renounce your own interests for your partner's sake."[10] Some other pieces of advice include: "Never give yourself up. Never try to conceal your strong points. . . . Don't let anybody boss you around. . . . Never give more than you can get."[11] "Be kind to him from time to time, grant him a favor or two—but never let him feel too secure. . . . Never let him notice that he is your everything."[12] "Go out on your own from time to time to make yourself more desired. . . . Make him just a little jealous every now and then."[13]

According to the model propagated in the journals, a modern Polish woman is liberated and unprudish. Sex is neither sex nor indissoluble marriage any longer. More and more often, public persons are interviewed, among other subjects, about their marriage, past and present relationships, sexual preferences, and opinions about sex. Reporting on female personages, the journals discuss not only their successful professional career but also their private lives, including, in some cases, the intimate details. It can be judged from the journals that a liberated and independent woman, able to express her erotic needs and preferences, has many sex partners during her lifetime and enters into many relationships—formal and informal, short- and long-lived alike. The heroines of press reports and interviews often mention their former marriages or relationships as stages in the process of acquiring life experiences and seeking happiness. Thus, the model propagated is not the traditional one of a family in which the husband is the woman's first and only partner and the marriage is a sacred and indissoluble union.

Despite the considerable social and moral transformations just discussed, the models propagated for Polish women of today traditionally attach great importance to motherhood, which is shown as the woman's paramount experience. Irrespective of professional ambitions and chances for success in a job, the woman should be a kind, caring, and loving mother. This is at least the model that emerges from the Polish women's magazines. Whether they live in a permanent relationship or not, a decided majority of the women such journals report on have a child or children. The heroines interviewed willingly tell about their children and mother-child relations; accompanying the reports and interviews are photographs of well-known women at home with their children. The women themselves also mention the great importance of motherhood in their life. The journals contain many declarations of the following kind: "When the children were born, my whole life changed. I gave them priority over everything else."[14] "What matters most in my life is my home and children. . . . I derive a lot of satisfaction from being with my children."[15] "The only indisputable sense of life are my children. All the rest becomes transformed with time."[16] "I have a husband and a son, which means I have somebody to live for."[17] The women's magazines present the charms of motherhood, multiple motherhood included. In recent years, over a dozen articles were published that dealt with women having their second child at an older age, as well as with the advantages of a child having a brother or sister. The approach to the problem is perhaps related to the stereotype of "Polish mother," still vivid in social consciousness, and to the traditional special importance of motherhood in Poland, where a woman has always been appraised in the context of being a mother and a good mother. This is why beside the model of a modern woman—a mother who is professionally active and set on succeeding in her job—the traditional model can still be found of the woman as mother and warden of the home.

Negative effects for the family of the woman's professional work are often mentioned in the journals. The communist system is accused of having destroyed the Polish family: with both parents working outside the home, the children being brought up by institutions (creches, kindergartens, schools, clubs), and each family member living a life of his or her own, lacking community spirit. This criticism of the present family model is usually accompanied by demands for women to initiate changes in this sphere. "For a long time now, Polish women have not been bringing up their children: the children are brought up on their own. . . . What the mummy earns is usually next to nothing[,] but working makes her feel good, that's all."[18] "The man has to earn enough to be able to provide for his family. The woman should run the house. . . . The fact remains: is that the home goes to pieces if not cared for by the woman . . . The good name of the HOUSEWIFE must necessarily be reestablished as soon as possible. She vanished with the rise of the communist system and should return with its fall."[19]

Housewives generally do not make heroines in the women's magazines; they sometimes appear in reports or interviews as the wives of popular men. The names they are given in such articles are "the bedrock of the home," "his Muse," "his better half," "the kind spirit," "his lady-love," "the mother of his children," "the perfect wife." Such women have no job; they help their husbands or run the house while the husband goes to work. The wife of a politician states, "I've submitted to my husband: he and his life have always mattered most."[20] Whenever housewives are mentioned at all in women's journals, their special talents at running the house or being the wife and mother are stressed, the activities involved are shown as both absorbing and attractive to the extent that the woman does not miss a job outside the home. Speaking of her decision to resign work, an actress states: "During rehearsals, the thought of having something to do at home oppressed me. Obviously I couldn't combine the two spheres. My home mattered more than the theater."[21] A politician's wife stresses the advantages of being a housewife: "I'd rather be a good housewife than an average chemist."[22] Admittedly, the women's magazines mention the successful, prizewinning, and title-bearing women more often; yet the other traditional model of the woman as wife and mother who runs the house and brings up the children does appear parallel to that of the successful career woman.

What the two models have in common is the fact that a woman should be active in controlling her own life; she ought to broaden her horizons, develop her interests, and see to her own improvement. Moreover, whatever her professional and social status, she ought never to forget that she is a woman. These periodicals offer a most explicit ideal of femininity. Thus, the Polish woman of today should take care of herself: her looks, dress, hair, and body. The journals contain a great variety of instructions telling women how to slim through exercise, cosmetic and medical procedures, and various diets. A lot of space in the women's magazines is devoted to face and body care; new beauty formulas and preparations of the well-known firms now entering the Polish market are discussed in detail. The journals also criticize the Polish women's former habits in the sphere of diet or fashion. Let me quote the following fragment by way of example: "The Polish women want to be attractive. They won't hesitate to spend considerable sums of money on clothes—the most expensive, latest fashion at that. The dress is to conceal all the defects of a woman's figure; it is in fact to work miracles, changing Cinderella into a princess. . . . Today, the foundation of health and beauty is a slim, well-shaped and compact body, peach-colored skin and a youthful face with no wrinkles."[23]

For this reason, the Polish journals print a great many articles on film or pop stars who manage to stay young and beautiful despite their age. Discussed with delight are the figures and faces of stars such as Joan Collins, Jane Fonda, Tina Turner, Gina Lollobrigida, Sophia Loren, and Linda Evans. But no mention is made of the fact that the looks of such women result from the work of teams of specialists. More and more space in the journals is taken by articles and ads concerning plastic surgery and other forms of beauty treatment. Each journal has a regular column devoted solely to such problems. The women are advised to take exercise, massages, special baths; to apply beauty masks; to learn antiwrinkle "facial aerobics"; to use special makeup. According to my estimates, a woman intent on taking care of herself based on such instructions would have to devote an average of 110 minutes a day to the suggested procedures (personal hygiene excluded). This seems hardly possible for the professionally active woman bent on making a career who is at the same time the perfect wife and mother. As shown, however, by analysis of the journals, she must necessarily cope with this task. Many of the instructions are formulated categorically: "You have to," "It's indispensable," "It's simply necessary," "It's the demand of our time," "Be modern," "Be a real woman," "You must find this much time for yourself. And don't make yourself believe you haven't the time."[24] The modern or "real" woman sees not only to her skin, body, and hair but also to her clothes: Her dresses must be stylish, smart, and carefully selected for the occasion. In addition to examples from foreign fashion shows, the journals present Polish fashion.

Women follow the journals' advice to feel better, to meet the demands of the modern world, but also to find and keep a man. As can be judged from the women's magazines, a man is one of a modern Polish woman's paramount values. Extensively discussed are happy relationships—the motive power of human activity and a sense of life. Single women are presented as seeking the partner of their dreams and waiting for their "other half." A relationship with a man—husband, fiance, or lover alike—is an ever-present element of the model propagated in women's periodicals. A lot of space is devoted to instructions on how to find a man, how to make him notice a woman, and how to keep his love. According to those suggestions, a woman should always be well kept and smart, at home as anywhere else: "Never wear hair rollers and a dirty dressing gown, and never go to bed at night with your face greasy with a facial."[25] A woman should do everything possible for a man to be confirmed again and again in his conviction that his partner treats him as the only real man in the world. Only then will he treat her as a real woman.

A woman should take care not only of her looks but also of her personality. Thus, the journals suggest books and films and prompt women to develop interests and activities in various directions as "the husband should see his partner not only as the wife but also as an interesting, attractive, and somewhat mysterious woman."[26] The perfect wife is also wise and tolerant, able to forgive her husband's weaknesses and even unfaithfulness and to stress his merits to satisfy his vanity. Most suggestions in this sphere are written from the woman's viewpoint, the woman being treated as the one who is more clever, reasonable, and able to compromise. Characteristically, however, none of the men's journals provides such advice to its readers; such periodicals never prompt men to be as tolerant, bighearted, and reasonable in their relationships with women. This confirms the traditional belief as to different moral norms, rules of behavior, and social expectations for men and women.

These differing norms are made quite explicit in these periodicals. In men's journals the problems of raising children or running a house are never mentioned; each women's journal, in contrast, has regular columns in which psychologists and educators give advice on parent-child relations. A lot of space is also devoted to furniture and interior decoration, maintenance of the kitchen, cleaning, and ways of caring for a partner's looks, hair, or choice of cosmetic preparations. What emerges from the journals is the image of a well-kept woman who successfully copes with raising children, cooking, and running a house and who sees to her husband's style, appearance, and happiness, making their home the place where he can find refuge from the stress and fatigue of his job.

What can be assembled from the preceding fragments concerning the values, character traits, and norms of behavior propagated by the press for the Polish woman? A Polish weekly publishes the following ardent appeal to women: "Get yourself lace bras and transparent blouses. Polish your nails and dye your hair whichever color you like. Take pride in being able to change into colorful butterflies in this hopelessly gray world. . . . Get an education and pursue a career. . . . Don't let anybody fool you into the alleged luxury of staying at home, having one baby after another, and waiting for your lord and master with dinner ready. . . . Be proud, reliable, wise, and conscious of your own worth."[27] Many feminist manifestos of this kind can be found. And yet the model propagated in Polish journals is decidedly antifeminist. Women are prompted to become independent and to score professional successes—but at the same time they are expected to square this task with household duties. It is quite obvious to all those concerned that nobody will ever ease a woman of some of her traditional duties related to the home and family. Thus, the perfect woman is one who reconciles the role of a wife and mother with a high professional status; who—despite the burden of household and professional duties—manages to stay beautiful, younger, slim, well kept, and smart, which means that she also finds time for herself. The extent of these requirements and the categorical tone of their presentation in periodicals make one suspect that the model is not really propagated but rather imposed on Polish women. Each of the journals that emerged in recent years tries to persuade its readers about their own imperfection; their chief aim should be excellence in all spheres possible.

The model propagated in women's magazines completely disregards reality. The suggested beauty formulas and procedures are most expensive, and the cost of all that is suggested by women's journals would exceed average monthly wages. Aside from the question of economic feasibility, a comprehensive realization of the propagated model seems impossible for other reasons as well: Twenty-four hours are too short a time to contain at least eight hours of professional work, nearly two hours of cosmetic procedures, eight hours of sleep (for health and beauty), time to help children with homework, time to cook dinner, time to read, time to go to the cinema or theater, and time to perform a variety of household chores. Therefore, it would be interesting to find out about the actual extent of realization of the propagated model by Polish women.

Late in 1992 a survey was conducted of more than one thousand Polish women over 18.[28] Unfortunately, it did not deal with all the problems discussed in journals; yet at least a part of the findings make it possible to compare the propagated model with the implemented one. Sixty percent of respondents were housewives and thus could not possibly be successful in their profession, which the women's magazines propagate so vigorously. This notwithstanding, most women (as many as 80 percent) were satisfied with their household duties. Professional work gave satisfaction to 25 percent of the working women; yet 70 percent of respondents would rather be a subordinate than a superior, which is against the propagated model. Few Polish women were active in the area of politics: A mere 13 percent, approximately, would agree to run for a seat in the commune or town council. And what about the average Polish woman's care for her looks? Against the propagated ideal of shapely and slim active woman, about 40 percent of respondents were overweight, and as many as 81 percent practiced no sports at all. The rest preferred hiking and bicycling (not the journals' favorites of calisthenics and aerobics).

In the sphere of erotic behavior Polish women failed to implement the propagated model, which assumes many sexual partners and extensive freedom of contacts within and outside marriage. Asked about the number of partners, many respondents (41 percent) admitted to having had just one; for 61 percent, their husband was their first partner. And 90 percent of the married women declared absolute fidelity. The traditional family values met with the greatest approval. Highly valued were a happy married life, a good partner, and mutual affection. For 97 percent of the married women, their marriage was among the things that mattered most in life.

No conclusion can be drawn from this survey regarding the impact of the propagated models on women's attitudes. Adoption of models propagated by the press is correlated with a younger age, whereas the sample included in the survey was composed of a large proportion of middle-aged and elderly women. Meanwhile, the new values and models have appeared in the Polish press only quite recently. For the time being, they may well be nothing but aspirations—the more so as their accomplishment is no easy task.

Notes

1. "Od redakcji" (From the editor), *Twoj Styl*, no. 1 (1990).
2. "Jej styl" (Her style), *Twoj Styl*, no. 1 (1992).
3. "Jak byc soba" (Being yourself), *Twoj Styl*, no. 5 (1993).
4. "Szczesliwy los" (Good fortune), *Twoj Styl*, no. 6 (1991).
5. "Kariery" (Careers), *Twoj Styl*, no. 8 (1991).

6. "Jej styl" (Her style), *Twoj Styl*, no. 2 (1992).

7. "Wolnosc smakuje jak poziomki" (Freedom tastes of wild strawberries), *Twoj Styl*, no. 10 (1991).

8. "Jej styl" (Her style), *Twoj Styl*, no. 6 (1991).

9. "Jej styl" (Her style), *Twoj Styl*, no. 1 (1991).

10. "Z malego flirtu wielka milosc" (A casual flirt turned passionate love), *Kobieta i Mezczyzna*, no. 22 (1992).

11. "Instrukcja obslugi mezczyzny" (Man: operating instructions), *Wszystko o milosci*, no. 7 (1992).

12. "Pokojowki jego serca" (A housemaid or lady-love), *Kobieta i Mezczyzna*, no. 16 (1992).

13. "12 przykazan dla zon" (Twelve commandments for wives), *Kobieta i Mezczyzna*, no. 6 (1991).

14. "Rodzinne wartosci" (Family values), *Twoj Styl*, no. 1 (1993).

15. "Jej styl" (Her style), *Twoj Styl*, no. 1 (1990).

16. "Jej styl" (Her style), *Twoj Styl*, no. 9 (1991).

17. "Jedno w zyciu przegapilam" (I missed just one thing in my life), *Kobieta i Styl*, no. 5 (1993).

18. "Portret intymny" (The intimate portrait), *Pani*, no. 5 (1992).

19. "Na dobre i na zle" (For good and all), *Magazyn Rodzinny*, no. 2 (1991).

20. "Przy mezu stanu" (Married to a statesman), *Twoj Styl*, nos. 7–8 (1992).

21. "10 pyten do obojga" (10 questions to a couple), *Zwierciadla*, no. 12 (1992).

22. "Przy mezu stanu" (Married to a statesman), *Twoj Styl*, nos. 7–8 (1992).

23. "Zainwestuj w siebie—ubedzie ci 10 lat" (Invest in yourself—and look ten years younger), *Magazyn Rodzinny*, no. 12 (1991).

24. "Porady kosmetyczne" (Beautician's advice), *Ona*, no. 3 (1992).

25. "Prawdziwa kobieta badz" (Be a real woman), *Pani*, no. 1 (1990).

26. "Porady dla pan w nowym roku" (New year's advice), *Twoj Styl*, no. 1 (1993).

27. "Nie palcie stanikow" (Don't burn your bras), *Kobieta i Mezczyzna*, no. 14 (1992).

28. Findings of a survey conducted by the Institute for Opinion, Market and Consumption Research GFK Polonia, published in the monthly *Twoj Styl*, nos. 1, 2 (1993).

Opportunities for Feminist Perspectives

Women's Studies in Poland

EWA GONTARCZYK-WESOLA

Much of the existing Polish research on women has obscured women's experiences of gender relations. This essay takes a look at how women have been lost in this research, what theoretical and practical implications follow from this silence, and how a feminist perspective might be relevant to the future conduct of research. A feminist perspective could contribute to the creation of a detailed picture of women's situation and to an understanding of women's experiences and gender issues. It could also help remove traditional patriarchal approaches, sex stereotypes, dated theories, and male/"neutral" biases. At the same time, a feminist-inspired research might provide conceptual tools for transforming society at all levels. In Poland, this seems particularly timely since so many changes are occurring in social and political life. However, despite evidences of the gradual growth of interest in feminist concepts and ideas, there are still many obstacles to the development of feminist scholarship. In this context, some solutions concerning the development of women's studies are suggested. Although the comments made in this essay relate specifically to research on women in Poland, I believe that this lack of specific research is not, in fact, a specifically Polish problem.

Since the end of the 1960s, a rapid development of research on women has taken place in many countries. This research has been greatly stimulated by the activities and concepts of the women's liberation movement, which has led to the recognition among academics that as a subject for research women have been neglected, overlooked, or distorted by existing scholarship. The activities of women in other countries have also led to the establishment of a new social science discipline and university courses in women's studies. With the growth of the discipline, a feminist perspective has been gradually adopted as a new approach to studies in other fields. Not only has the subject of women been included in research, but it has become possible to articulate radically new theories within mainstream disciplines based on feminist principles (DuBois 1987; Duelli 1984).

Nowadays, the growth of women's studies, broadly conceived, is evident in various perspectives developed in the great deal of research on women carried on within existing disciplines, such as anthropology, sociology, education, psychology, philosophy, and history. This growth is also visible in the great number of books and articles published on women's issues. Consequently, both the women's movement and women's studies make contributions to the development of various disciplines and to the construction of a new discipline—and hence to knowledge at large. They also effect great changes in women's condition, gender relations, and society as a whole in terms of progress toward gender equality and equal opportunities for women.

However, such great changes have not yet occurred in Poland. In this context, it seems inevitable to pose questions concerning Polish research: What kind of research on women is carried out? What perspectives are adopted in this research? Is there any evidence of trends toward the development of women's studies as a new discipline? Why has feminism as a perspective in science received relatively little attention?

It is not my intention to classify or assess Polish research in detail. I simply want to highlight the similarity between science and constructionism in Poland and elsewhere in the universality of male bias and the "inevitability" of women's position. I also want to point out a great difference: In Poland little attention is paid to feminist research; in other countries the necessity for radical scientific, social, and political changes has to a great extent already been recognized. Moreover, despite some resistance to feminist concepts, the complex and various forms of androcentrism in science have been demonstrated in many studies included in feminist critiques of science (Harding 1986). I believe that many concepts also have relevance to Polish science.

In general, women and gender issues are omitted in studies conducted in Poland (Gontarczyk-Wesola 1989). They focus only on neutral/male concepts, needs, experiences, values, achievements, and attitudes and include only men in research. But it is usually assumed that they represent "a whole society." Consequently, generalizations are made with regard, for instance, to "students," "teachers," and "workers." In fact, science maintains and transmits only male issues and concerns. Moreover, it even omits and distorts many facts, phenomena, and processes. In this context, already the question emerges, Is it possible to explain and understand the facts, phenomena, and processes pertaining to women? It seems obvious that not everything that concerns men also concerns women in one way or another. Besides, there are also issues with no equivalent existence in the experiences of both sexes. But because of the male/neutral perspective in research, the majority of issues, needs, and experiences of women remain unknown. They also remain unknown in cases where women are included in research because the analysis makes no distinctions according to gender.

There are some studies that focus on women or distinguish between men and women in analysis. They provide very valuable information concerning various issues related to women. But this research constitutes only a minority and is mostly subsumed with "neutral" science at large. Traditional attitudes toward women and sex stereotypes are still evident in many analyses. In most of these analyses women are presented in the context of their roles as mothers, wives, and homemakers. Some research does acknowledge the difficulties women face as women, particularly in living with traditional attitudes and habits, but these problems are then dismissed with references to improvements made under socialism. In fact, there are almost no references to the impact of gender as a social and cultural construct; hence gender relations, inequalities, and stereotypes remain unquestioned. Moreover, mention of feminist concepts is rare, and there are no calls for radical change.

"Sexist problems, concepts, theories, method and interpretations" remain intact; and the feminist "calling for more radical intellectual, moral social, and political revolution" (Harding 1986) remains almost without response. Indeed, the sexist perspective evident in research reflects the prevalence of traditional patriarchal attitudes in Poland and at the same time reinforces commonly held views. Moreover, women's traits, domains, and social roles are generally considered to flow naturally from women's psychology, which is seen as determined by biology. Thus, to a great extent women's needs, interests, potentialities, possibilities for self-actualization, and view of themselves as human beings, not just mothers, wives, and homemakers, are not taken into account. These omissions notwithstanding, in 1928 Polish sociologist Florian Znaniecki indicated that the roles of mother and father are social and cultural constructs, that the functions assigned to each change, and that in some cultures the roles were, and in some cases still are, assigned by society irrespective of biological ties. Moreover, he claimed that there are cultural differences in the definition of male and female roles, and he stated that women are particularly constrained in their roles because of patterns transmitted in education.

The omission of feminist concepts in Polish research is an obstacle, for instance, in the understanding of women's experiences, sex differences, and inequalities and in the creation of a clear picture of women's condition. In effect, it is difficult to suggest any ways to change their condition. In fact, there are a lot of difficulties in the recognition and development of a feminist perspective in research. This may be attributed to a variety of interrelated factors: a lack of accurate information on feminist studies and their impact on the transformation of science in other countries; few books and no journals on feminist studies from other countries available in Poland; weak and ineffective efforts to spread feminism in Poland. Feminist issues and activities are seldom discussed in scientific works or in mass media. The powers that be also claim that feminism would not be accepted in

Poland. Nevertheless, feminist questions are sometimes raised, but without explicit reference to feminism.

There is also reluctance among women who might be drawn to feminism to investigate it because of the distorted and negative images of feminism already in circulation in Poland. Feminist issues and activities have been presented very selectively and ridiculed often. Public opinion claims that "Western women are of a different kind and have different problems." Women's liberation movements have been associated with small and extreme groups of women engaged in the sex struggle. Feminists have been identified as man-haters and lesbians or as women who want to be men. Feminism has been connected primarily with the sexual liberation of women, and there has been almost no information about the issues of social and political liberation. At any rate, antifeminists claims that the situation of women is much better in Poland than elsewhere and that therefore these issues are of no relevance to Polish women's condition. In addition, feminist concepts have been considered a priori irrelevant because of the commonly held view that sex equality has been achieved and that there is no discrimination against women in Poland. Consequently, there has been a tendency to reject any distinction made between the sexes. Such distortions hinder the proper understanding of feminism and its aims. Thus, some researchers consciously or unconsciously avoid feminism as a term, along with its concepts. Some female researchers may be afraid of being labeled a feminist or faced with the question "By the way, do you hate men?" Or, paradoxically, these women may fear being accused of adopting "the emotional, typical, feminine approach in research, instead of the only proper, neutral, objective, male one."

In fact, much conceptual confusion remains to be cleared away in Poland. There is evidence of contradictory ideas of women, as well as traditional and progressive attitudes toward gender roles. It seems to be a result of manipulation and mystification concerning the usage of many notions despite the absence of their reflections in a social reality. The situation of Polish women is a consequence of policies and decisions previously made at the government level. Perhaps women were deluded by the presence of a women's organization established by order of the party to represent women's interests, as well as by universal assertions that gender equality had been implemented and women's position had improved.

Despite some gains, women's needs and issues were treated superficially and subordinated to other priorities. In fact, women were not able to articulate their claims because they were not aware of the impact of gender on their condition. They were not conscious of inequalities; their experience seemed to them natural and inevitable. In Polish society the roles and position of the sexes are seen as inevitable and desirable, and therefore there is little pressure for radical reform. Even with the current changes in social and political life and the promise of a democratic state, conditions are not favorable for feminism. Women are faced with the pressure to resume their traditional gender roles.

The principles of sex equality and women's emancipation are fundamental issues for both socialism and feminism. And feminism is sometimes identified with socialist principles and equated with changes that were previously brought about in Poland. Nevertheless, sex equality and women's emancipation were not achieved. Policy was based primarily on slogans and not on actions. As a result, professional roles were simply added to women's roles as mothers, wives, and homemakers. Women's condition was particularly hard, and sex inequalities and gender relations remained intact.

But many people are convinced that there was sex equality and that women were indeed emancipated. Since many Poles were not satisfied with such a social order, they prefer traditional patterns and reject feminism. These preferences affect the attitudes of researchers. Some researchers may be very traditional, some may prefer to avoid feminist issues, and some argue that the distinction between male and female is not necessary. In Poland, "there are more important issues than women questions" (Duelli 1984). It is evident that patriarchal and socialist systems caused many contradictions and paradoxes concerning the issues of gender and sex equality. Inevitably, women have to disentangle these confusions to liberate themselves. As yet only feminism offers methods and concepts to cope with this task.

Finally, despite evidence of the gradual growth of interest in feminism, there are still many obstacles to the development of feminist scholarship. Polish women have to face a feminist challenge because there is an urgent need for a feminist perspective in Polish research. They may follow the women of other countries by researching, teaching, establishing centers, making networks, and communicating with each other. All these may provide premises for the attachment of real meanings to distorted and absent issues and the reconstruction of knowledge, as well as for activities to change women's (and men's) condition and transform society at all levels.

References

DuBois, E. C. *Feminist Scholarship*. Urbana: University of Illinois Press, 1987.

Duelli, Klein R. "The Intellectual Necessity for Women's Studies." In *Is Higher Education Fair to Women?* ed. S. Acker and D. W. Piper. Guilford: SRHE & NFER-NELSON, 1984.

Gontarczyk-Wesola, E. "The Restructuring of Women's Education for New Forms of Work and Lifestyles." *European Forum of Socialist Feminists*. Internationella Konfernsen Rapport No. 5 (1989).

Harding, S. *The Science Question in Feminism*. Los Angeles: Open University Press, 1986.

Lesbians in the Middle

Lesbian Organizing in Poland— an Interview with Romana Ciesla

TANYA RENNE

My name is Romana, and this is Violeta. We are lovers from Krakow and the organization Lambda. I have been involved in Lambda two and a half years, but Violeta has been there since the beginning—three years.

We try to be active members of Lambda; for two years we have organized lesbian meetings—gatherings, trips. We correspond with lesbians all over Poland. We gave an advertisement in the gay newspaper *Enache*—a short letter of appeal about lesbian women with the main question "Are there any lesbians in Poland?" "If there are, please write to us"—please appear, please let us know that you are out there, let's make connections in Poland between different towns and different women. Do not let divided groups and isolated lesbians exist in Poland. Let's be together. It was our idea to let lesbians know about each other.

From this first appeal we got thirty or forty responses; that was 1991. We organized the first meeting in Krakow for those women who wrote letters. They wanted to meet with each other, so we organized our first meeting in Krakow in June 1991. It was a very nice, a very good meeting, a very useful three days. We spent the time discussing and getting to know each other. Our main purpose was to let them all know we exist—that we are all similar in spite of the fact that we are different; we have so much common. It taught us self-confidence and power. This was the best thing for lesbians in Poland because we are so isolated and living separately, especially in small towns and villages. Some are so poor and completely uncertain of their identity.

For the second meeting, in autumn 1991, not all of the women from the first meeting came; it was in Zakopane. Twenty-eight women were there; it was our first meeting in the mountains. We had a wonderful time (with wonderful weather) talking and drinking wine and beer, and again we spent time discussing with each other and getting to know everyone. But when we wanted to discuss our problems more seriously—roles, responsibilities, anything, on radio, newspaper—some of them thought we were too small to organize such a big enterprise.

Our goals are to coordinate a community to encourage other women to contact each other, as well as to meet and edit a lesbian newspaper. Maybe to organize some other events, like trips or something like that. The worst thing is that we still have no activists in Polish lesbian groups. Most of the women are passive—they are still waiting, waiting for something to happen. Truthfully speaking, we, too, are passive, not true leaders. We would like to do something but together with others, or support somebody who would like to make things happen, but people only look around and ask what is in it for them. So the situation is very difficult, sometimes too difficult for us.

We write for our newspaper because our first activity was started this way (by writing to *Enache*); we were trying to change this newspaper a little bit, trying to get more lesbian pages (*Enache* is a monthly gay magazine, issued out of Poznan). The editors are all men—four or five of them—and they are very kind to us. They often repeat, "Please send us your materials—please give us what you have about lesbians." They send us pictures, and we write about our own experiences, these meetings we organized, and we also send them pictures of our own. But it takes two or three months to edit and publish each issue, so often the materials are very dated when they finally appear. And these men print pictures of naked women because, according to their sense of justice, they think that we like to watch naked women; so they put completely stupid illustrations with our articles. We are not very happy because it is still a gay newspaper with naked men on the front side, naked men on the back side. It is possible that lesbians living in small towns are afraid to buy such a pornographic newspaper; perhaps they are ashamed to take such a magazine to hand.

There were also initiatives in Poland to issue a lesbian newspaper. It was called *Sigma*. It was a unique initiative by two women from a small town in the south of Poland. They wanted very much to edit a lesbian newspaper, but they weren't prepared; they didn't collect many materials. With a lot of effort and money they printed two thousand copies and then had big problems with distribution. After the first issue they distributed them by official means, but in the end the official distributor refused, so the whole enterprise went down the drain, and we still have no lesbian newspaper. We think the only way is to occupy more and more pages in *Enache*, try to take over more and more space until we can do it alone.

Enache is important because it is a resource for information—the lack of which is a very important and a very big problem in Poland. Some lesbians can't be confident human beings because of a lack of information about themselves, about their rights, their possibilities. They are so afraid that this fear minimizes their lives.

Part Two

 # Slovakia and the Czech Republic

Importing Ideology?

I believe that women are the eyes and ears of
the world; we see everything, hear everything,
feel everything; there are no secrets among us.
        —Member of the Skopje Women's Movement

First and foremost in the minds of many feminists in Slovakia and the Czech Republic is the reeducation of the citizenry to an awareness of rights and responsibilities in the new democracies. Abortion is indirectly restricted by high costs and further aggravated by the rise of unemployment among women. Just as most other Eastern European communities have lost women in parliament and other avenues of influence, so have the Czech and Slovak Republics (although it is questionable that the influence in the good old days, when 20–35 percent women held seats in government, matched their real numbers). The Czech Republic faces special problems with a wave of tourism and thus a rise in crime, an explosion of the free market, and a backsliding of attention to women's concerns. The Czech economy is still struggling, now to keep up with expansion and demand both economically and infrastructurally. This great economic pressure on Czechs and Slovaks is especially hard on the women who bear the double burden of occupational work and domestic work. In a piece entitled "Women's Priorities and Visions," Jirina Vrabkova addresses the low percentage of women in government and the "hypocritical proclamations on women's artificial emancipation" that the past forty years have placed on women and the present women's movement. She, like her Polish counterparts, expresses fear of old communist ideologies replaced by new ideologies.

Jirina Siklova addresses the difficulties with Western feminist approaches more directly in her essay entitled "McDonald's, Terminators, Coca Cola Ads—and Feminism?" In it she discusses many of the blossoming women's organizations in the Czech Republic and the reasons for their aversion to feminism. She creates a very clear analysis of the effects of the last forty years of nonparticipation, forced ideologies, and indoctrination.

Jirina Siklova and Jana Hradilkova talk about the growing awareness of violence against women and the reasons this violence is so difficult to combat. The observations in their essay "Women and Violence" are true not only for every country in the region but also for most of the rest of the world. The rise of crime in the street, as Jirina Vrabkova states in her earlier essay, has been a result of "freedom." People are not afraid of being sent away now for crimes against the state—they feel that if this is a democracy, then they can do what they please.

In "The Change in Reproductive Behavior in the Czech Republic," Alexandra Buresova looks at the work of reproductive rights and the legislative changes affecting women in this regard. She includes information about the most recent abortion law proposal and attitudes concerning abortion.

Jana Stepanova talks bluntly and humorously about coming out as a lesbian feminist during and after the revolution in "A Lesbian." She speaks about her relationship with her mother and the ways in which she has formed her identity as a woman, a lesbian, and a feminist in groups of women, around women's issues and individuality. Jana and so many women like her give a picture of what feminism and feminist discourse are likely to look like in the very near future as they organize and realize their own issues as women, daring to make them a reality.

Also included in this part is a piece by Eva Hauser, a feminist science fiction writer, entitled "Men Are Burglars of Extraterrestrial Origin!" She writes about her journey to feminism and describes how the genre of science fiction can be a vehicle for social change and awareness during periods of oppression.

❖ Women's Priorities and Visions

JIRINA VRABKOVA

Since the collapse of the totalitarian regimes in the countries of Central and Eastern Europe, Czechoslovakia included, a set of changes in the political and socioeconomic field has started. Forty years of communist patriarchal rule and its hypocritical proclamations on women's artificial emancipation, motivated by the need to employ the cheapest labor force, have caused their reluctance and aversion to politics, both national and international alike. In addition, this aversion has been multiplied by activities of the Czechoslovak Union of Women, one centralized women's organization working closely with the Communist Party. The Federal Union of Women has been closed down, but the Czech Union of Women continues to conduct business on behalf of all women.

Indeed, a long period of isolation from information about women's movements abroad has also been a reason for Eastern European women's reluctance to emphasize their feminine identity. Which, on the contrary, has been founded in response to Western feminist movements. The feminism in the 1960s and 1970s, as it was known in Western Europe and the United States, did not surface here. It was unfeasible because women here were "building socialism" and simply were not acquainted with feminism.

In practice, these conditions meant that women worked very hard to bolster the family budget, receiving one-third less salary than their male counterpart, taking care of the family, visiting compulsory political training and meetings. It is no wonder that Czech women, living for many years with the stress of being good workers and good mothers at the same time (this sexist division of roles was supported and sustained by men and their mothers) are fed up with engaging in any form of social or political activity.

Feminism and emancipation are despised words here. There is a widely held opinion that our women are emancipated enough "thanks," but no thanks to the previous regime. We therefore must also emancipate men. Meanwhile, women have been hustled into leading roles of mothers and housewives, while men have become passive and neglectful of their roles as fathers. But this dominating role of women in the family is limited to the private sphere only. Outside the family, as a rule, they accept more subordinate roles, particularly in the workplace.

Feminism here means just another "ism"—one ideology replaced by another one—or a vision of a militant, frustrated, unsuccessful (usually ugly) woman who is hostile and man-hating. Czech women do not believe that the Western form of women's struggle has brought something positive to them. They cannot understand, for example, the demands of Western women for more kindergartens and day care centers. In our country some women think that the behavior of their children in a group is one of the bad influences that causes increased criminal activity.

Women in Czechoslovakia have the option of maternity leave for three years, which is considered, controversially, an advantage, on one side, but, on the other side, a disadvantage as it prevents contact with their profession and the larger society. There is "a cult of motherhood" but at the same time no possibility for earning money during maternity leave. Thus, a woman on leave is dependent on her husband and loses career opportunities in the process. The situation of single mothers is very difficult, but there are also opinions that the children of divorce should not be given exclusively to their mothers.

It is not my intention to cite all phenomena of inequality together with the reasons they occur in our society. Instead, I simply want to point out several examples. Girls marry at a relatively young age (between nineteen and twenty-one, very often as a result of an unwanted pregnancy), an increasing divorce rate (in Prague nearly one-third of all marriages end in divorce), an increasing rate of abortion, greater unemployment, and thus a feminization of poverty (women represent about two-thirds of the total 190,000 unemployed in the Czech Republic).

Women's passivity in regard to participation in politics is matched by their underrepresentation in the economic reforms of privatization. The political arena is absolutely and undoubtedly dominated by men: The number of women in the Federal Assembly has decreased from 24 percent to 9 percent. (A quota system is not a possibility here because it would stimulate too many memories from the communist past.) Furthermore, that 9 percent is hardly for the advancement of women. These legislators are recruited from church circles or represent their party's interests or both. They intend to make a political career rather than promote women's rights. They therefore must adjust their behavior to a male way of doing things. It is not fashionable to make a political career and at the same time deal with women's issues. Even so-called independent women members of parliament urge women to undertake typical women's activities, such as creating small local health groups to educate children and men in habits of personal hygiene (perhaps the wrong idea was meant in the right way—to start with ecological awareness and mental hygiene—but this approach is reminiscent of women's way of thinking in the 1950s).

With regard to involving more women in a grassroots movement, in other political activity, and in efforts to increase their influence, there was an attempt to form our first lobbying structure, "Initiative of Women 91." This lobby addressed members of parliament but broke up several months later. Indeed, there are no intentions or proposals to form a club of women parliamentarians or a council of equality within the republic governments. Rather, opinion favors having the appropriate institution or ministry deal with family issues instead of equality. (The Government Council for the Questions of the Women and Family, in Slovakia, and the Confederacy of Women's and Family Initiatives, in the Czech Republic, have proved quite insignificant for the advancement of women.)

In the field of Czechoslovak diplomacy, a successful step forward has been made in the representation of women: There are now six women ambassadors. But they represent the exception rather than the rule. There is no systematic effort to prepare women for political participation or engage them in it.

Closely bound to women's weak political influence (and that of men as well) is their insufficient knowledge of law and citizen legislation. For example, a number of international documents and conventions related to the status of women (and ratified by our state) are being neglected, often because of ignorance and unfamiliarity. (Unfortunately, members of parliament lack knowledge of these documents, thereby making their implementation very difficult and sometimes leading to misinterpretation.) Unfamiliarity with such important conventions may preempt appropriate discussions about their provisions (as in the case of the right of the life of an unborn child during disputes on the text of the Charter of Principal Rights and Liberties, a document similar to a bill of rights). In this regard, the Initiative of Women 91 has tried to distribute copies of the U.N. Convention About the Elimination of Forms of Discrimination Against Women to parliamentarians in the Czech Republic since the shameful debate on amendment to the abortion law took place.

Another problem for women is forced prostitution. (This theme does not get much press because of insufficient statistics as well as the assumption that prostitution is a "profession." I tackle this problem from the perspective of growing tourism in Eastern Europe.) "Czechoslovakian girls are pretty, snugly, educated, cultured, and, at the same time, cheap," remarks one customer. In Prague alone, there are about thirty thousand prostitutes (detailed data are unavailable because of lack of registration—an increasingly dangerous omission in the era of AIDS). New business law has not clarified this "profession" and has not determined the conditions under which it may be performed (since the women are not registered, they do not pay income taxes). "High-class" prostitutes are cultivated, speak several languages, and earn about DM 300 ($200) an hour (a fantastic amount compared to the average monthly salary of DM 188). "Low-class" women who step in the streets are unmercifully exploited by pimps. Women's motivation to work at this profession is predominantly economic ("My husband does not like it, but he agrees with it, knowing that nowhere else can I earn such a high salary"). To continue this joyless paragraph, I should mention trafficking in women—a phenomenon associated in our minds with the Third World but nevertheless occurring here. Hundreds of these cases are listed in police statistics, but because of an absence of relevant laws and an insufficient enforcement of the few laws that do exist, the police are quite helpless to stop this crime.

A conference on the traffic in women and forced prostitution was organized by the Committee for Equality Between Men and Women of the Council of Europe in September 1991. However, despite the fact that Czechoslovakia became a member with full rights and received a proper invitation, it did not take part in such an important event.

Given the essential political and socioeconomic changes occurring within Slovakian and Czech societies, and the fragility of a newborn democracy, a review of values is advisable and vital. How do we deal with the past but at the same time handle increasing nationalism, xenophobia, anti-Semitism, racism, and ethnic conflict, all of which slow down economic reform? The role of women and their status need deep, sustainable research, and the women's movement needs more time and space for self-identification within reoriented economic, sociopolitical, environmental, and cross-cultural dimensions, as well as with international women's movements.

"Gender studies" has been introduced into the curriculum of the Department of Social Work and Applied Sociology at Charles University in Prague. There has also been an attempt to collect a women's library. We are especially lacking in a women's publishing house and positive advertising.

Keeping in mind all these facts and realities in light of the hectic and unexpectedly fast pace of change, I am very skeptical about whether women will be able to form a new and positive awareness of their need for emancipation. Perhaps a new wave of feminists will be recruited from the next generation, a generation exposed to new discriminatory and aggravated conditions and limited access to the labor market in particular. Women are still manipulated to fit into certain stereotyped social models (in spite of the fact that young girls behave in very democratic ways). According to some woman intellectuals, "We must first learn democracy and thereafter try to do something for women," or "It is necessary to turn back in order to begin to strive again."

McDonald's, Terminators, Coca Cola Ads— and Feminism?

Imports from the West

JIRINA SIKLOVA

The views expressed here bear the mark of more than forty years of the Iron Curtain and the subsequent isolation of the women in the former communist states from the rest of the world. Thus, women from the West and women from the former communist countries react to different experiences, and our knowledge of each other is distorted.[1] We frequently use the same words, the same terms, yet their content is different because different historical experiences underlie the same concept. This difference holds for all East-West negotiations, including our attitudes toward feminism. Please realize that our rejection of many of the ideas supported by feminism is primarily a reaction to our own recent past, as well as to the indoctrination we were subjected to for decades.

The intellectual movement of Western European and North American feminists between the 1960s and the 1980s bypassed the whole of Central and Eastern Europe. In Czechoslovakia the feminist movement was developing—just like everything else—under the trusteeship of the Communist Party, as part of the national ideology. The only women's organization—the League of Czech Women—was openly called "the prolonged hand of the party." The social and economic conditions experienced by women living under communism were also different from those of their Western counterparts. Since one income was not enough to live on, it was necessary for women to enter the workforce, and thus the majority of women did not regard the involuntary "choice"—the possibility or necessity of gainful employment—as an opportunity for self-realization or self-assertion. Consequently, we lost the illusion that the mere fact of being gainfully employed, of having a job, can "liberate" women. Most of the men working by our

side were not self-confident bosses but people similarly "downtrodden" by
the overprotective party and the government. Thus, men were not our rivals but humble partners working at the next desk or machine. Women did
not have to conform themselves to the political regime as much as men did
because, as a rule, they were not the main breadwinners of the family and
their professional work was not the only form of their "career." Women
could also use their duties to their children and their family as an excuse to
get out of paid work, or they could even "escape" to maternity leave.

For these reasons, women today in postcommunist countries do not feel
such an aversion to men as is the case with a great many Western European
feminists. As women we were suppressed not by men as such but by a political system that lacked distinct sexual characteristics. This is also why, for the
moment, proclamations of patriarchy under capitalism tend to evoke memories of political indoctrination. The hatred, the militantly ideological manifestations of some feminists, and the ideological character of feminist trends
make us feel the same nausea that we used to experience with references to
"class struggle." Today we are unfortunately at the stage of aversion against
every "ism." And "feminism" regrettably has this ending. Moreover, for the
most part we know next to nothing about the genuine feminism of our time.
Our knowledge ends with Clara Zetkin,[2] where we usually switched off our
attention. In this respect, we have a total gap—literally, an abyss.

For the time being, we in this country are not aware of our essential interests as women. This awareness will, however, emerge hand in hand with
our society's endeavor to create, or assimilate itself to, a capitalist social
order. I believe, however, that our feminist movement is going to develop
not on the basis of taking up some great ideologies but rather on the basis
of solving concrete, nonpolitical, and primarily practical tasks.

Women and Politics Today

Prior to the elections of 1990, forty-two political parties were registered in
the Czech and Slovak Republics, but not one of them had a program specially aimed at solving women's problems. Not one political party is
headed, or even vice-chaired, by a woman. After the elections in 1990, 8
percent of the deputies in the government were women. In the Czech Republic today, not one woman is a member of the government. Hence, the
"visibility" of women in politics is null.

The number of new, small, spontaneously arising women's organizations
is, however, increasing, and this is what I personally consider important.
These organizations are—and will continue to be—the actual roots of further development of the women's movement and of feminism in postcommunist Europe.

Until the overthrow of communism in 1989, there was only one women's organization, the Women's League, whereas at present there are twenty-seven new women's organizations registered in the Czech Republic. Only seven of these are focused on politics or form a part of a political party, such as the Social-Democratic Women, the National-Social Women, the Club of Christian Women. However, not even the politically focused women's organizations have their own, independent political platforms; they merely support political parties in which 90 percent of the leading positions are occupied by men. Five of the new women's organizations are focused on professions, for example, the Association of Women Entrepreneurs; four are religiously oriented; others are particular groups of women, such as the Organization of Lesbian Women. Finally, there are groups organized around ethnic and national identities; for example, the Union of Romany Women strives to raise the cultural and educational levels of the Romanies (Gypsies), publish their own periodical, and cooperate with and stimulate other Romany organizations.

Women also occupy important positions in ethnic and national organizations of various kinds. For instance, the Polish minority is headed by a woman who was previously a member of parliament. Within the framework of the thirty-four national associations, there are presently thirteen Romany organization, in all of which women play active roles. Although these and other women's organizations are not interested in feminism, and explicitly refuse it, the work they are doing for women is important. It is on this basis that the women's movement will eventually develop in this country—not as a movement directed from above, controlled by some party, but as a movement deriving its existence from the interests of women.

Captives of the Past

Given all of these factors, Western feminists must not regard the verbal rejection of feminism that they might encounter in contemporary Eastern Europe as a reaction to their views. It is primarily a reaction to our recent communist past. As an example, let me mention the organization Prague Mothers. It is one of the first really informal, spontaneously arisen organizations of women who are interested in ecological problems and stand up for the interests of women. Prague Mothers even organized demonstrations during the communist regime and was subsequently persecuted. However, the organization outright rejects feminism and even refuses to discuss it. Members consider it an area that is of interest only to university-educated women or else regard it as a kind of intellectual deviation. In spite of this, or perhaps because of it, these women, with assistance from women in Germany, have already established a network of "centers for mothers," presently comprising twenty centers located in various small towns all over the republic. Other groups of women have organized assertiveness training for women, seminars in management for women, art exhibits and women's theater, and summer sojourns for Romany girls and offer crime prevention counseling and help for women victims of crime. All of these socially active women, however, verbally reject feminism, and for this reason are in turn frequently rejected by Western intellectuals.

We are, without a doubt, captives of our past. I am afraid, however, that at times Western European and American feminist intellectuals are captives of their own ideology. When Western feminists ask us how many times we have demonstrated against our government, against the discrimination of women in employment, or against lower pay, we are at a loss as to what to say. We have not demonstrated; we do not revolt as women. In this country, the political struggle for women's rights has not yet been included in our program. Czech women were obligatorily organized for too long; hence, they tend to connect liberty with the liberty not to be organized in any way. They regard as positive anything related to the forbidden past, anything "retro." If it were economically possible, Czech women would perhaps prefer to stay at home for some period of time and just play the role of hausfrau, of which the West is so scornful.

The small, politically uninterested women's organizations, which are established and dissolved in the course of a few months, frequently make Western European women politicians smile. They have no ideology, they lack political profiles, and they defy all examination and sociological analysis. Their protagonists are not interested in the philosophy of feminism and will not play any role in future political elections. Yet now, right now, they are of extreme importance to us. Women, both as women and as citizens, learn through them to organize themselves and to become conscious of and stand up for their own interests. Through these activities people turn into citizens.

Let me introduce an analogy: If there are large burns on the body, it is necessary to implant small bits of skin in the burned places and then patiently wait and attend to the implants. Some implants wither away, while others heal up and expand, giving rise to a substitute skin covering the burned area. In our republic, and I think in the other countries of postcommunist Europe, we are at the stage of developing a "new skin." That is, we are at the stage of forming citizens—citizens, for the present moment, irrespective of sex differences. If we were to thwart this process through impatience, the "healing" would be delayed. This is why I ask Western feminists not to recommend that we fight for something. Do not ask us what political program we have. We have none. We are suspicious of all the isms. At this stage of our development, feminism is no more than another ideology to us.

Feminism Meets Skepticism

Feminism is more or less unknown to us, but we object to its being frequently presented as a new, global ideology of liberation suitable for the
whole world, as a new messiah. I have even heard slogans such as "Communism is dead. Today it has been replaced by feminism, for women are a
group that for centuries has been exploited, kept down, and exposed to oppression." We have unfortunately become certain that someone who has
previously been exploited and oppressed is not necessarily the best leader of
society. Socialism was a failure; the working class did not prove competent
as a leader and bearer of revolution. Party bosses who allegedly led the
working class simply introduced ideology to it and spoke for it. Every now
and then I have the impression that something like that is going on in
today's feminism.

We also resent the forthright leftist air that feminism has assumed—or
maybe that is its actual orientation. In our country, leftist policy is regarded
with aversion. And so the sins of the communist past are being transferred
to feminism. Pardon us for it, and please try to understand rather than to
explain and condemn. Moreover, we object to some of the Western feminists' insensitive conduct toward us: As those who "already know everything," they class our arguments and counterarguments among "teething
troubles" we will soon get over. This sometimes reminds us of the attitudes
of apparatchiks or of those imparting political indoctrination.

Furthermore, we consider certain issues of feminism to be problems that
have their source in luxury. A great many questions propounded by feminists are at present pointless for us. They are, for the time being, a luxury
for which we have neither time nor the right conditions to think about.

For all that, we are not poor creatures, or victims—we are just different.
Take the differences as they are, and tolerate our diversity. Accept that for
the moment women in Central and Eastern Europe will not be a dynamic
factor in the transformation of society. We must first reach a stage of being
able to identify ourselves as women, not just as members of the downtrodden—only then will it be possible for us to take more interest in feminism.

Frontiers have been opened, and we are experiencing a kind of psychic
shock, an agoraphobia. We are at a loss about what to do with liberty. We
need an orientation. Give us time for our self-discovery. Only then can we
be partners in dialogue and in the movement. According to what Western
feminists themselves say, Western European and North American women
were subjected to oppression as a consequence of capitalist patriarchy. We
were enslaved by the omnipotent Communist Party.

Throughout the years Western European and American feminists have
had the opportunity to seek and define their program, to choose and dis-

cuss it. We could only accept or, in exceptional cases, reject the political program given to us. That being so, please give us time for our self-discovery. I would not like to see the women of Central and Eastern Europe merely taking over Western feminists' views and again imitating someone else. I would not like for the new Europe to be uniform in its thinking, for the bygone uniform decoration in the form of red flags and the hammer and sickle to be replaced by an analogous uniformity in the form of McDonald's restaurants, or Schwarzeneggers in the role of Terminators, or Coca Cola advertisements, or other homogeneous, maybe even feminist, symbols. Harmony always arises from a multitude of different tones; beauty lies in diversity. If we proceed from both Western feminists' experiences and our own, from the different types of oppression and stress, then something new may arise not only for feminism but perhaps also for the whole of Europe. I would welcome this. Please tolerate our dissimilarity. Give us time and space.

Notes

1. This essay was originally written for presentation at a conference in North America and thus addresses a Western audience.

2. Clara Zetkin (1857–1933) was an East German feminist and one of the founders of the German Communist Party. For many years, she led the international communists' women's movement.

▦ Women and Violence

JIRINA SIKLOVA
JANA HRADILKOVA

People in postcommunist states are currently beginning to learn their rights, as well as learn how to be citizens—how to take care of their own interests and make their own decisions. Along with this process there is a growing awareness of human rights and the rights of women. Just recently we have begun to discuss whether force is part of sex, whether sexual relations are possible without force, when force is "still normal," and when it is pathological. This essay is one such exploration.

Before the revolution, domestic violence was heavily influenced by the fact that people lived in constant fear of threats and repression and that a large part of the population had to, or thought it had to, conform to the regime. Families became places where people were able to act naturally, without conformity. Thus, the family was where people usually reacted to stress and to feelings of being demeaned at work or during political meetings. Men were more likely to be in leadership positions and therefore were subject to more public pressures, which they often released within the family setting. In relation to their wives, they acted "typically macho."

Today both men and women are used to such more-or-less accepted behavior, which is furthermore reinforced by the fact that men are more likely to be the founders of new businesses and to have incomes that are substantially higher than those of women. Increasing, violence in the Czech Republic is also encouraged

- by the letting loose of the control and repression that under totalitarianism were normally applied to anyone who committed crimes
- by the shift toward a new structure of power and decisionmaking
- by contemptuous feelings toward the previous police regime
- by the fact that the police force and judicial system were misused under communism
- by the dilution and transformation of the police
- by the opening up of borders and the possibility of international criminal gangs entering the Czech Republic

Women's Attitudes Toward Violence

Women in postcommunist states often accept brutal behavior, including sexual harassment, as obvious reflections of "manhood," and so far they have not protested against it. Under totalitarianism, questions of men's and women's behavior were not explored in sociological studies or in the popular press. Until recently, sociology was reduced to mere state ideology, which is why it did not pay attention to these questions. Therefore, men and women today do not realize some of the unreasonableness of certain reactions and attitudes. Citizens of postcommunist countries have an even harder time reflecting on their own behavior. Presently, more attention is given to economic questions, issues of consumption, the free market, and political transformation, than to questions of gender.

People generally don't know what is classified under the category of "punishable crimes of rape." Even among specialists this classification has been defined only since the beginning of 1993. Most people do not accept the fact that a woman has the right to refuse intercourse even after giving the offender the idea that she is interested in having sex with him—for example, if she willingly goes up to his apartment for a glass of wine—and that nonconsensual sex in such a circumstance constitutes a crime. Men refuse to believe this, and women do not know their rights.

Sexual harassment, about which so much is written in the West, is not discussed very often here; most women do not know what it is. Obscene comments about women, women being criticized for their appearance, various "playful" smacks, and pseudoflattery are routine in most workplaces, and it even sometimes seems as if women welcome them. For example, kissing a woman's hand is considered a sign of being a modern gentleman and is seen as challenging the previously required relation of "comradeship" between men and women. Sexual relations between bosses and their subordinates, verbal allusions to sex, and sexual jokes at business dinners (previously at team meetings) are routine and no one—to the surprise of Americans—objects to it. Only recently have these problems been discussed and written about. But hardly had we encountered the term *sexual harassment,* which can be translated as sexual bothering and unwanted sexual attention, when some comic twisted this term into *sexual rattling* (a pun on the Czech word *haraseni,* which sounds like harassment but has a different meaning) and the whole issue had its backbone broken.

Legal Codes on Sexual Violence

Rape, according to the Czech legal code, is defined as the use of violence, the threat of immediate violence, or the misuse of a woman's inability to defend herself to force a woman into sexual intercourse. An offender's punishment depends upon a victim's age and on her relationship to the offender. The object of this law is the right of the woman to make independent decisions with respect to her sexuality. The crime of rape can be committed only upon a woman (and not upon a man) who is not the offender's wife. The offender can only be a man, but a woman who hurts another woman through violence or threat of violence in order to help a man in forcing the victim into intercourse can be considered a co-offender. Included under rape is sexual violence against a woman with whom the offender lives but who refuses to have intercourse with him. Her physical maturity and sexual experience are not taken into consideration.

Coercion into intercourse, according to the law, means that the offender used violence, that is, physical force, with the object of overcoming or preventing serious resistance from the woman and forced her into sexual relations against her will. Intercourse is defined as the joining of the male and female sexual organs. As long as forced copulation occurs, the crime is considered rape, whether or not the offender experienced sexual gratification. Contact of the sexual organs is not, however, considered sufficient.

The definition of coercive intercourse is restricted to situations in which the woman gives up the possibility of resisting only because she sees her resistance as completely hopeless. She gives in to the attacker because she has no other choice. If the offender considers her resistance weak—that it is only a pretense and that in reality she does want to have intercourse with him—legally his behavior would be considered a factual mistake, and the offender would not be held responsible for committing an intentional crime. Included in this case are situations in which the offender did not know that the situation fulfilled the legal definition of rape.

The laws demarcate conditions under which the victim is limited in her freedom of choice and can't act independently because, to a certain extent, she is dependent in a substantial way upon the offender's power—for example, if he is her father. If she was not dependent upon him, she would not choose to take part in this action. Women who in such cases submit to sexual relations are in fact being violated; this even includes cases where the offender is the woman's ex-husband. This is a fact that most women who are undergoing divorce proceedings are unaware of. Because of a lack of available apartments, many women are forced to live with their ex-husbands during or after divorce. Even when the ex-husband forces the woman to have intercourse, the woman does not usually consider using this as evidence before the court or reporting it as rape.

This law also applies to situations in which a daughter is sexually abused by her father or stepfather (perhaps with the agreement of her mother, who by these means thinks she can hold onto her partner) and who doesn't have the opportunity to move out or doesn't have anywhere to go and doesn't have money enough to support herself. So far legal awareness that the victim of abuse from a father or a stepfather has the right to report this to the court has been limited. Protection of victims of sexual abuse has also been ignored; even victims of legally recognized abuse have had to remain living with those who abuse them.

This law and its interpretation have not been sufficiently used in the interests of women. The primary problem for the victim during the judicial proceedings is the interpretation of what constitutes "serious" resistance on her part. The victim faces verification that her resistance was not just pretense, that the amount of resistance she showed was proportional to her strength, and that her resistance occurred as soon as possible; she also faces inquiries into her behavior preceding the rape and the context in which the crime occurred. During these inquiries, a woman who decides to report a rape is practically blamed for the crime. She is interrogated, and her words and arguments are scrutinized by the attacker's lawyer, who attempts to show that she would have protected herself better if she hadn't really wanted the sex. The attacker's lawyer also tries to show that the attacker was not aware that he was committing the crime of rape. The victim can't very well disprove this since rape usually occurs without witnesses. Thus, those who accuse the rapist often end up themselves being accused.

Reasons Women Don't Report Rape

There are a number of reasons that women don't report rape:

- There is still an overwhelming distrust of the authorities and of police.
- Harsh investigations of rape cause further psychological and sometimes even social injury to the victim. Court negotiations last a number of months, during which the victim's name and all the details of her personal life are made public, causing her repeated social damage.
- The satisfaction the victim might derive from seeing the rapist punished is minimal, whereas her moral and psychological pain can be considerable and incalculable, and neither the victim's psychological damage nor her loss of prestige in the workplace can be replaced or compensated.
- Reimbursement of material damage is minimal and problematic since the court often requires the victim to collect evidence that damage was done to her, to prove that the damage was done by the offender, to discover the offender's address and place of work, and to pay for the legal costs of the trial.

- The offender is not only treated courteously but also given a lawyer, while the victim is left on the sidelines. The court case can even theoretically proceed against the will of the victim, even though she has to pay for all of the legal costs. Once proved guilty, the offender is often given psychological therapy, usually psychotherapy and resocialization, as a means of softening his sentence. Meanwhile, the court ignores the needs of the victim.
- Even if the victim wins the trial and the offender is sent to jail, she must still rightly fear that after his release he will attempt to revenge himself.

This situation will be even more complicated in the future with increased legal and health care costs.

The recent period has, however, seen a sprouting of spontaneous self-help groups for women and organizations that want to solve these problems. The White Circle of Safety was begun in the Czech Republic in 1991. This organization, which primarily does counseling for victims of violent crime, is run on an all-volunteer basis and includes psychologists, psychiatrists, criminologists, lawyers, judges, and social workers. In a year's time, it has given out personal advice to 84 people, written to 135 victims of sexual violence, and fielded 200 telephone calls relating to these issues. The White Circle of Safety also sponsors seminars and weekend meetings in which participants learn how to recognize the danger signs of sexual violence, practice self-defense, and study their legal rights. Along with the Gender Studies Program, the White Circle of Safety coordinated with the private television company Allegro a successful televised discussion on sexual violence.

The most important aspect in all of the research and counseling work is that it breaks the silence about violence against women, speaks out on international laws protecting women against wartime rape, and calls to the attention of the courts and the police the necessity for them to learn about this topic and to educate specialists who will deal with these problems in ways that are more sensitive than those previously used. It is necessary to write about these problems so that victims no longer feel that they are the "only one," so that the public will blame the attacker rather than the victim, and so that women will recognize their rights on these issues, both in the workplace and in relation to their husbands.

◈ The Change in Reproductive Behavior in the Czech Republic

ALEXANDRA BURESOVA

> The State, its laws and its machinery of power should not have the authority to decide whether a woman is to have a child or not. The right of a woman to dispose of her own body is indisputable. The real respect for life means the respect for the woman being an entirely free subject and not an apparatus producing, regardless of her own will children, future citizens, in case the State needs them.
>
> —Robert Merle, *Les Hommes Protégés*

Shortly after the gentle revolution of 1989, a campaign, initiated mainly by Christian communities and advocates, against the current abortion law began to form. Since then, several new bills have been submitted, always proposing a law more restrictive than the current one. The recent bill was submitted by a board of gynecologists in spring 1993. Although some provisions of the bill prevented women from free choice regarding pregnancy, the bill itself was reasonably liberal. At the same time, women's groups met with the minister of health service to open the bill for public discussion. Their demand was met, and a set of suggestions to improve the bill was made available, none of which was adopted. During 1993, there was a successor to the ministerial post who did not submit the bill to the government and commented on it thus: "At present we do not conceive of changing the legislation in the area of interruption of pregnancy. A general discussion might, as the example of many countries shows, cause a considerable split within society. And such consequences may inhibit the transformation of our whole society." Thus, it seems that our politicians do not exhibit much will to influence the domain of reproductive rights, either in liberalizing or restricting it. The experience and the results of the general election in January/March 1993 in Poland have proved this caution wise.

And what is the most recent situation in the Czech Republic? In autumn 1992, the charges for abortion were changed by the decision of the Ministry of Finance. The charges were raised and raised again in 1993. At present the cost of an abortion is CK 2,831 (approximately $166) up to the eighth week of pregnancy and CK 3,460 ($203) between the eighth and twelfth weeks (a minimum living allowance for an adult in the Czech Republic is set at CK 1,360 per month, approximately $80). This price represents a maximum; it can be reduced by individual institutions, although reductions are uncommon. Furthermore, it is not legal to perform an abortion on foreign women lacking permanent residence in the Czech Republic; this restriction prevents women from neighboring, more restrictive countries from coming to the Czech Republic for abortions (this factor is due in part to cooperation with the Polish government).

The spectrum of available contraception has grown considerably; the market is also supplied with more expensive drugs from Western countries. The Czech medication Neogest is fully covered by medical insurance, as is a similar Hungarian drug. All other drugs, however, are covered by insurance companies at only CK 20 per month, while the actual cost of imported contraceptives is more than CK 100 per month. RU 486 has yet to be registered. The mass media have discussed RU 486 several times, and the public has been informed, but the responses have been contradictory. On the one hand, some citizens welcome the possibility of another form of abortion; on the other hand, others reject it absolutely on the basis of the Hippocratic Oath, among other moralistic reasons.

Available information concerning modern forms of contraception and possibilities of abortion has improved since 1993. The media, however, remain silent or present opinions based on "pro-life" positions. Some organizations with extensive funding are founding a network of consultation centers for so-called natural methods of contraception and "women in distress." In these centers women with unwanted pregnancies are made to comply with the pregnancy in order to give the child up for adoption after birth.

Prescriptions for contraceptives are still controlled by gynecologists; it is thus their attitude that determines whether they will meet the requirements of women's demand. Abortions may be performed exclusively in state institutions, not in private clinics—a restriction that prevents the establishment of competition in pricing for services. Family planning clinics, which could feasibly offer modern contraceptives at lower prices, still do not exist. The Czech FPA committee's opinion is that this republic has enough gynecologists to prescribe contraceptives; there is no need to found family planning clinics. The committee sees the core of its activity in spreading information about planned parenthood. In autumn 1993, coverage of abortions for poor women was rejected by the Ministry of Work and Social Affairs. The Women's Commission of the Helsinki Citizen's Assembly sent a letter condemning this decision to the minister.

Statistical data convey the influence of the political system in the Czech Republic on the pattern of reproductive behavior of its population. In a comparison of the first six months of 1993 with the first six months of the previous year, data showed that the number of abortions dropped from 50,208 to 37,237, but at the same time the number of live births dropped as well, by approximately 7,000—especially among women in the youngest age group. This is mainly due to the use of hormonal contraception; in 1992 the number of women on the pill increased by about 52,000. Therefore, it is possible to say that in spite of an atmosphere unfavorable to groups involved in pro-choice activities, changes in the attitudes of the population do take place. No legislative changes represented by a new abortion law are to be expected; the political parties in power are well aware that issuing a restrictive law might cause a loss of part of their electorate. Nevertheless, they do not want to antagonize the allied Christian-oriented parties, which are part of the ruling coalition. The registration of RU 486 is sure to bring more disputes.

We continue to see the question of free contraceptives and abortions as a heated issue. However, women in this country are passive in this domain, and with the exception of a handful of women's groups, they do not show interest in activities that might bring change. Compared to previous years, then, our situation in the area of reproductive rights is not as dramatic as it once was; but there is no reason to be satisfied with the present state of affairs either. Because of the high charge for abortion, it is more economical to pay for contraception, which costs less. The drop in pregnancies among women in the youngest age group is proof of more responsible behavior. This responsibility is also reflective of the increasing financial burden of maternity compared to the benefits of finishing school and finding a job before marriage and motherhood.

Public Opinion and Contraceptive Use

A public opinion poll on abortion conducted in April 1991 showed that 61 percent of citizens recognized women's right to choose, with only 4 percent favoring absolute prohibition. Among women aged eighteen to thirty-nine, as many as 93 percent supported the right to choose. The high abortion rate in the Czech Republic is undoubtedly connected to the limited use of contraceptives. Sociologists state that the current abortion law is one of the reasons for this pattern of contraceptive use. When the current law was introduced, modern contraceptives did not exist, and women became used to solving unwanted pregnancies by means of medical intervention. This way of thinking probably still prevails today. Low-quality sex education, which introduces a negative point of view toward sex, is undoubtedly another reason. People are informed that modern contraceptives (oral contraceptives and IUDs) are harmful to their health, that coitus interruptus has a pernicious influence on male potency, and that mechanical contraceptives reduce the pleasure of sexual intercourse. Thus, many women, when asked why they do not use any contraception, say that they do not see any reason to destroy their health and that they can always choose an abortion as a last resort.

A number of gynecologists who have the monopoly on prescribing contraceptives support these attitudes. Gynecologists have no financial motivation to urge contraception (their services are state funded), and in practice it is easier for them to fill in a form and carry out an abortion than monitor a woman's use of contraceptives over several years. The moralizing attitude of some gynecologists and their hostile manner, especially toward young girls, who are being ordered from waiting rooms on the grounds that they are "too young for things like that," also play a role. The shortage of modern contraceptives completes the problems. No wonder only 15 percent of fertile women use IUDs and 5 percent use oral contraceptives.

Currently, the advocacy of reproductive rights appears to be "work in dissent." Reproductive rights are not discussed in public, and it is necessary for activists to use personal and unofficial contacts with parliamentarians and other authorities. The mass media are silent on these issues, and the public has not even been notified of the contents of the new abortion bill. Although our new society calls itself a democracy and emphasizes the observation of human rights, it is evident that not all human rights are included and that the state wishes to keep control over some of them.

Notes

A slightly different version of the section "Public Opinion and Contraceptive Use" was published in Alexandra Buresova, "Public Opinion and Contraceptive Use," in *Bodies of Bread and Butter: Reconfiguring Women's Lives in the Post-Communist Czech Republic,* ed. Suzanna Trnka and Laura Busheikin (Prague: Prague Gender Studies Center, 1993), pp. 42–48.

A Lesbian

An Interview with Jana Stepanova

TANYA RENNE

My name is Jana Stepanova. I'm from Prague in the Czech Republic. I am twenty-three years old. I work as a graphic artist for a newspaper.

I think I realized I was a lesbian three years ago when I started to date my girlfriend. I always had the feeling that in the society in which I found myself there wasn't anything for me. I felt very strange there, that I was different—somehow I am different. I didn't know how or what it was. I felt uncomfortable around people because I needed something else; I didn't know what. I saw that they were different and that I wanted different things from them, things they weren't able to give me.

When I was in high school—a very alternative school for artists—I found there a friend and had a wonderful, beautiful relationship—we call it the "beautiful relationship"—for all those four years I was there—we had everything but the sexual act. We were kissing, caressing. We went out together and weren't ever with anyone else. Then she found a boyfriend, and I was very disappointed because I thought, "Why does she have to have a boyfriend when she has me?" Of course, there were "lesbians," and I heard something about it from friends and family, who were all saying, "Don't do it because there is something wrong with it and wrong with you if you were a lesbian." I didn't think of myself as lesbian because the word *lesbian* was very dirty.

So I tried to have relationships with men. My girlfriend told me I should find a boyfriend, so I did. I showed her this relationship, and she was like "okay" (*laughed*); it was crazy. We went our separate ways: she to the art university and me to work. Two years later I moved away from my parents, and I was really shaking between two worlds—right, left—I wanted to try everything. Then after the revolution I met a woman who was a friend of a friend. She told me in our first conversation, "Maybe I am a lesbian" between some other sentences and I just said, "Maybe I am, too" (*laughs*). A week later she came to me and said, "I was at a meeting for lesbians. It was really nice, and one woman shook my hand, and it was really beautiful," and I thought, "Hmm, I should try it." Then she was really in love, always thinking, "Should I sleep with her or not?" And a gay friend of mine told her, "Try it and you will be clear." Afterward she told me, "Well, I'm a lesbian." I thought WOW—she was younger than me, and I didn't think it was possible to make myself as clear as she had. So I went to one of these meetings, and I met a woman who later became my girlfriend. I just figured I was a lesbian because she was the person whom I wanted to live with, whom I wanted to be with, whom I wanted to share everything with—she was my life. She was a person to me. She wasn't a woman or a man; she was a person. I was so relaxed—so comfortable—I wasn't, of course, from the beginning, but I had never felt that feeling before. It was so natural. After the first night I thought, "I will be always with women because of this, this, and this—because with men it doesn't work—I have never had this feeling with men." So it was clear.

Being Czech and lesbian, I had two choices—I could have figured out that I love women—that I prefer women and I prefer women's feelings and behavior—just women, and still be "normal." I could think for the rest of my life that I'd get married to have a baby and so on. And the other choice is to really feel and act like a lesbian. This is what I do because I think that this tendency for a different orientation may be genetic or something unchangeable, but the way of life everybody has to deal with it—everybody has to decide for themselves.

If I had known some model of lesbianism when I was young, maybe I wouldn't have been afraid to touch that friend of mine. Maybe I would have felt more comfortable, and I wouldn't have taken so long, but it's only if if if, you know. The fact is that after this revolution I was allowed to meet a group of homosexual people, and when I went there, I wasn't sure if I was or wasn't a lesbian, but this group helped me to make myself clear. These support groups are very important. I came out because I loved my girlfriend. The revolution affected it because the revolution allowed us to form this group. When those people got together, it was very important—it was power. They needed to find contacts—to find some self-confidence. If I hadn't gone into the group, I wouldn't be as sure of myself. It was so powerful to even get involved with her because I knew that she was a lesbian and she was clear. She was seven years older than me, which really helped me. She was very active, the first person who was showing her face on TV to give interviews as a lesbian.

First people have to feel comfortable about what they are doing; then the power just comes. It was very easy for me to take on a lesbian lifestyle. So it was easy to show it to others. I felt very comfortable in society.

I am a feminist. Lesbian and feminism in our country are separated. Feminists don't think about themselves as lesbians, and lesbians don't automatically see the connection to feminism. They need to think about it. It doesn't mean that a lesbian has sympathy for all other lesbians, but the feeling that I am around lesbians means I can do a little bit more than if I am just in larger society. It feels good.

After maybe two or three months, I told my mom, and she said that I'd get over it. She said it was only another "scream" in my life because I am always screaming. I get into something and afterward, nothing. After three years, when I told her that I had broken up with my girlfriend, she said that it would be okay and that I would get over it—it's true—my mom knows me (*laughs*). Now she believes I am a lesbian; she doesn't have anything against it; she just accepts it. She never said to me, "That is bad; I don't like you"—she always tried to accept me. I was always close to my mom, except those four years when I was in this high school—we moved away from my father (whom I never liked), and she married my stepfather and had a baby. Before that I was the youngest. So after this baby was born, it took my place, and I didn't like my mother. I remember her as a person in my early childhood. I just love her always, unconditionally. I always want to say that she is a wonderful person, and I always should be stronger than her because she was very unhappy with my father. He is very clever and powerful, successful, but he is disgusting. My mother is an angel here in the world. And she has a sister who is like a twin, but she is five years older, and sometimes I stayed with her. I remember those two and how they affected me.

I haven't clear goals. Maybe I am too young for clear goals. I know that for the next five years I don't want to have a baby. I want to do something for women. I want to do something for myself, I want to do something for myself so I will be clear, honest with myself—to know myself.

◈ Men Are Burglars of Extraterrestrial Origin!

Women Writers and Science Fiction in the Czech Republic

EVA HAUSER

Although the history of the science fiction genre is usually considered to begin with Mary Shelley's *Frankenstein,* science fiction was for many years a male domain. The "classical" American science fiction of the 1930s and 1940s consisted primarily of technological adventure stories about spaceships, robots, and battles with evil extraterrestrials and didn't leave much room for the realistic depiction of human relationships or sophisticated female characters. In contrast to the literary mainstream, science fiction usually portrayed its female characters as either passive, beautiful women, wicked witches, alien queens, or (in the best possible instance) ugly spinsters who hadn't been able to marry and so became devoted to their careers.

In the past twenty or thirty years, this situation has begun to change in response to the influence of feminism and to the genre's need for new subject matter, new ideas, and new horizons. Science fiction authors have started to use more of the so-called soft sciences (sociology, biology, psychology) in their stories. Among Western science fiction authors, there are now quite a few women: Their science fiction often imparts new qualities to the genre, new perspectives on the possible directions of social development. Sometimes they even create feminist utopias in which they attempt to envisage the way that a "women's" world (or matriarchal society) would work in practice.[1]

Czech science fiction in the past did not suffer from the objectification of women as much as American science fiction did, perhaps because the whole character of Czech science fiction was much closer to that of mainstream literature than was the case in North America. The science fiction of Czech authors such as Karel Capek (1890–1937), Jan Weiss (1892–1972), and Josef Nesvadba (b. 1926) was rather humanistic and psychological, focused on political and sociological problems, and much more concerned with the aesthetic quality of the text than were the texts of their American counterparts. Women were generally regarded by them as the bearers of life, of new hope for humanity, of better moral values. Ludmila Freiova (b. 1926), the leading Czech woman science fiction writer of her generation, had a similar view of women, and her stories had a strong didactic element.

The only Czech science fiction novel from totalitarian times that has something in common with feminism is Vladimir Paral's *Zeme zen* (The land of women), published in 1987.[2] Paral was originally a mainstream author who was attracted to science fiction for the same reasons as many other Czech writers of the 1970s and 1980s: In science fiction, he could use metaphors to express more freely the truth about our society. Paral had probably heard something about Western feminism, but not much, since the image of feminism created by our media was very deformed and utterly negative. Women in his novel create a military regime and oppress men in a way that is typically masculine (in reality, the book describes the way that Paral suffered during his military service, with only the gender of his officers being reversed). Ultimately, the book has nothing to tell us except that a woman's life can be happy only if it is "natural," with natural meaning, as is so often the case in the official rhetoric of our media, "identical to the present role model."

The basic questions posed by Western feminist science fiction authors— Who or what are women? What is their identity? What do they find fulfilling? What is the true nature of gender roles (what could they and should they be)?—were not asked in our science fiction literature in totalitarian times at all. Generally, people rejected feminism as they believed that the status quo was "natural," and that the difficulties evident between the sexes were caused by the "overemancipation of women" under the communist regime.

In the early 1980s when the political situation became more relaxed, there suddenly appeared a lot of local science fiction clubs. These clubs gave young people the opportunity to read not only scarce official editions of Western and domestic science fiction writers (which often sold out very quickly) but also homemade samizdat editions of material that was otherwise unavailable. In Western countries, science fiction fans come to science fiction clubs just to have fun and socialize, but in our country science fiction fans joined clubs because they wanted more information and more literature to read.[3] In the beginning, most of the members of these clubs were students of mathematics and technical subjects, so it might be expected that the proportion of women science fiction fans would be rather small. In reality, however, the ratio of women science fiction fans to men was even smaller than the ratio of women science students to male students, so it is evident that at the start of the 1980s science fiction was not considered an attractive subject by most Czech women. This, too, has started to change somewhat with time.

In the science fiction clubs, there evolved a group of writers who for some reason couldn't or didn't publish officially—either their work was unacceptable (too experimental, nonconformist, politically incorrect), or they deliberately opted for this alternative form of publishing because they felt more at ease with the smaller, but friendlier and more immediately responsive, science fiction audience. These new authors were often middle-aged (Frantisek Novotny and Josef Pecinovsky, for example, the two most popular science fiction writers to emerge from Czechoslovak fandom, were already in their forties), and in a sort of throwback to the American science fiction classics, they tended to write old-fashioned science fiction adventure stories, full of technology, gadgets, and long space voyages. However, there also appeared one woman of their generation, Carola Biedermann (b. 1947), who immediately started to experiment with the possibilities of the science fiction genre. She calls herself a "radical feminist," and in her curriculum vitae, she lists "shocking the bourgeoisie" as one of her hobbies.

Biedermann caused the first of her feminist "scandals" when she published her story "Oni" (They) in the March 1991 issue of the science fiction magazine *Ikarie* (started by a group of science fiction fans in summer 1990, after the revolution). The story contains only very slight science fiction elements, but it is full of naturalistic descriptions of how various perverts and annoying relatives (ranging from random flashers to the protagonist's mother-in-law) molest the unnamed heroine, first as a young girl, then as a teenager and an adult. The best-known and most controversial of her works, however, is a collection of feminist essays, *Mstiva Kantilena* (1992), in which she humorously states that men are so rough, rude, swinish, and inhuman that they must be extraterrestrials (probably convicts expelled from some other planet) who at some point in the distant past conquered the earth and stole it from its original inhabitants, complete with everything it contained (including women, who became slaves). She goes on to "prove" her theory in a series of witty observations on aspects of male behavior, such as the inclination of men to spit and piss in public and their tendency to collect utterly useless objects. There are many other traces of the alien origin of men in their psyches and their behavior, says our "female von Daniken."

Although the book draws attention to the fact that it is "deliberately nonscientific," many book reviewers, both male and female, reacted to it with deadly serious anger. Perhaps the real reason for this reaction is that it is the very first book by a contemporary Czech writer to be labeled "feminist" on the cover, but whatever the true cause of the explosion, the debate it provoked is only for the good because people here are still very reluctant to think or talk about feminism.

Another important female figure in our recent science fiction history is Vilma Kadleckova (b. 1971). In her early twenties now, she began to write and publish in samizdat while she was still in her teens (during the second half of the 1980s), when she represented a kind of "prodigal daughter" of Czech science fiction. Kadleckova writes something midway between science fiction and fantasy—her worlds are close to the harmonic worlds of Ursula Le Guin—and she was an immediate hit with our science fiction fans. Kadleckova belongs to the generation of young women who are enchanted by traditional gender roles (which, rightly or wrongly, people believe were denied them by communist ideology). These young women have not experienced any oppression themselves, have had free access to education, and have not yet gone through the drudgery of household chores and childbearing, and so they express a sincere regret that they grew up in a society where they were expected to be emancipated.

To finish, perhaps I should mention some of my own experiences with science fiction writing. Until the 1970s, I always wanted to be an author of mainstream fiction, especially of experimental fiction, but it proved to be extremely difficult in the oppressive conditions of totalitarianism, when nobody could write a single word without the ideological supervision of the editor ("That's not optimistic enough," "This theme is too absurd," "Your vision of the world is too grim," "What about showing some young, positive characters in your stories?"). In the end, every author developed a form of self-censorship, the worst possible block for creative writing. So I started to write and publish science fiction in the fanzines, which after all the years of struggling with the official media came as a liberation—finally, I had some contact with readers; I had an audience. After a while, I even managed to publish my stories in a few official science fiction anthologies whose editors had connections with fandom and from time to time used authors from the science fiction clubs.

Shortly after the revolution, in 1992, I published a collection of stories, *Hostina mutagenu* (A feast of mutagens), with the official publishing house Svoboda. This book was contracted in 1988 and had been in the process of preparation since before the revolution (a delay of four years between delivering the finished manuscript and having a book published was routine). Unfortunately, the book didn't draw as much attention as it would have if it had been published in the times of the totalitarian regime, and this apathy was symptomatic. Many science fiction authors suddenly started to suffer from a loss of reader interest about this time: Now that everyone could speak openly, nobody was interested in metaphoric stories dealing with totalitarianism anymore.

The texts of my early stories, such as those collected in that book, display a sort of "spontaneous feminism": The heroines are women who, under disastrous environmental conditions (an extrapolation of the catastrophic environmental situation in the Czech Republic), struggle to care for their children and simply to survive. Like most Czech women, however, at the time I wrote these stories I didn't consider feminism to be anything more than the frivolous, crazy, extremist activity of some bored American women.

My attitudes began to change after the revolution. In 1992 I wrote and published my second book, a science fiction novel called *Cvokyne* (The madwoman), in which I described life under totalitarianism in a more open way. I also try to analyze the conflicts caused by the double burden of an ambitious woman scientist who tries to play the role of mother, housewife, and professional all at once. This novel, which is largely based on my own experiences as a molecular biologist in the end of the 1970s, is already, in part, "deliberately feminist." After the Velvet Revolution, my access to information about Western feminism changed dramatically, and like an increasing number of Czech women, I came to the conclusion that feminism is something that would be quite useful for Czech women as well.

Notes

1. For a discussion of the feminist utopia in Anglo-American science fiction, see Sarah Lefanu, *In the Chinks of the World Machine: Feminism and Science Fiction* (London: Women's Press, 1988), chap. 6. (The U.S. edition was published under the title *Feminism and Science Fiction*, in 1989.)

2. Vladimir Paral, *Zeme zen* (Praha: Eskoslovensky Spisovatel, 1987).

3. The science fiction underground is a worldwide phenomenon. Although originating in the United States, the network now extends virtually all over the world (including Latin America and parts of Asia and Africa). Known as *fandom,* a term coined by American fans in the 1930s from fan + domain, the underground publishes small-press periodicals and critical magazines about the genre, or fanzines (another American coinage). Fanzines have had a continuous history in Britain and America since the 1930s. In Eastern Europe, SF fandom and fanzines were always regarded as suspect by communist authorities, though an organized network of science fiction clubs nonetheless existed in every country of Eastern Europe, including Albania. In Czechoslovakia, the first regular fanzines began to be published in the early 1980s. Although some fanzines managed to operate at least semilegally in the gray area of "internal publications" for officially sanctioned hobby organizations, most were published illegally and may be regarded for all intents and purposes as samizdats, or underground materials.

Part Three

 # Hungary

Fending off the Conservatives

We were trained to be hypocrites. There was an official point of view and an informal point of view. You were obliged to speak in two different languages—to think in two different ways.

—Mihaela Miriou, feminist philosopher, Bucharest

It is said that Hungary is particularly isolated as a non-Slavic island in a sea of Slavs. The common history it shares with its neighbors, however, indicates that there are many of the same digressions and progressions. Women's rights, positions in society, and employment are at stake, and feminism is making a statement among women's organizations. Self-proclaimed feminist groups are few, perhaps only three—in Sopron, Budapest, and Seged. But progressive women's groups are plentiful. Although this situation appears progressive by any standards, public opinion toward feminism is dismal. The fact that Hungary has always been a child-centered society means there is a great number of youths, and typical of youth in former socialist countries, they lean toward progressive change. However, a child-centered society is also a family-centered one. As changes in social and political structures affect Hungarians on a personal level, organizations of women are changing to meet the demands of the day and trying to resist the pressures to conform to traditionalism.

The existence of a historical Hungarian feminist movement at the turn of the century was undoubtedly connected to parallel movements in Czechoslovakia and Romania, not to mention elsewhere. But information has largely been sacrificed to the archival gods of dust and decay. In "The Construction of Women's Case," Judit Ascady documents the rise of a women's movement active before and after the turn of the century.

Where Ascady leaves off with the banning of independent groups and organizations, Agi Hochberg takes up in "The Feminist Network," outlining the beginnings of the first self-proclaimed feminist group since the Association of Feminists was disbanded in 1949. In this manifesto/history, Hochberg considers violence against women, society's acceptance and perception of sexuality, and concerns over threatened abortion rights. Reka Pigniczky takes up the abortion issue in "Hungarian Abortion Legislation," an afterword to parliamentary decisions. Antonia Burrows, an English activist living in Budapest, describes in an interview, "Protesting Porn," the Feminist Network's action against pornography.

The presence of a Gypsy movement and Gypsy parties in East-Central Europe is not uncommon. However, representation of all Gypsy needs is rare. The Gypsy Mother's Association in Hungary is the only such organization in the region representing women's concerns. Iona Zambo, in "Gypsy Women," makes a case for why Gypsy women are underprivileged and multiburdened.

Concluding this part is an essay by Reka Pigniczky, "The Making of a Women's Movement in Hungary After 1989," which reports on the Hungarian Women's Foundation, a foundation created to provide a link between official politics and women's groups in Hungary.

The formation of groups is a big step for such a repressed society; the use of the word *feminist*, even bigger and political action, nearly inconceivable. The women of the Feminist Network, Sopron, and Seged are working furiously to overturn the annals of public opinion—according to which women are not to be taken seriously except in matters that concern sexual possibilities. Equality is far from a reality in contemporary Hungarian society—but unlike other Eastern European nations, save those that formerly made up Yugoslavia, the grassroots movement and the intellectual/academic movement of feminism in Hungary are developing together, if slowly, to form a solid front among youth, and planned activism is spreading the principles of political activism.

▦ The Construction of Women's Case

Turn-of-the-Century Hungarian Feminism

JUDIT ASCADY

Feminism or the situation of women in general is not among the leading concerns of Hungarian society. For more than one hundred years now, since women began to organize, they have never been able to prevent public opinion from making the assumption that women's interests mean interests against those of the family or society at large. This is one of the many reasons that women's emancipation and feminism are dirty words and largely misunderstood, if not completely neglected. Women today do not like the idea that their activities, ambitions, and organizations are interpreted as selfish, destructive, and even unnatural. So if they want to be accepted as women, they will not combine the struggles of everyday life with the general notion of women's struggle. They hope to manage as individuals whose problems have nothing to do with the structural inequalities and oppressive features of a patriarchal society.

Another reason feminists have such difficulties making their point understood is that people's minds have been successfully brainwashed by the promises of previous ideologies. As a result, Hungarians are used to thinking that every social criticism provides a wholesale set of guarantees that follow the people's suggested lines and value systems, that the ideal society is close at hand. In this way people expect every political thought to have universal claims of truth as well as solutions to every problem of social, economical, or political life. Obviously, feminism does not meet, much less want to meet, these demands. On the one hand, people expect feminism to present itself as an ideology, but on the other hand, they also fear the power of ideologies and get hostile toward any mode of thought that presents itself as an ideology or that they perceive as one.

Rather than list the reasons feminism has not made a significant impact in Hungary, as well as in other Eastern-Central European countries,[1] I want to point out a factor that could be easily changed: the lack of contemporary feminist thought, activism, and history of feminism and the formulation of women's demands. Very little research has been done on the emergence of feminism in Hungary, even though one can find in national archives a rich collection of publications, letters, and other documents of feminist activists and the public debate around women's demands. The official history written in the state-socialist era did not make an effort to include feminist initiatives in the history of movements. The main focus was always on workers' class struggles, and the role of communist approaches was constantly overemphasized. It was in this context, and only in this context, that women were mentioned.

On the basis of writings by Agnes Horvath, Katalin N. Szegvari, and Anna Fabri,[2] and upon my own research and observations concerning material not yet known to the public at large, I wish to preview the history of women's emancipation in Hungary. The first event to be documented about women's awakening and their growing interest in public life is a petition to parliament in 1790, just two years before the publication of Mary Wollstonecraft's *Vindication of the Rights of Woman*. This petition was written "in the name of Hungarian mothers" by, in fact, a man, Peter Barany,[3] and contained much more modest demands than Wollstonecraft initiated. It addressed the most respected gentlemen of parliament with the request that they let women (the women of the noble class) participate in parliamentary sessions as spectators. The reasoning supporting this request is remarkable, especially because it became one of the basic arguments for women's emancipatory endeavors for education or for their participation in public, political, or cultural life in the nineteenth century: namely, that by listening to the debates, women would be better informed and more open-minded. More important, better-informed and more open-minded women would be better equipped to educate their sons in a patriotic manner. In fact, by giving this right to women, parliament would be acting in the "interest of the nation."

For a very long time this kind of justification was needed when women's demands were formulated. To be given a certain right, women had to prove that they would be given it not solely for their own sakes but always for the interests of others, preferably the family or the nation. In fact, the interests of the family were always seen as synonymous with a woman's own interests. If the interest of the family is met, then the interest of the woman is also satisfied. Unlike men, women in these traditional approaches did not have an independent existence; they were assumed to exist as bound to the family. There were very few alternative contexts within which women were mentioned other than the context of motherhood.

The earliest reported women's organization, the Women's Charity Organization, was founded in 1817 in Pest. It was followed by a large number of similar groups. The women who participated were generally upper-middle-class ladies who felt solidarity with the poor or found amusement in having a company of lady friends involved in activities other than "empty-minded chats to pass the time." The general public and men's societies welcomed these charity groups. In addition to the charity groups, different clubs and literary circles run by women appeared. These early women's organizations did not challenge any of the good-old norms and values, nor did they question power relations. In fact, this was the only form of acceptable activism for proper, upper-class, urban women.

In the provincial countryside there were women of nobility who were in a different situation and had responsibilities in running estates. Some historians interpret this fact as women enjoying equal rights, as in the cases where women inherited land and became feudal landowners themselves. If the family did not have any more male heirs, it was possible for a woman to own an estate because the family fortune and its maintenance were of more importance than preventing a woman from owning property.

Hungarian historical writing does mention a few famous women from the past centuries, respected for their patriotic deeds or for their position as mothers of famous kings or heroes of wars and battles. These women became symbolic figures of women's glory.

Women writers of the 1820s who wanted their own voices in public life were not respected in the same way. Instead, they became the focus of a huge public debate. The mid-nineteenth century saw the emergence of women's literature in Western Europe (for example, Jane Austen, Mary Godwin, and Mme. de Stael). The first article ever published by a woman in a "scientific" magazine in Hungary, in 1822,[4] was met with grave disapproval. The debate continued for decades as to whether women could take part in cultural and scientific life at all, if it is or is not against nature and God's will for women to write, if women should be allowed to do intellectual work, and if they should be educated at all.

Education itself was the next important milestone in the history of the construction of women's case. When the idea to open schools for women became accepted, there was no consensus on what should be taught. The defenders of traditional values wanted to limit the range of subjects for girls to household skills, childrearing, and perhaps languages and art. An important event in the struggle for women's emancipation in education occurred in 1885 when a bill was passed to let women into universities. But only ten years later, under pressure from conservative deans and university professors, the number of female students was strictly limited. These restrictions were among the many reasons that feminists of the period decided that the time had arrived for organization.

The first feminist organization in Hungary, called the Association of Feminists, was founded in 1904 as a part of a larger organization, the International Women's Suffrage Alliance. The membership of the association grew from three hundred at its founding to more than one thousand a decade later. The association had local chapters in twenty-eight towns throughout the country. The association published the monthly *Women and Society* (later *A Woman*), which was distributed widely. The members of the association were from different strata of society, with varied professional backgrounds: white-collar workers, teachers, intellectuals, urban upper-class housewives, and factory workers. Their most active period was in the years before World War I. Later they joined social movements opposing the war. After the war, the right-wing, conservative government associated their activities with leftist organizations and made the continuation of their work impossible. The most important personalities of the association left the country, including Rozsa Bedy-Schwimmer, who worked later as a peace activist and died in New York. In 1946 the association was founded again and existed for three years until the authorities banned it together with hundreds of other civil society organizations.

The central aim of the association at the turn of the century was to represent the cause of women's suffrage in Hungary. Association members wanted women's "liberation as individuals," "equality before the law," and "votes for all individuals." These were the most important claims that connected Hungarian feminists to international conferences such as were held in Copenhagen (1906) and London (1909), where they gave reports about their own activities.[5] In 1913 the Seventh Conference of the International Women's Suffrage Alliance was held in Budapest. Many of the leading liberal and radical intellectuals and politicians of the time participated.

Feminists in Hungary organized big campaigns, including demonstrations, public forums, discussions, and publications, for the reform of the right to vote in the years 1905, 1908, and 1912, when (partly as a result of their pressure) parliament put the reform bill on the agenda. Thanks to a strong conservative line, this bill was not passed then,[6] despite support for feminists in political and public life from such groups as the Men's League for Women's Suffrage, formed in 1910.

In addition to political aims, the Association of Feminists was very sensitive to different social, educational, and occupational issues. One of its first activities in 1904 was to set up a consultation service to help women choose professions. The office provided the most recent information about jobs and educational opportunities, including universities or vocational schools already accepting women. The office also gave personal encouragement and advice and in its first five years helped more than two thousand women. The city helped the office financially.[7] That the City Council of Budapest had good relations with the feminists always engendered hostility and little support and understanding. This cooperation enabled the initiatives of the women to be realized. Another prime example of common effort is the story of the first day care centers, set up with the active contribution of the feminists as experts and volunteers.[8]

Publications by feminist authors, aside from their monthly periodical, contributed to the rise of public awareness and understanding of women's demands in changing social frameworks. Feminists would get the most important books by Western feminist thinkers translated (for example, Charlotte Perkins Gilman's *Women and Economics* was translated by Rosie Schwimmer).[9] Hungarian women authors published works analyzing the socialization of individuals, marriage, and women's work (see the works of Szidonia Willhelm, Sarolta Geocze, and their male colleagues Andor Maday and Geza Kenedi).

Feminism, this hidden thread in Hungarian women's history, is still to be discovered. Its impact can be understood only after the historical documents are brought to light. If attention is not drawn to this historical background of Hungarian feminism, all the efforts of those who once devoted their energies to this cause will be wasted, and modern-day feminism will be seen as alien and unconnected.

Notes

1. For a complete list of reasons, see Ann Snitow, "Feminist Futures in the Former Eastern Bloc," *Peace and Democracy News* (Summer 1993).

2. Agnes Horvath, "A nok elso politikai mozgalma" (Women's first political movement in Hungary) (unpublished manuscript); Katalin Szegvari, *Numerous clausus intezkedesek* (Numerous clauses between the two wars) (Budapest: 1988); and Anna Fabri, "Az elso magyar ujsagirono" (The first Hungarian woman journalist), *Az irodalom maganelete*.

3. Peter Barany. A magyar anyaknak . . . (Request of Hungarian mothers . . .) (1790).

4. Eva Takats, "Egy ket szo . . . " (A few words on women and marriage), in the Tudomanyos Gyujtemeny archive (1822).

5. Women's Archive of Amsterdam (Vrouwenarchive).

6. The reform bill to grant women the vote was introduced by the revolutionary Karolyi government in 1918.

7. The correspondence between the Association of Feminists and the City Council can be found in the Budapest Archive, IV.

8. See the letter from Vilma Glucklich to the City Council in 1905, Budapest Archive, IV.

9. Charlotte Perkins Gilman, A no gazdasagi helyzete (Budapest: 1908).

The Feminist Network

A History

AGI HOCHBERG

Antecedents—the Need for New Organizations

In Hungary before the change of the political system, there was one sole organization, the Magyar Noi Orszagos Tarsasag (Hungarian Women's National Council, or MNOT) working under the administration of the Magyar Szocialista Munkas Part (Hungarian Socialist Workers' Party), that was supposed to represent women and stand for their rights. This organization, entirely dependent on a male-dominated party, did not try to mobilize women; it refused to accept a conspicuous state of affairs as far as women's social position was concerned, which could have influenced its politics. The fact is that Hungarian women were (and still are) experiencing a crisis concerning their roles.

This "confusion of identity" was the outcome of the "forced emancipation" of women by the socialist regime. This process started after World War II when Hungary, seriously damaged and demolished, badly needed cheap labor to rebuild the country and launch heavy industry, nonexistent and incongruous in a traditionally agricultural society but strongly recommended in a budding communist system. Consequently, women have found themselves ever since trapped in the double role of mother-wife and new worker doing paid work in the public sphere. The MNOT did not fight adequately against a social discrimination that was manifold in many spheres and could very clearly be demonstrated. For instance, the principles of "equal pay for equal work" and "equal opportunities in politics" remained only in theory and were never realized in practice. As a consequence, during the political changes of 1989, even though the MNOT endeavored to renew itself, it manifested neither awareness of the need to reconsider its political stands nor an intention to adopt a wider feminist perspective. On the whole, until now there has been little alteration in its overall mentality.

Despite the traditional views of the MNSZ (the Hungarian Women's Association, the new name of MNOT), about twenty women organized a "tea party" for women on the premises of MNSZ in autumn 1989. The main topic of discussion was "a classically feminine one": beauty. "Why do we women conceive our physical appearance as a basic need and expectation?" At this debate some of those women got to know each other who later attended the tea party of 1989.

A series of lectures entitled "Woman in Society" was organized at the Department of Sociology at ELTE University, Budapest. This course was initiated and started in spring 1990 by students and professors of sociology aware of an acute lack of women as "subjects of serious academic study" within Hungarian scientific life. The course turned out to be quite successful and proved the existence of interest in and a need for discussion of women's issues. That was where the core of the would-be Feminist Network got together. We began to hold regular meetings at a university club. There we exchanged our impressions and experiences as women living in Hungarian society. Our social backgrounds, our professions, our ages, our ways of life, were all different. Nevertheless, it seemed quite obvious to us that as women we had experienced the same kind of discrimination: Each of us had already met the tangible limits of female existence in some ways—at work, in career opportunities, in financial or moral fields, or in our private lives.

On June 8, 1990, twenty-five members founded the Feminist Network in Budapest. Ever since then we have tried to maintain several basic aspects of our group. It is a social movement independent of parties or the government. In our declaration of intent we stated that in current Hungarian society the political changes of the recent past have had no positive effect on women whatsoever. Male values and categories continue to prevail and determine the functioning of society: Power, competition, and profit keep dominating the fields of politics, economics, and increasingly, culture. Women are confined to the periphery. They see themselves becoming a minority, despite talk of progressive democratic methods of change by male leaders of the new parties.

In the current of the economic changes between 1989 and 1991, we have witnessed an "inevitable" increase in unemployment among women; suddenly women are reminded overtly of their "principal" function as mothers, indispensable to the home. This conservative political discourse serves as a convenient pretext for justifying a high number of dismissals: Raising children has always been solely a woman's holy and unquestionable task. The Feminist Network believes, however, that motherhood is only one of innumerable possible activities that can and do interest women.

That is why one of our main goals is to launch a process of consciousness-raising among Hungarian women. To realize this, we intend to resort to various means; including the publication of books, organization of public debates, publication of our own newspaper, and visibility in the mass media. One of our main purposes is to assure that women can start on the difficult road to self-realization having the same opportunities as men at their disposal, and to this end we consider the establishment of support and solidarity between women indispensable.

Our main actions have been as follows:

- We joined a citizen's initiative to protest against the preparation of a bill to restrict abortion rights in Hungary. We collected about seven thousand signatures in the streets of Budapest and in rural areas, and we also sent a petition to the minister of welfare and to the media.
- We organized a public debate to discuss abortion issues and invited several social movement organizations, different parties, and journalists to participate in the discussion.
- We organized a solidarity demonstration in front of the Polish Embassy against the proposed outlawing of abortion in Poland.
- On the international day against violence against women we organized a public debate about the issue. It was followed by another debate (we intended to hold a regular debate around the issue of violence), a taboo in Hungary. On the second occasion some policewomen, working in the field of crime prevention, and some psychologists also contributed to the discussion.
- We organized a demonstration against the Gulf War together with the Budapest Anarchist Group (the only antiwar protest in Hungary) in front of the Iraqi and American Embassies.
- We formed a pro-choice campaign, the first grassroots political campaign since the beginning of the transition, to fight restrictions against abortion.
- We held demonstrations in solidarity with Women in Black against war in Yugoslavia.
- On International Women's Health Day, we held a public forum to discuss the consequences of the new abortion law, interviewing state counselors (under the new abortion law a woman who wants an abortion must be interviewed by a state counselor) and discussing what women can do to combat discrimination and humiliating practices at the gynecologist.

Violence Against Women and Sexuality in General

Socialist morality never brought about any significant change in the consideration of such taboo subjects as sexuality or violence. It defined what were to be considered deviant, undesired, or punishable types of behavior: Homosexuality, lesbianism, masturbation, exhibitionism, voyeurism, sado-masochism, fetishism, and transvestitism all counted as sins against "social-ist morale." In lawmaking the issues of who could be considered a rapist, victim of rape, or pervert, at what age, and in what situation were dis-cussed. The protected age is up to twelve, and rape is recognized only as a sexual crime and not as a crime of power or violence; nor is it considered to have any connection with the rapist's psychology, such as a need for domi-nance. Rape in marriage has never been considered an issue, and the police deal with intrafamily rape only if "blood flows." In the public mind, women ask for violence and rape through their behavior. It is going to be a very hard and long process before social mentality understands and accepts a deeper analysis of this issue. We consider the following issues as vital sub-jects of concern:

The right to control our own bodies
The right to give birth or not
The right to abortion
The right to different sexualities

Sex education is all but absent from education; this has been true across all generations. Often there are misconceptions. There is very little litera-ture available about rape that accounts for an increase in rape figures. Re-cently, the media have covered rape cases in more detail. Women often en-dure various forms of violence, not recognizing them as violence; they go on bearing different forms of humiliation silently. Battering has tradition-ally been considered a useful way to punish women; "women are good when battered." These are some of the reasons we believe there should be more awareness concerning violence and sexuality and hope to encourage such awareness through public debates and discussions.

Abortion Issues in Hungary

In Hungary about 90,000 abortions are carried out every year (in 1989, there were 90,508 abortions for a population of about 10.5 million). In of-ficial quarters this number, compared to the European average rate, is con-sidered too high. Nevertheless, in the hard economic situation of these years it is reasonable for people to avoid having more children if they can still find a way to interrupt unwanted pregnancies. Even though there is only a narrow range of choice, Hungarian women can get contraception quite easily with a medical prescription. Sex education, however, is very limited, and consequently so is information about sex and sex-related is-sues, such as birth control and sexually transmitted diseases.

Among those who ask for an abortion today in Hungary, there are a lot of young women struggling with housing difficulties. Today both prices and availability make housing inaccessible to the majority of young people. In Budapest alone the number of homeless was estimated at several tens of thousands in 1991. The rate of unemployment has soared severely from an official 0 percent pre-1989 to 5 percent in 1993, which is a relatively enormous change, and the process has only been deteriorating since the free-market system was introduced.

Since 1956 abortion has been legal in Hungary. There was a restrictive law passed in 1972, but it was modified by ministerial decree the following year to be less restrictive. According to the decree, the main conditions for the interruption of an unwanted pregnancy are the following:

- An abortion can be obtained if it reduces the harmful effects on the mother's health.
- An abortion can be carried out only in hospitals, by trained experts, and in cases determined by regulation.
- A committee must decide about the righteousness of an abortion as it relates to the interests of society and the protection of mothers' and children's health.
- A fee should be paid for abortion services.
- In the case of a minor, a legal representative should be consulted.

The law of 1992–1993 reflects the mechanisms of the party-state and not people's opposition to abortion out of religious or moral considerations. Nowadays, "pro-lifers," Christian and nationalist movements, and parties that particularly miss white Hungarian children would like to make use of the restrictive law (1972), which has rarely been applied.

In Hungary the Society for the Protection of the Embryo has continually attacked abortion rights since 1988; another organization, Pacem in Utero, has been active since 1989. The latter group collected more than ten thousand signatures in support of its demand for legal modification. The Feminist Network, despite its modest membership, collected about seven thousand, and on the basis of the data and opinions heard in the media, it is clear that the majority of the Hungarian population is for free abortion. This was also confirmed by the results of a survey carried out in May 1991, which demonstrated a clear 70 percent of the population against abortion restriction.

In summer 1990 a fiery social debate broke out around abortion issues in Hungary, but those most concerned (women) were absent from the media. The debate was further heated by a bill proposing restrictions on abortion. At the beginning of 1992, the Constitutional Court decided that the current legal situation concerning abortion is unconstitutional, which means there would be legal modifications. In light of the overwhelming and predominantly conservative nature of all the changes that have taken place in Hungary so far (in politics, economy, and social welfare), the curb on abortion rights was imminent.

In the words of one of our members:

> The ferocious battle against abortion that basically aims to deprive women of their rights to self-determination (their human rights) regards women's bodies and organs as the property of the prevailing [political] power; it completely neglects women's projects and intentions with regard to their own lives. . . . The phenomenon that during political upheavals the fight against abortion comes into full swing is peculiar but inevitable. It usually serves as a way for male politicians to score points. . . .
>
> Most women, whether feminist or not, take up motherhood with pleasure at the right time of their lives. Enforced motherhood, however, gravely disrupts women's lives. . . . Antiabortionists—and at the same time those who are in favor of population growth—only think of quantity, not quality of life. Why do we love those "who" are but germs of life so much? Why don't we dedicate our efforts, our resources, deeds and goods to the amelioration of the lives of those already born? This would undoubtedly involve more sacrifice than just airing principles and protests. . . . Demographers worry about the diminishing number of Hungarians. . . . It is flabbergasting that right now, when our country is in such a catastrophic economic state, the word of antiabortionists and growing population fans should gain such weight and attention.
>
> Have they ignored the soaring inflation and unemployment rates? The fact that there are no more flats, that the number of the homeless is ever increasing, and that those who still have flats can no longer pay the bills? . . . Is this really the moment when we should be multiplying?

Hungarian Abortion Legislation

An Afterword

REKA PIGNICZKY

As the countries of the former Soviet bloc make their transitions toward democracy, each new parliament in turn addresses and makes new regulations about women's reproductive rights. Hungary, too, has its own act in the abortion drama of the region. In 1992, after the initiatives of several antiabortion organizations, which were followed by the counterinitiatives of pro-choice organizations, the Hungarian Constitutional Court canceled the existing legal regulations on induced abortion and set a deadline for parliament to pass a new abortion law. This deadline was December 31, 1992. Before I go on to outline the current situation for women opting to have an abortion in Hungary, I first explain the previous legal environment concerning women's reproductive rights.

The abortion question was regulated only once by parliamentary law—in 1978. Abortion has never been fully denied, but the right to one was modified several times by decisions of the supreme court and ordinances by the governments in power in the 1930s, 1950s, and 1970s. The law in effect until a decision was reached that December was a pragmatic compromise outlined and formulated in 1956 among certain political and ideological circumstances. This regulation might be called "moderately restrictive." It permitted abortion until the twelfth week; however, the woman had to explain her reasons (health, social, etc.) to an abortion committee, which had the exclusive right to condone abortion. In practice, this committee was treated as only a formality. The result of the most recent abortion legislation in Hungary yields a law that is quite similar to the ordinance of 1956 and may be said to be quite liberal in composition—although it still presents various restrictions for women wishing to terminate their pregnancies.

The Hungarian National Assembly had to choose between two versions of the Law on the Protection of the Fetus, proposed in fall of 1992 by the governing coalition (which included the Hungarian Democratic Forum, the Independent Smallholders' Party, and the Christian Democratic People's Party). The largest liberal opposition party in parliament, the Alliance of Free Democrats, submitted its proposal for a law on "the termination of a pregnancy" in spring 1992, but this proposal was not released for debate in parliament.

The "A" version of the legislation stated that abortion would be illegal unless the pregnancy (up to twelve weeks) endangered the woman's health, the fetus was at risk of being unhealthy or deformed, or the pregnancy was a result of rape. The "B" version stated that abortion would be legal up to twelve weeks with certain restrictions, which I will not list here since the final version of the law contained almost all the significant restrictions that had been originally proposed.

Here I must make mention of the propaganda of those who wrote the legislative proposal—Dr. Laszlo Surjan and Dr. Erzsebet Pusztai of the Hungarian Democratic Forum and Ministry of Health, respectively. By including the possibility of a quasi-total ban on abortion in the "A" version, they set the panicky, black-and-white tone of the public abortion debate: Either abortion will be legal, or it will not. This antiabortion angst arose despite the fact that such a legislative outcome was nearly impossible: Over two-thirds of Hungarian citizens were polled in summer 1992 as being *against* such a restriction of abortion and thus the government would be committing political suicide by passing the "A" version Thus, choice "B" seemed "liberal" in comparison. The media attention on the "A" variant masked the reality of the not-so-liberal "B" version, which itself was not without considerable restrictions on women's reproductive rights. Therefore, when the crucial moment arrived and the "A" version was discarded, the "B" version remained, a seeming hero of women's reproductive rights— after all, abortion could have been entirely banned.

The final decision was to disregard the "A" version and to consider passing the "B" version with possible modifications. The current restrictions on women in Hungary who choose to terminate their pregnancies are the following:

- Parental consent (or the consent of a legal guardian) is mandatory for women under eighteen years of age. There must be a signed statement from this person that she or he permits the abortion, and the person giving consent must submit the request for the abortion personally.
- There is a mandatory three-day waiting period after a woman has requested the termination of a pregnancy.
- After a woman has requested an abortion, there is a mandatory "counseling/enlightenment" about the procedure of the abortion; its possible dangers and postabortion infertility rates; the alternatives to abortion, including adoption; and information about contraception.

The official title of the law itself remains: the Law on the Protection of the Fetus. This legislation is therefore in principle an antiabortion, "pro-life" law. The opposition's proposal to title it the Law on the Termination of a Pregnancy was voted down. With respect to the title, the authors of the law intended, in Dr. Pusztai's own words, that the law would "bring about a change of perspectives, and . . . create more of a sense of familial obligation and respect for human life." Furthermore, very recently Dr. Laszlo Surjan, also the president of the Christian Democratic People's Party, stated that in retrospect his party is not satisfied with the current law and that if and when the Christian Democrats take the majority of the seats in government, they will change the law to be more moralistic. Therefore, today Hungary enjoys a "liberal abortion law," which to most pro-choice groups is really a wolf in sheep's clothing, not to mention the fact that it is structured so that antiabortion groups have a potential upper hand in implementing further restrictions on abortion procedures in Hungary.

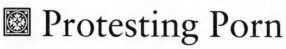

Protesting Porn

An Interview with
Antonia Burrows

TANYA RENNE

I am Antonia Burrows. I am English and forty-four. I have been coming to Hungary for twenty years as a visitor and living here since 1988. I came five years ago when I had a suitable gap in my life and started to teach at an English-language school, where I taught for two years and then joined the university's Social Policy Department, where I teach English, women's studies, and media studies.

In my spare time I work with the Feminist Network. We have been in existence since June 1990. Our first campaign was against pornography, and for that you have to know that in 1988–1989 the communists liberalized, not by giving the people any real power but by giving them pornography. In other words, buying off the men to keep them quiet at the expense of women. People kept defending it, saying, "We can't have censorship because we have had it for the last forty years." We can absolutely see this point, but then you just run up against the same brick wall everywhere.

It was really hard-core pornography, and there was just a slug of it all over and at a child's eye level. There was just nowhere you could go without it. We had a huge graffiti campaign and made stickers, and we had a wonderful time going round night after night sticking these things all over. We sprayed all the windows and shopfronts of stationery shops hanging pornographic calendars. We told them why we did it, of course: "We have done this because it degrades women and this kind of licentiousness is not freedom. It only means men's freedom to dispose of women's bodies." We stuck them all over the metro, on the walls, in the streets, and stuck them on the books and magazines, too. We even started telling the newsstand salespeople that we were going to sue them for contravening public decency. They used to laugh at us, and so we would get a policeman to say something, and for a while they would remove it from public view. But not many people were actually prepared to do that because people had been intimidated for years into not complaining about anything in any official way or anybody selling anything because anybody who was in charge of goods was actually in a position of power—shortages gave middlepeople power. I was always told never to go in to a shoe store and say, "Have you got these in a size 36?" but to say, "What size have you got these shoes in?" because otherwise they would say, "Well, we have them in 35 and 37 but not 36" and expect you to pay more. You have to develop little tricks to adjust to the power people have over you. That's why people wouldn't dream of complaining to newsstand people even if they thought that all this pornography was a bad thing. We had other sheets as well saying, "Hungarian mothers for feminism" and "Hungarian feminists for the family."

About the same time, there were a lot of articles published by old men that said feminists were destroying the family and murdering motherhood and that the Hungarian nation was dying out and that it was all these selfish women's fault who were too keen on having their own lives instead of devoting themselves to their duty, which was, of course, to produce lots of Hungarian babies. They all considered feminism to be a communist aberration. It is either a communist aberration or a Western imposition.

At that time, there was a very clear renaissance of nationalism in Hungary. You have to know the extraordinary euphoria of being allowed to fly your own flag for the first time; up until then they were only allowed to fly the red flag or their own with a hammer and sickle in the middle. I remember being told about how it felt to see the flag in 1956 with a hole burned in the middle where the hated hammer and sickle had been. You have to understand what this meant to be allowed to be a nation again, how important that was for them. The result of all this was to go back to the last system where they had been allowed to rule themselves. The solution of the nationalists was to tell the women to have lots of babies: The nation was dying because the communists had allowed abortion; after all 5 million Hungarians had been murdered since World War II (through abortion).

The communists had allowed abortion, but they had done absolutely nothing about contraceptives and sex education. The communists were held responsible for allowing this terrible "slaughter of the innocents" (read: abortion), with the complicity of women, who had fallen for this complete confidence trick of communism. Of course, they had lost the respect in which motherhood had previously been held, and how foolish they were if they were so evil to have believed all those communist lies.

So this is what Hungarian women are facing now: a constant attack against their rights and the way they lead their lives. In a lot of ways, they are dealing better with the restructuring of the system than their husbands. This means pressure to keep them out of positions, limiting their rights and responsibilities, and using just about anything against them to get them back where they belong.

 Gypsy Women
Barriers to Citizenship

IONA ZAMBO

All over Europe reemerging nationalism aggravates the situation of minorities. Research shows that in the region, specifically in Hungary, prejudice against Gypsies has grown. Social and economic crisis and a spread of poverty were followed by a dramatic increase in segregation. The prevalent ideology, held by politicians and common people alike, is that Gypsies are culturally, morally, and intellectually inferior. Let me quote a few lines from an article that appeared in the November issue of *Cigakritika* (Gypsy Critic). A reporter asked random Hungarians on the street about their opinion of Gypsies. A taxi driver replied: "It's the easiest thing in the world to recognize a Gypsy. I hate them in principle, but I still have to give them a ride because they are the only social group who can afford taxis. You don't have to ask where their money comes from; just read the police reports." An unemployed skinhead answered: "They should be wiped out—every last one. Hitler's biggest sin was starting this job and never finishing it. We skinheads will do it and defeat all inferior races." Of course, there are a few positive voices as well, but the forgoing examples describe the general attitude. Out of Europe's Gypsy population of 15 million, eight hundred thousand live in Hungary. The Gypsies are the biggest losers in the transition process. Neither the country nor the Gypsy community was prepared for the effects of the transition. It caught the Gypsies unprepared and without economic resources.

Because of a lack of basic living conditions, Gypsy families that are multiply disadvantaged can't join the market economy. Most Gypsies live in extreme poverty, have large families, and are unemployed and unskilled. Their housing is unhealthy, dark, damp, and crowded. It doesn't meet basic hygienic standards. Gypsy settlements, *putri,* are often located near garbage dumps or swamps far away from infrastructure.

Our state of health is radically deteriorating. There is not much hope that it will improve in the near future. Infant mortality as well as premature birth is very high. Children's physical and mental development is slowed, which presents serious problems in education. They are behind their peers and can't keep up with the rest of the class, a factor that affects their whole lives.

As the very survival of Gypsies is becoming threatened, more Gypsy representatives have begun to speak out, but we are still not participating in the political decisionmaking process. We are tiptoeing in front of the walls surrounding the economic and political system. Our actions remain invisible. It is a fact that Gypsies do not have resources, financial or social, to make their own representation more effective. There is no mother country or politically and financially strong international Gypsy organization to rely on or get support from.

The transition created a new social situation that gravely affected Gypsy women. Most Gypsy families are single-income families. The man's income, which is becoming increasingly deficient, is the sole income. Binding tradition, many children, and lack of training keep women from joining the workforce in spite of the need to do so. Gypsy families are known for having many children (families of ten or twelve are not uncommon). Family planning has never existed; women become mothers as early as age fourteen. Therefore, a sharp decrease in the birthrate cannot be expected; only better living conditions could bring the rate down and ensure an escape from poverty.

The Role and Rights of Gypsy Women in the Family

Families are multigenerational. There are two things that control the community: the *patyi,* or the regulation of traditions, and the *krisz,* or the ethical and moral codes. These are unwritten laws mandatory for everyone. For example, these rules ensure unconditional respect for the elderly and assign women a secondary place within the family. Women are present but can't control their own lives. They are subject to traditions and their husband's arbitrary power. Adultery is a forgivable sin for men but not for women. A woman who cheats on her husband has to face the contempt of the whole community and very often physical violence from the husband.

The Hungarian Gypsy community is characterized by a kind of social stratification that is similar to a caste system. A young person beginning a relationship with someone from a lower caste is scorned. Relationships, however, are based on emotions and not prearranged; eloping is very common for young couples. When a woman joins a man in marriage, she becomes part of his family as property. Before then it was her own family that controlled her; now it is her husband's. She has obligations to fulfill toward them. Women who rebel against family traditions and try to break out of this one-way street most often become prostitutes. Their fate is determined by their lack of education and training and their naivete. Most of them look for shelter in big cities and end up in the hands of pimps.

The process of transition will be a long one for Gypsy women. We have to break out of a double bind, first by struggling against restrictive traditions in the community and then by proving ourselves as women in society. The key question here is whether Gypsy women have equal opportunities to make free choices in the future. A lot of tolerance is needed for us to define our needs, to learn to take our own lives into our own hands.

The Making of a Women's Movement in Hungary After 1989

REKA PIGNICZKY

In Hungary, as well as in the rest of the region, political and economic transitions show a marked tendency to wipe out the legacy of the previous, communist regime. A poignant example of this retrogression is the situation of women in Hungary, where the gains of the previous regime (for example, full employment, education, participation in political and public life, and family protection) are continually in danger of being revoked and/or restricted. Although it is true that the inclusion of women in political and economic life was the result of coercion by a quota system initiated from above (and therefore not the product of a grassroots women's movement in any sense), Hungarian women found themselves in an advantageous position in that they could try their hand at political life and also win economic independence by joining the labor market. Despite the fact that today we know that the rhetoric behind the "emancipation" of women was in reality meant to serve the goals of industrialization and development of society, today women still find themselves in advantageous positions in the sense that they do not have to fight from absolute zero to gain their economic and political rights. This situation is already quite natural and irreplaceable. The many decades of women's movements in the West have still not been able to achieve these gains completely.

Therefore, without the momentum of a real women's movement, the cornerstone of women's equality was successfully laid in the previous regime in Hungary. Unfortunately, however, the movement for women's equality is almost completely nullified by its association with the communist past, which forced women (but not men!) to become equal. In this sense, the movement is a relic of the communist era. Thus, there is no acceptable ideological approach to the women's movement; we cannot speak of emancipation, the economic and reproductive rights of women, or the legal equality of women (this liberal approach has already been achieved.)

Nevertheless, it is quite obvious that after the transition we find women in Hungary in a disadvantaged position. Even though they are protected by

the law, they do not enjoy societal equality: Compared to men they are un-
derpaid, they do not occupy a fraction of the positions of economic and political leadership, family leave and maternity leave (until now the most favorable in all of Europe) are in danger of being reduced drastically, and
conservative leaders are promoting a return of women to the traditional
homemaker/mother role. Today we can observe the retrogression of
women's status, whereas women won considerable leverage under the
rhetoric of emancipation during the previous regime. Currently, women try
without the aid of infrastructure and ideology to preserve what they have
gained and further develop their positions. It is indeed difficult to react politically to small steps taken backward; it is difficult to rally around seemingly insignificant negative changes (first slight restrictions in reproductive
rights, a chipping away of the family leave subsidies, changes in educational policy that preserve the traditional status of women in certain professions, etc.). For this reason, every step of the political and economic transition must be accompanied by a comprehensive feminist analysis. But
because at this point "gender politics" is not officially embraced (and
barely embraced on a grassroots level, where there are only thoughts about
a possible women's lobby), it is possible that ten years from now, Hungarian women will find themselves starting a movement from a much more
disadvantaged position than they were ever in.

The Hungarian Women's Foundation

MONA, established in November 1992, is a nonpartisan, nonprofit foundation that has taken on the ambitious goals of redefining and improving
the role of women in Hungarian society. Many decisions have been made,
in both the public and private sectors, without input from over half of the
population and without study of the impact these decisions would have on
women. Channels of communication must be opened with those persons
whose policies and decisions affect women, and women must learn to effectively advocate their own needs.

The main goal of the foundation is to promote a more active participation by women in both political life and the civil sphere. MONA seeks to
educate women on empowerment strategies for participation in a wide variety of public roles. More concretely, MONA is currently at work on developing its main project, Women in Civil Society, which extends from
April 1993 to April 1994. This project is a series of meetings designed to
serve as a catalyst for the cooperation of existing women's groups and for
the possible integration of new interest groups into Hungary's women's
movement. The first of these "meetings" was the National Women's
Roundtable.

MONA's future plans include the remainder of the Women in Civil Society project; the third meeting will be the Conference of Women Mayors, to be held on September 30–October 1.[1] The purpose of the conference is to provide a forum for women mayors to network, to relate experiences, and to participate in specialized training at the municipal level. Recently, the director of MONA and a project coordinator traveled nearly two thousand kilometers throughout Hungary to personally speak with women mayors interested in attending the conference as well as compiling a synopsis of regional problems. The preliminary program of the conference includes one day of networking, presentation of regional reports, and discussions by experts on the situation of the local governments. The second day will consist of a "training" session for women mayors. The mayors will divide into four groups and simulate the functions of a municipality. Experts from the Interior Ministry will facilitate these groups as well as provide constructive criticism of the performance of the mayors.

Topics remaining within the Women in Civil Society Project include:

- Women in advertisement
- The women parliamentarians of Hungary
- Women's studies in Hungary
- Women's legal status in postcommunist Hungary
- Women's employment, unemployment, and retraining
- Hungary's role in the Women's World Congress of 1995
- The role of women in party platforms
- Women in leadership, politics, and business
- The National Women's Roundtable II

The National Women's Roundtable

On April 24, 1993, MONA convened the National Women's Roundtable; this was the first meeting of women's organizations since the transition of 1989 and possibly in the history of the women's movement in Hungary. In attendance were 150 women representing twenty-four women's groups that spanned the wide spectrum of Hungarian civil society.[2] Despite the rhetorical title of the roundtable—"Why is there no women's movement in Hungary?"—many women's groups emphasized that the number of participants and general success of the roundtable did indeed point to the existence of some type of women's movement in Hungary today. The spirit underlying the roundtable was best summarized by Maria Nemenyi, who gave the opening discussion for the afternoon debate:

> We believe that the rhetorical nature of the title of the first roundtable of women's organizations in Hungary simultaneously touches upon a profound

problem, which the existing women's groups themselves have already recognized. It is well known that the parties, movements, and organizations, developed along the lines of divergent ideological, economic, political, ethnic, or even personal human values, which have mushroomed since the transition of 1989, have only occasionally included the unique issues that women, making up over half of society, represent. In both public life and politics, women undertake even fewer roles than previously. Most recent legislative proposals and measures which are directly related to women's lives have hardly shaken those affected from their passivity.

Presumably this phenomenon is related to the unique development of Hungarian society since World War II, and the distinctness of the societal role of Hungarian women. Possibly because of these specific societal factors, "feminism," the female perspective, has a negative connotation in Hungary, and not only in male circles.

We think that it would be educational for the existing organizations to try together to find an answer to the question posed, albeit in a poignant fashion, in the title of this roundtable.

Of the many civic groups (grassroots organizations and other special interest groups) at the roundtable, five stand out as likely to play a determinant role in the future of the Hungarian women's movement. Following is a detailed description of these five groups.

The Gypsy Mothers' Association

The Gypsy Mothers' Association was formed in 1991 by its current president, Iona Zambo. She began by describing the Roma organization as the most disadvantaged of all because Roma women must fight discrimination not only as women (with traditionally difficult conditions within the family) but also as an ethnic minority living within Hungary. Furthermore, the name of the association is meant not to reinforce the traditional family-centric role of women as mothers and wives, but to address conditions specific to the Roma community, where it is common for a woman to marry and have children as early as age fourteen. Therefore, the concept of Roma Mothers is all-encompassing and addresses a broad range of women. The main goals of the Gypsy Mothers' Association are education and representation of the legal rights of Gypsy mothers.

Furthermore, the association seeks the healthy integration of Roma mothers and their communities into society by focusing attention on folklore, education, and successful survival strategies. The association's activities include organizing open debates on issues such as the welfare law, which, instead of alleviating the difficulties of Roma mothers, is making their lives more difficult.[3] The Gypsy mothers organize training in technical skills and work with local governments to provide secure workplaces, as the vast majority of the Roma population is made up of unskilled, unemployed labor. They have formed a wide information network that extends to all smaller communities throughout the country, which generally receive very little information about the possibilities for social mobility.

As one of the main concerns of the organization is the education of Roma youth, the Roma mothers have developed a plan for a restructuring of the educational system. Because Hungarian law assures a normative compensation for national/ethnic minorities,[4] each municipal government receives a fixed sum for each Roma child. This financial support, however, is oftentimes not used for the advancement of these children but instead serves to alienate them further from their schoolmates, as a "different." The Roma mothers' educational program would include a type of schooling in which the children participate in special training for elementary school and high school. This program would include all necessary training that the current system does not provide for Gypsies. Furthermore, the Roma mothers have organized summer camps (called lifestyle camps) and established a foundation, For a Better Future, to provide Gypsy high school students with a brighter future (the dropout rate among women especially is very high). For this new system to work, however, the association stresses that it needs the help of local governments. Finally, the work of the organization includes plans for a regional information base that will provide cultural, social, pedagogical, and institutional support for Gypsies, mothers in particular.

The Feminist Network

Nilda Bullain spoke mainly about the background and current activities of the network, and Judit Ascady addressed the reasons for adopting the name and goals of feminism. The leaflet that the members of the network passed out at the roundtable included a comprehensive description of the network, as well as the meaning of feminism, stated briefly as "the establishment of equal opportunities for women in all sectors of society, the fight against all forms of discrimination against women, the encouragement of the participation of women in political life and the civil sphere, the representation of women's issues in legislation, and the raising of consciousness with respect to women's unique problems and needs within Hungarian society."

The Feminist Network is an officially registered voluntary association. It was founded in June 1990 and now has an active membership of around fifty people from a wide range of social backgrounds, with a pool of around one hundred additional volunteers for specific campaigns. During the pro-choice campaign (from April to December 1992), there was one full-time campaign coordinator, funded by a grant from the Global Fund for Women; all other work was carried out by members on a voluntary basis.

The network has a record of two and a half years of grassroots activity, mainly concerned with raising awareness of women's perspectives in culture and politics. Its most important work has been the campaign for free choice. The seed money for the pro-choice group has allowed the network to introduce campaign methods new to Hungary, including

- Planning and completing a mass mailing of postcards to lobby individual members of parliament
- Working with political parties in the Hungarian parliament (e.g., the Alliance of Young Democrats, the Alliance of Free Democrats, and the Hungarian Socialist Party) to formulate modifications of the restrictive law on abortion proposed by the government in fall 1992
- Producing and disseminating position statements by the campaign group to all members of parliament
- Holding three press conferences to inform the media and public about the status of the abortion legislation in Hungary, thereby raising public awareness of legal procedures and parliamentary process
- Meeting with Gyorgy Szabad, the president of the Hungarian parliament, to hand over thirteen thousand signatures (thus passing the ten thousand–signature minimum for parliamentary and media release, collected by the campaign from pro-choice supporters)
- Using activist techniques to create publicity on the parliamentary abortion debate
- Releasing two half-page political ads in a prominent Hungarian daily newspaper, the *Magyar Hirlap,* to focus public attention on the issue and encourage greater citizen participation

The most innovative aspect of the campaign was the door-to-door distribution of sixty thousand lobbying postcards that included a form that could be returned to respective representatives of parliament. Furthermore, through a Feminist Network initiative, the European Network for Women's Rights for Abortion and Contraception sent an open letter to the Hungarian parliament to demonstrate international solidarity with Hungarian women.

Future plans of the Network include creating a public law center in Hungary to provide political training for women; cooperating with other grassroots movements in Hungary on issues of interest to women (e.g., promoting the Feminist Network in Nyiregyhaza); establishing a public education outreach program to involve citizens in the legislative process and media; and setting up a telephone hotline for women victims of violence (training of those who will be staffing the hotline will be conducted by women from similar hotlines in Croatia and Serbia).

The Association of Hungarian Women

The Association of Hungarian Women was developed in July 1989 as a nonpartisan and independent citizens' group. The association is actually the successor to the Women's Council, which was the official women's organization during state socialism.[5] The fundamental goals of the organization are the realization of women's human rights and the achievement of actual equality and actual equal opportunity within society. The association places great emphasis on ending and preventing all forms of discrimination against women. The group has seven hundred registered members and thirty-five to forty-two member organizations, which claim to support up to ten thousand members. One of the largest member organizations is the women's section of the steelworkers' union, which includes members from other unions as well.

The association emphasizes pragmatic activities. It formulates opinions on the impact of all major pieces of legislation on women. All of the information gathered and written by the association may be utilized by any member of parliament, committee of parliament, or government ministry. The association organizes forums on such topics as women's identity and self-esteem, the electoral participation of women, the analysis of party programs with respect to women, the problems women face in employment, sex education in the schools, and the situation of women in agriculture. With support from an Austrian foundation, the association organized a training seminar for women working within local governments. The association also fosters international relations, especially with the United Nations, thereby promoting the advancement of Hungarian women toward European norms.[6] The association performs charity functions by visiting the elderly, the homeless, women in refugee camps, and women who live below the poverty line. The association has a free "mental hygiene" service, which includes consultation with a lawyer, a psychologist, a sociologist, and a family-protection worker, free of charge. Finally, the association offers scholarships to young women entering higher education who wish to write their thesis on the situation of women in Hungary. The association publishes various pamphlets and short books on issues that concern women in Hungary today (e.g., women's unemployment).

The Ombudswoman Program

The Ombudswoman Program is a nonprofit, nongovernmental, service organization envisioned by and for women in Hungary. Adamik Maria, the creator and director of the project, stated that the overall goals of the program are to address and implement hands-on solutions to specific social, economic, and political problems facing women in Hungary as it enters the international community.

More specifically, the Ombudswoman Program is a conglomeration of three parts: a women's center that will treat the actual needs of women on a day-to-day basis, a nonprofit women's research center and library that will house all data and research based on the activities of the women's center, and an academic germanium that, fed by the research center and library, in the long run will elaborate the field of gender studies in Hungary. The over-all purpose of this conglomeration is to fuse the theoretical with the practical, to have an academic base and a practical source from which a strong women's movement may emerge.

The first phase of the program, the Women's Center, is already under way. This will be the first women's center in Hungary; no other broad-ranging service-oriented institution exists for women. The center will include direct social services, an information referral center (although many of the institutions that women may need, such as a battered women's center, family counseling, employment retraining centers for women, and alcohol and drug treatment centers for women, rarely exist, if at all), and a public meeting place where women's groups and other actors within the public sphere may meet and debate issues concerning women.

The Women's Club of Sopron

The idea to form a women's club in Sopron (a midsized city on the Austrian border), as Beata Devenyi, the leader of the club explained, was initiated by a U.S. Peace Corps Volunteer, Nancy Picard, in 1991. An English teacher for the Peace Corps, Picard picked up on the feeling of unrest among some of her women students and suggested that they meet a few times a month. Thus, the club was founded and served as a forum for women in Sopron to discuss their roles as wives, mothers, and, possibly, independent women.

Through Picard's contacts with U.S. funding agencies, the club raised enough money to plan and organize a women's conference in May 1992. The club invited prominent politicians, other women's groups (at that time there were only a few), and some government representatives from the United States to address the conference. This was the first such grassroots "women's conference" since the transition of 1989, and according to both the press it received and the participants, it was a success.

Why Is There No Women's Movement in Hungary?

Maria Nemenyi mentioned that many of the women's organizations were present at the roundtable because of "outside need"—that is, women's groups and researchers from the West have prompted a type of women's movement, a type of women's perspective in Hungary that would otherwise be missing.[7] Nemenyi outlined three possible reasons for this missing perspective. First, there is no women's movement because there is no need for one; women achieved both legal and social equality under state socialism. Furthermore, if women suffered from societal hardships, those were not considered to be related to their gender (that type of discrimination was eliminated for them by the state), but instead had to do with larger class issues that were not gender-related. Second, no women's movement developed, just as no other civil movement could develop, since the authoritarian nature of the state undermined all such initiatives. Third, women may not have felt an internal need to define their problems in relation to their existence as women; that is, women have accepted their status as something predetermined and natural, and they have no desire to change this, not that they could.[8] It is this third possibility that Nemenyi focused much of her later discussion upon—the sociohistorical and sociopsychological aspects of the Hungarian women's movement.

Nemenyi went on to disprove the aforementioned reasons for the lack of a women's movement in Hungary by explaining that (1) despite the fact that women enjoy almost full equality before the law, they are still at a disadvantage in leadership and management positions with respect to pay and social recognition; (2) there were quite a few civil groups during the 1980s in Hungary—for example, the various Roma organizations, environmental groups, and alternative groups—that did receive public recognition; and (3) although women may not feel that they are disadvantaged by the sheer fact that they are women, this perspective may have deep roots in the type of gender socialization within Hungarian society.

This third point was a very important one, and Nemenyi underpinned it by briefly addressing why the word *feminism* has such a negative connotation in Hungary today (many of the women's groups at the roundtable stated that they were not feminist in nature; the only group that took on this label was the Feminist Network). She explained that there were at least three types of feminism that should be mentioned—liberal, Marxist, and radical feminist—and that if we would look more carefully at the definition of these, not a few of the groups present would agree with the underlying concepts. Unfortunately, this term is still pejorative here, and therefore she suggested that it may be wise to just use the term *women's movement* instead.

The reason for this negative reaction toward feminism may be lodged in the reality of socialization itself; that is, the socially determined role of women in Hungary does not mesh with the ideals of feminism and emancipation. The images of women in the mass media, in the schools, in churches, and in the family define the roles women will take on in their lives. The traditional role of women in Hungary, it may be said, is socialized from a very early age to take on the dual burden of motherhood and paid labor.

Nemenyi went on to explain that the reasons for this socialization of the family and its members may be found in the history of rapid industrialization and state socialism in Hungary after World War II. The most common family type became those with two breadwinners and few children—the nuclear family. The reconstruction of the economy, and within it the status of individual family members, was both negative and positive with respect to the possibilities it lent women: Women won a larger range of social mobility while simultaneously taking on the double burden of family and paid work. For this reason, with the development of the "second economy," it was mainly men who were able to work two jobs (because they did not share the responsibilities at home) and thus benefit from a better economic status and, ultimately, from a smoother transition in 1989. Women, however, were always somehow producing less than men, and the responsibilities of the family were unilateral. Thus, the two "traditional" roles defined for women after World War II proved to be to their disadvantage.

In conclusion, Nemenyi briefly depicted the lines along which a women's movement in Hungary might develop in the future. The first could be a turn away from those dual roles that women have had to adopt as both mothers and workers and toward a movement that promotes a family structure in which men are the sole breadwinners. As Nemenyi noted, however, families in Hungary have never had this "traditional" construction and, with respect to economic reality, cannot afford this now either. It is also unsure whether women would like to step out of the workforce and public life and retreat to the family.

The second type of women's movement might organize itself around the modernization of women's roles in Hungarian society. Nemenyi mentioned that in a survey conducted of women and men about the nature of the family and the roles of family members, women seemed to provide more "modern" responses concerning integration, the sharing of familial responsibilities, and a more egalitarian relationship. Thus, this movement might address the restructuring of the family and redefine the positions of women and men with respect to society.

In the discussion that followed Nemenyi's presentation, almost all of the women's organizations present spoke. A lively debate grew around the role of women within the family, with obvious conflicts of interest arising between those women who want to define the sphere of women vis-à-vis the family and motherhood and those who believe that women should also be active in the civil and political spheres in equal numbers with men. We could also say that there was a third, "midlevel" group, which advocated that women should join the labor force, accept leadership and management positions, and be able to juggle the responsibilities of caring for the family. A few members of this middle group advocated the redefinition of familial responsibility to include men as well, although these were few in number.

A few women's groups commented on the importance of the wide range of opinions present at the roundtable, including the presence of all the major political parties, and in particular lauded the calm and nonconflictual nature of the discussion among these groups. It was widely felt that one of the major achievements of the roundtable discussion was that, although there were quite divergent opinions about what role women in Hungarian society should assume in the future, all of the women's organizations agreed that women are in a disadvantaged position in Hungarian society and that there is a need for a stronger representation of the special interests of women within the public sphere. From women's health issues, parity of pay, and equal opportunity to a stronger political representation on both the national and local levels, all the women's groups present felt that women's issues per se do exist, and that is why they have formed their organization as something aimed at women.

Notes

1. Since the roundtable, MONA has sponsored the second "meeting," on June 5, 1993, a one-day seminar on Women and the Hungarian Media. Similar to the roundtable, the conference was broken into two main topics. The morning session addressed the question "What image of women does the media portray?" and in the afternoon the panel addressed the question "What role do women play in the Hungarian media?" For the morning panel, MONA invited the editors of three Hungarian women's journals; for the afternoon, MONA invited noted journalists and reporters to discuss their experiences as women within the Hungarian media. After a heated debate, approximately twenty-five out of the sixty women who attended signed a petition to initiate a new type of women's club that will focus on the representation of women within the public realm.

2. These groups represented close to three hundred thousand women in Hungary.

3. The reason for this is that the new regulations require a woman to have (or have had) a registered workplace in order to receive welfare support; most Gypsy mothers are unemployed or illegally employed.

4. This compensation guarantees a fixed sum per month per minority student.

5. The seat of the association, as well as the president, Judit Thorma Asboth, has remained the same, although now the organization, just like other organizations, must submit a proposal to the state budgetary committee in order to receive funding each year.

6. The U.N. Convention on the Prohibition of All Forms of Discrimination Against Women was signed by Hungary in 1983. The Hungarian Women's Association distributed five thousand copies of this agreement to various women in Hungary.

7. Although it may appear that Western women's groups (as well as individual actors) have done much to initiate a women's movement in Hungary, as well as in other parts of Eastern Europe, it is problematic to assume that for this reason there is no internal need for feminism (or a focus on women's issues). Instead we might say that because of the previous political environment, social issues are not identified as gender oriented and specifically women's needs, such as women's health,

child care, employment and pay equity, and violence against women, are left un-mentioned as such. From this perspective, we may say that Western women's groups, as well as the new influx of gender studies literature, may help redefine and redirect the same issues into a gender-determined analysis. Thus, a different under-standing of the importance of Western women's groups would be to call them "fa-cilitators" that shed light upon existing women's issues in Hungary but are not identified in this way. (For more on this, see Maria Adamik et al., *Gender in Post-Socialist Countries* [Budapest: Routledge, 1992].)

8. Nemenyi also briefly mentioned that there might be a fourth explanation: that there is a women's movement, but we do not know about it because the mecha-nisms of public communication and power are in the hands of men, who don't allow the expansion of any type of movement or ideology.

Part Four

 # Romania

*Feminism in
Unchanged Hardship*

Women will realize the tragedy of their retire-
ment from public life the moment they attack
us directly from the constitution.

—Maria Antoaneta Ciochirca, Romanian
Association of University Women, Bucharest

Whereas the private sphere held the most safety in other Eastern European countries during the communist regimes, in Romania personal lives and issues were discussed outwardly and openly at workplaces and in the street—resulting, for whoever was in the wrong, in quarrels, frustration, and political marks against them on their personal record (a kind of report card detailing parentage, political affiliation, etc.). The risks to personal safety mentally and physically were so severe in Ceausescu's Romania that little remains today of Bucharest, once a thriving city of the East.

In the 1980s Ceausescu and his wife, Elena, implemented projects of national socialism and with them, severe restrictions and isolation. The goal was to make Romania completely self-sufficient, self-determined, and free of debt and dependency on foreign powers. The results were an impoverished state, where little was available to the people, and forced homogenization, which created a loss of self that was to be replaced by a new socialist people—without identity. Ceausescu's policies included the regulating of how much space each Romanian had to live in (meaning the destruction of most historical buildings and their replacement by rows and rows of identical apartment blocks), plans for regulating how many calories each individual would consume (based, scientifically, on how much activity members of each profession performed), and, of course, regulations on motherhood and the termination of unwanted pregnancies. In 1966 when the population began to decrease in Romania, a new law was instituted to reverse this phenomenon. Women were encouraged with maternity leave, monetary benefits for more children, and national "valor" awards for raising six, eight, and ten children.

Elena Ceausescu is often considered more brutal than her husband. This fact has proved detrimental to the progress of women in public life—fearing association with her and negative public opinion, women avoid public life and leave the project of reform up to men. Reform itself is hampered by a lack of motivation as Romanians begin to suspect that the revolution staged to depose Ceausescu and his family was a false one, meant simply to place his former advisers and colleagues in greater positions of power.

Within this part is the namesake for the anthology itself. When I approached Mihaela Miroiu for her contribution, entitled "Ana's Land," she decided to write a text about women's suffering by philosophically analyzing a legend about the sacrifice of women. The piece has been deemed the namesake because it is about a perfectly ordinary Romanian woman—Ana. Nearly every country has similar legends and Miroiu sites: "in Estonia, the sacrifice of a virgin for the building of a church; in Russia, the sacrifice of a pregnant woman for Novgorod's walls; in Wales, the sacrifice of an orphan;

in Japan, the sacrifice of a slave." I also interviewed five high school students studying philosophy, becoming familiar with feminism, and organizing their thoughts. The interview, called "The Future Is Feminist," speaks directly to their age and their hopes, demonstrating that these women are like any other women introduced to feminism, yet specific in the situation from which they approach it. That these women are getting the opportunity to think and talk about women's issues demonstrates the need for more role models like their teacher Mihaela Miroiu.

Lastly is a composite of several interviews, "Maria Antoaneta Ciochirca," with the lively and obscure character Maria Antoaneta Ciochirca, the founder of the Romanian Association of University Women. The daughter of a persecuted anticommunist, Ciochirca fought for her right to be educated and now organizes to influence the system in Romania, a system she says has changed since the so-called revolution.

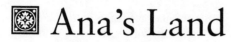# Ana's Land

The Right to Be Sacrificed

MIHAELA MIROIU

The Legend of the Arges Monastery

The legend of the Arges monastery is a masterpiece of Romanian folklore in poetic form. The legend tells us the story of the building of a very old, though still existing monastery. One day Negru Voda (the black king) decided to rebuild a ruined old wall in the Arges valley, and he hired ten builders, who were led by their master, Manole. Negru Voda promised them a large reward to build the most beautiful monastery: glory, titles, money. But if they failed, they would face a terrible death. The ten builders started their work. But they soon realized that everything they were building during the day was collapsing during the night, so their work would never be finished.

One night Master Manole had a dream, and it was suggested to him that the monastery could not be built unless one of the wives or sisters of the builders was walled in. The first woman who arrived at noon with food and drinks had to be the one. Manole told the dream to his men, and they pledged to follow the instructions of the dream but to tell no one. However, only Manole kept this promise. As he was working on the walls, he saw his wife, Ana, in the distance carrying food. He prayed to the forces of nature to stop her, and nature listened: A terrible wind blew up, and heavy rains lashed. Ana, however, forced onward through the tempests and reached Manole.

Manole told her he was going to play a game with her, and it would consist of walling her in. Ana, trusting her husband, believed in the "game." Step by step the wall was raised around her body, and she began an anguished cry. Manole ignored her as she told him that she was carrying a baby, now also in pain. Still the ten men continued, brick upon brick.

With the instructions of the dream fulfilled, the monastery was soon completed. Negru Voda marveled at the beauty of the building. He asked them if they could make a more beautiful building than this. When they answered affirmatively, Negru Voda was furious. For if they could build a better one, why had they not built it first of all for him? He forced them to the roof, where they could not escape. But Manole tried to reach the ground with wooden wings. And a small spring rose up in the place where he tumbled to his death, close by the monastery he had built.

One cannot claim that there is anything absolutely original in this legend, concerning, as it does, myths of sacrifice. Similar myths are found in other cultures: in Estonia, the sacrifice of a virgin for the building of a church; in Russia, the sacrifice of a pregnant woman for Novgorod's walls; in Wales, the sacrifice of an orphan; in Japan, the sacrifice of a slave. Sometimes the beings sacrificed are birds, horses, dogs, or cats.

In a study of this legend, Mircea Eliade commented: "The idea of creation is connected in the popular mental universe with notions of sacrifice and death. Man can't create anything perfect unless he impoverishes or diminishes his own being. As a creature, man is barren, he is unable to animate what he has fashioned except by a sacrifice—his own or his neighbor's." Eliade noticed that the Arges monastery tale does not suggest that Ana died. Instead, it tells us that one can still hear a small cry of pain from the monastery, reminding us that the baby is suffering. Thus, Ana remains alive within the walls in the same state as when she was bricked in.

Eliade also assumed that Ana accepted being walled in with serenity and resignation. Ana was sacrificed, but it was not her choice; she was duped. Think of her struggle against the phenomenal forces that waged to prevent her reaching Manole. She came to bring victuals; she was not asked to sacrifice herself. She was traditionally dutiful, but there was no duty that required her to offer to die for her husband's glory. Manole loved her but was unable to consider her like himself: She was "fond property," a possession. He was moved by craving for glory and fear for his life. Of course, he was honest—honest in keeping the secret, honest to the king and to his comrades.

Eliade was honest, too. He agreed that glory needs sacrifice, and he tried honestly to justify Manole's actions. But it is obvious that Manole behaved immorally and that the textual evidence does not support Eliade's interpretation. However, he still claimed that Ana accepted her fate with serenity and resignation.

For many years, generations of children were taught in the same blind way that the significance of the legend lies in the craving to create something and that the creation requires us to sacrifice the things we love more than any other things in the world, even to sacrifice ourselves. This legend is strong evidence for this thesis: Manole sacrificed for his king, and Ana sacrificed for her husband. (Note here an implicit analogy: The relation man bears to society, his king, is the same as the relation woman bears to man.) Eliade's "ideological blindness" prevented him from realizing the fundamental relationship involved in this legend: one in which the master had power over others. Indeed, Ana was not a free person, for she was bound to submit to her master-husband; Manole was not a free man, for he was bound to submit to his master, Negru Voda; and, in turn, Negru Voda was not a free man, for he was bound to submit to his master—his passions. Man must be an end in himself. However, this Kantian imperative could hardly seem like anything other than a dream for billions of people in the contemporary world who are slaves of the slaves, as Ana herself was. So many of us are Ana people, or Anas, for short.

Sacrifice for Others' Goals

The usual term for self-sacrifice in feminist literature is *supererogation.* An action is supererogatory if, first, the agent is morally permitted to refrain from performing it—in other words, it is not his or her duty to perform it—and, second, if the action would be a very good thing when performed. Heroes and saints perform supererogatory actions. Their actions are important for the communities they live in and point to significant human values. Now, heroes and saints have something in common: their actions. Their sacrifice is conscious and voluntary. Their choice is free.

But heroes and saints should be not paradigmatic for an understanding of the nature of supererogatory behavior. A huge but anonymous amount of supererogatory actions might be discerned in the behavior of the anonymous members of different societies. Think, for example, about the way people live and think and feel and desire in totalitarian societies—fascist, communist, or patriarchal ones. The point is, however, that something perverse happened in all of them: Supererogatory actions became regarded as duties.

In such societies, powerless people face the need to sacrifice themselves for powerful ones. Like Ana, they are walled in for the sake of a goal or a glory that is not theirs. Non-Nazis, people who do not belong to the communist *nomenklatura,* women in patriarchal societies, are all Anas. Their sacrifice is, of course, rewarded: The masters and the propaganda glorify their actions. But their actions are not valued more than the actions of anonymous people lacking personal identity. Those who sacrifice are glorified not as individuals but as people, proletarians, wives, or mothers. The master is seldom individualized; the ones who fulfill their all-covering duties, never.

Romanian women experienced this sort of training in viewing supererogation as self-sacrifice and duty. While in the Western world women struggled to assert themselves as individuals, as powerful and creative people, as different and able to create specific values, we experienced our self-creation in the walls of monuments built for the glory of a totalitarian megalomaniac power. (I must emphasize that our condition could hardly be regarded as essentially different from that of men!) Like many other tyrants, Ceausescu believed that during his reign a new Romania would be born. He ordered the destruction of many ancient historical monuments, churches, and private houses. In all the cities and in some villages, others were built according to his tastes and whims. Planning became the favorite slogan of his propaganda: planning where to work, how to live, and what to eat; planning the number of children for each family; and even planning the thoughts one is to think. Uniformity was an essential value: uniform buildings and uniform people, uniform food and lodging, uniform newspapers and thoughts.

However, behind this artificial but overwhelming "reality" the real intention was: to be forced. Forced to live in a definite place (village or city), forced to marry and to have at least four children, forced to work (not only paid work but also "patriotic," unpaid work), forced to enroll in ideological courses and learn about the "Carpathian Genius," the "Champion of Peace," "Romania's Hero"—in a word, forced to glorify the "supermaster."

Nation, people, state, and other collectivist entities were reified. Their oppressive force was directed against individual lives, which came to be regarded as nothing but the means by which to attain the "goals" of these phantasmal creatures. Our consent and our free choice were out of the question. To make people consent to their own walling-in, Ceausescu's propaganda devoted a great deal of energy to developing a new concept of man: the New Man, an ideal person trained to ignore self; to ignore personal needs, desires, peculiarities; and to be devoted entirely to caring for the final goal, for nation and state, for others, not for her- or himself.

Ana cared for her husband. She did all her best to come to the monastery with victuals, in spite of all obstacles. She took her caring for Manole not as a supererogation but as a duty. For Manole, caring for Ana was supererogatory. The standard interpretations of the legend of the Arges monastery admire Manole for the fact that he sacrificed the one he loved most. He was a hero. One might argue that Ana was a saint, for she freely consented to be sacrificed. But that is not true: Pace Eliade, Ana was not a saint since her sacrifice was not supererogatory. She was sacrificed; she simply behaved as her duties required of her. The distinction between duty and supererogation can be meaningfully applied only to Manole's actions, not to Ana's.

Like Ana, people in totalitarian systems are bound to do their duties. For them, the distinction between duty and supererogation collapses. It is those of us who try to understand them, or conceptualize our own experience, who make the distinction and claim that supererogation can characterize their behavior. I think, therefore, that the workplace in the former communist countries and women in patriarchal societies did indeed perform supererogatory actions. But this is a conceptualization of their behavior, an analytical way of looking at them, rather than a real distinction they actually experienced.

Identifying supererogatory actions with duties was a malefic consequence of the attempt to create a New Man. I have the terrible feeling that this will be one of the most perverse and long-standing remains of totalitarian societies: people who did not belong to the *nomenklatura* or women still consenting with serenity to their walling-in, to the devaluing of their being, to the belief that what really matters is the master's will or glory. I have for years been persuaded to think something like this: "What is important—to have such a beautiful building as the Arges monastery, which worked for centuries, or to save the unimportant lives of people like Ana and her unborn baby?" My answer was automatic: "Of course, the building is more important; Manole made the proper choice." We, all Anas, gave the same answer in the same manner.

In Eliade's view, there is a very close connection among creation, sacrifice, and death. He accepted a very well-known prejudice in Romanian culture: Romanians are not in search of death and do not want to die, but they are not afraid of it. In the case of ritual death, they meet it joyfully. But this is not the point with Ana and with all Anas. For we might ask, "If someone has the power to establish the rituals, are they also manipulating the joyful death?"

I cannot stop thinking about our condition in Eastern Europe under the totalitarian regimes. And it seems to me that in that context the answer is bound to be affirmative. (Of course, Eliade was not concerned with this context. But even if he was right that for centuries Romanians have been subjected to that myth, we can still contemplate those empirical expressions stemming from our recent communist experience.) During the popular uprising against Ceausescu in Bucharest in December 1989, the slogan "We who die shall be free" was, in my view, a paradigmatic form of our subjection to the myth of a joyful death. To die for a high ideal was regarded not as a supererogation but as a duty. But one obeyed this duty not because it was promulgated by the master but because it was enforced by one's own will. The autonomy of will, so much praised in Kantian ethics, found its expression in the consent to die. Paradoxically, that was Ana's first free choice.

One might object that this kind of option is consistent with a necrophiliac ideology. I think that this point, so forcefully argued by Mary Daly, is correct. Communism generated a necrophiliac ideology, a lack of joie de vivre. People were less willing to struggle for their self-expression, self-individuation, respect, and dignity (analogously, think about feminists' claims about patriarchal societies).

This essay can hardly be described as a description of what happened to women in Eastern Europe during the past half century. Consequently, my conclusion is moral rather than descriptive. I think that all of us have to fight against masterhood: against the master of man, against the master of woman, and against the master of nature. To reject Ana's condition is a moral right; to banish in ourselves and others Manole's way of thinking, feeling, and willing is a moral right. Ana's condition is, first and foremost, women's condition. But the moral right to reject this sort of condition should be shared by all people.

The Future
Is Feminist

An Interview with Five
Young Romanian Women

TANYA RENNE

We are in an indistinct, typically small apartment in Bucharest at the end of January. The atmosphere outside is oppressive and depressing. The lines for food stretch for hours, the lights on the subways are dim or nonexistent, but here in this apartment, with these five young women, we are smiling. They are bright, articulate, and complicated, as eighteen-year-olds tend to be. They tease each other and bask in the attention of their teacher, Mihaela Miroiu, who is the endless philosopher asking them questions, challenging their responses. The following is a short interview I did with these women, so willing to talk, so enthusiastic and confident.

Mara   I am Mara. I'm eighteen years old. I am a student. I will finish high school this year. I want to study philosophy at the university here in Bucharest. I have a sister.

Camillia   I am Camillia, eighteen years old. I haven't any ideas about what I will do, I am only preparing myself for something. I want to do the same—study philosophy and sociology. I know something about feminism, and I want to do something about that, too.

Christina   I am Christina. I am also eighteen. I study philosophy here in Bucharest. I also want to study classical languages. Right now I am just preparing to finish high school and to take my exams this summer.

Anca   I am Anca. I am also eighteen and preparing to study philosophy. I love cinema very much, and I would like to be a film director—not now, in ten, in twenty years, not very soon. And I like to travel.

Anda   My name is Anda, eighteen. I will also study philosophy, and then maybe I will go on to become a doctor. I am very interested in psychiatry.

How did you find out about feminism?

Mara I first learned of it when our teacher Ms. Miroiu talked about it in class. We studied its connection to sociology—feminism is very connected with sociology—and about feminist theories in philosophy.

Camillia Well, I found out about feminism first without a name when Ms. Miroiu talked about the condition of women. Really, every time she had something to say about something else. Our classes started four years ago, and she just told us things not about but rather from a feminist view. After that she told us how much she admires feminist philosophers and that there are male philosophers who are feminists . . . and, well, a lot of funny things.

Christina I can add that I know it is a new way to think old problems. I haven't read feminist books, but I am willing to think about new ideas. I don't know if I am especially into feminist philosophy but instead into this context of new ideas and trying to find new ways to live. This is what interests me.

Anca In learning about feminism, I have learned some very interesting things, but because I don't know a lot about it, I only have some ideas. The relationship between men and women has attracted my attention lately. I have some ideas which are hazy in my mind right now. I hope learning about feminism will clear them up a bit.

Anda I found out about feminism in school, just like my classmates. I am interested in it because it is a reevaluation of philosophy up until now— with very important ethical implications.

What is your personal definition of feminism?

Mara For me, feminism, the word, is related to the way of thinking about philosophy. For me, it is more a philosophy, a theory about problems, and, to be more specific, it means to change the point of view of thinking about problems. The first point is in something like the Chinese yin and yang— two ways of being that are complementary. I understand feminists think that philosophy until now is made up by extrapolating only the yang way of being and thinking for all problems. I mean the yang in terms of the masculine way of thinking, and they [feminists] want to think through these problems as they relate to yin worldviews.

Camillia I think that first of all I see in feminism a way of getting away from passivity.

Christina Feminism, for me, defines me—is strictly related to the way I am. This is a problem that became very interesting for us in the six months, in the first three grades of school—sexual differences were ambiguous.

There wasn't a strict line difference between boys and girls—we tended to have the same, let's say, mentality. Now we are beginning to separate, and I am very interested in the differences. I have always thought that being a girl and then a woman—well, you have to be yourself—well, this is a kind of cliche. I have always considered that being a woman is very different. Women have always had the power to caress, to be friends, motherly—that isn't a very good word for it—but this is a quality that men do not have. While without too much accent on feelings—this attitude is very important that women have the power to take care of things in a very different way.

Anca I think I am quite interested in an old philosophical problem—what is our nature? Our cultural determination? I think feminism is a new way to look at an answer.

Anda I think that feminism is a way to rehabilitate the feminine way of life. Reevaluation in the sense of giving it a new sense, another sense—a sense different from the male way. So I think that feminism is valuable and worthy in itself, not as a copy of something else, like a copy of a male model.

What is the best thing about your life and the worst thing?

Mara For me now in Romania, I am not very interested in politics. For me, Romania is a collection of places where I have been in my childhood and in my life. So I think the best thing for me in Romania are the friends—the people and the places where I have grown up. I spent my childhood on the seaside. The hardest thing is to not be able to travel and meet people from other countries; that is how one learns other ways of thinking. Of course, there are a lot of people to know here; it is also difficult not being able to know a lot of people here. I want to know places and art and people, too.

Camillia The worst thing in my life up to now has been me, myself. The best is something that others have given me. There are also good things I have managed to do lately to get out of a kind of depression—a very long depression, full of ups and downs.

Anda The most difficult thing for me right now is money. Not having money means I cannot travel as much as I would like to. It also means I cannot be on my own, independent from my parents. The most beautiful thing is life with my friends and the people I love.

Christina The hardest and the most beautiful things are quite complementary. The hardest thing is the constant way in which the intellectual potential ruins itself in this country—it is very painful to see. Very bright people cannot get what they want. This is not ambition but rather a reinstallation of values. I think I am quite optimistic at this age, and I am not sure if I will have the same opinion in ten years. The most beautiful thing is quite complementary because it is my friends. Americans have a word for it: great. Great from both points of view—intellectual and human. They are a great comfort to me always, and this is why it is painful for me to see how they fail. It is also their lives at stake, and you cannot forget that.

Anca For me, Romanian, it is my language and a kind of relation to the people which I haven't had outside (I spent two weeks in France). There are other problems as well—the economic situation is very bad because I need money to travel and to have books and music. I have begun to understand that it is a very important problem. I am afraid of a kind of Romanian fatality, our pathetic situation and position. The best thing—I don't know—this relationship with people and my language.

What is the first thing you would change if you could change anything?

Mara I would like to be independent economically from my parents. This is related to our situation in Romania. I would also like to have other kinds of friends.

Camillia The first thing I would like to change is giving to young people after more than eighteen years old the possibility not only to have a job or to earn money but also to have a house of their own.

Anda I would always be materially independent so that I could work and travel. I'd also like to have more friends.

Christina I'm not really quite sure if I can change anything. But if I could, the first thing I'd change would be myself. It is quite a selfish point of view, but I'm not quite pleased with the way I am, and I would change myself if I could. What would I change about Romania? Well, this would be a very altruistic—I would change everything except what I have right now. I mean, I would change everything but my friends. I wouldn't change them—they are unique, and I wouldn't want something else.

Anca Of course, material independence. I would like to have it, too. And for myself I would like to be able to do everything I want—to have the energy not only to make plans but to realize them.

How do you imagine your future and the future of Romanian women?

Mara I am not very optimistic at this point, though I am generally an optimistic person. I think it is hard to change something like this—the way of life in Romania and women, too. Maybe I am wrong; I hope I am wrong. I think, for me, it is possible to avoid the same life my mother and grandmother had. Maybe they liked it, but I don't. With my grandmother and my mother I doubt they really wanted to change anything. That is the worst thing: Romanian women don't always want to change their lives. I could never do the same.

Christina I don't imagine my future as being something small and bright. I imagine my future as being something huge and indefinite. I don't really know if I can do anything about my future. I would like to become something, but I don't know what. So I will wait. This is my philosophy right now: Wait and see.

Anca I think that my chance would be to travel—to meet a lot of people. Because when I am changing lifestyles, I have a lot of energy. Changing gives me energy, and I think I could think and be very social if I could travel.

Anda There are certain things that occupy my mind at present. It is about men—I am going to be a woman who gets the man she wants. It is also something about the moment—living the moment, feeling the moment.

What do you feel is your responsibility to the future and to yourself?

Mara My professional future—I am responsible for that. I don't trust the future very much, but I think that because there were people who told me I had a chance in this field, I can do it. At least for that I am the one who is responsible for doing something important and new. About the rest of my life—I think I am also responsible for being friendly with others and to make them, if I can, happier, but certainly not making them unhappy.

Anca I am trying to choose, in my life things for which I feel I have the whole responsibility. Like trying to express myself or being happy.

Christina For me right now, the future is very hazy, and I just don't think that I know very well what depends on me. I don't know what I will be doing in ten years, but I think something very important I have to do is to give. This is very romantic and idealistic, and I don't know if it is a very practical point of view. It is quite a foolish point of view to give and not to receive. But I like it quite well just now. I hope I will like it in the future—whichever future I have.

Maria Antoaneta Ciochirca

A Testimony

MARIA ANTOANETA CIOCHIRCA
TANYA RENNE

Maria Antoaneta Ciochirca is the founder and president of the Romanian Association of University Women. An activist as well as an educator and a surgeon, she restarted the association in 1989 (it had been banned in 1944) with the purpose of reforming education and getting women a better education in Romania; she hopes "to allow women the opportunity . . . to keep their heads up and their feet down." Her work on the association has made it clear that little has changed in Romania since 1989. "My phone has been disconnected by the police, and my mail takes three weeks to reach me from the other side of Bucharest. I'm having problems with the police even now, after the reforms." When asked about women's activities and progress in Romania she says, "Romanian women are inactive from ignorance. Just ignorance. We are not able to think in another manner. . . . It is a kind of strange illness, like a sort of HIV."

In this account she describes how she survived the years her brother and father were arrested as traitors. "My reasons for being an activist (as opposed to a theoretician) come from my childhood and my father's life before me. My father died in 1951 in prison not like a theoretician but like an anticommunist militant. He was also a very active person, and he died for that."

I was nine years old. The Securitet's agents came to arrest my brother. When they came searching, I hid beneath the staircase on the way to the cellar. An officer gave me candy to tell him where my father was. No response; he made me walk along the yard as he pointed his gun against my neck. Angry they couldn't find my brother, they took my mother to their car. Crying for her, I lay down in front of the car, desperate. The officer ordered the driver to "run over the dirty rat." But the latter had kids of his own, and he drove around me. When they left, they sealed the house we were living in, so my grandmother of seventy-eight and I had to live in the stables. The house was changed into "an official room" for the delegates coming from the center. Mother returned after two weeks. It was winter, and she had no warm coat and was nearly unconscious in the cart they brought her in. She had been bitterly beaten and kicked; she was vomiting blood. They had wanted to know where my brother was. My grandmother, who had lost both of her sons in World War II on the same day, paid no heed to the communists and took down the seal they had put on the house and put my mother to bed in the house. She had been watching and nursing her for a month, praying to God to save her, with no medicines and no doctors at all. In order that we might survive, we sold almost everything we had in the house, keeping for us one bed for the three of us, a wardrobe, and a table. I was imploring God to have the snow melt in order to look for stinging nettles to eat and keep soul and body together.

My brother was caught and arrested, so the terror intensified. In 1951 I sat for an entrance examination for high school and ranked second. But I was not accepted on the account that I was the "daughter and sister of 'great enemies of the people.'" Desperate, I left for Bucharest, and there I applied to the Ministry of Education, where I was allowed to attend high school, but only as a private student.

In the summer of 1951 Mother went to the Securitet to inquire about my father, about whom she had heard no news since 1947. He had had no rights to parcels or visitors. She was told that my father was all right and advised to leave the parcel there.

That very same day I found out that my father had died in February; the news was brought by a man from the country who had been set free from Gherla's Prison. He barely disclosed the truth about my father because it was forbidden and he was very frightened. That very evening my mother came home, happy that my father would receive a parcel. I was not able to tell her the truth; I couldn't spoil her happiness. However, my mother learned of my father's death much later. For years she had hoped, and it was not until 1957 that she accepted the truth. Six years had passed since his death, and she received his death certificate together with inheritance charges and formalities. In the death certificate, number 414477, the cause of death was listed as "myocarditis." Who knows what "cause" broke his heart? He was fifty-eight years old.

I graduated from high school and sat for the admission examination to the medical faculty. I promised myself that if I got accepted, I would go to Gherla's Prison and look for my father's grave. There I found the detainee graveyard somewhere on the outskirts of the town—a barbed-wire enclosed meadow surrounded by a ditch full of water. I sat near the grave site and stayed there until dark, wondering how much humanity and kindheartedness lay beneath the heaps of earth without gravestones or names at all. There was one big wooden cross with one arm broken. No one passing by would have known that that place was a graveyard where people had been buried after dying for the sake of truth and justice. Somewhere, there under the ground, my father's body lies.

Many thanks to the Ex–Political Detainees' Association for building a memorial to those who died at Gherla's Prison—for our heroes.

But I cannot forgive the communists who let them die and buried them cruelly without permitting their families to do so with honor and tradition. I can no longer forgive those of today either, these leaders who further hold back the truth from us. The hated communists who today pretend to be anticommunists unscrupulously lie on the graves of the young, who died for freedom and for the death of communism. Romania's governors of today are an insult to our heroes, and the surviving people are still afraid of them and thus allow them to retain their power.

Part Five

 # Bulgaria

Dependency and Reform

Perhaps if we convince all the women, the men wouldn't be such a problem.

—Feminist playwright, Budapest

Bulgaria was closest to the USSR and perhaps most assimilated with Soviet rule and policy. Progressives in Sofia today consider themselves lucky for not having been completely consumed by the Soviet empire as the Baltic states were. This close relationship meant great dependency, and contemporary, postchange Bulgaria is feeling the crunch of the loss of Big Brother. Bulgaria was one of the last socialist countries to make reforms and turn over its government to democratic principles. The time that it took Bulgaria to reach the same level of social change as its neighbors was spent watching what others were experiencing. The wisdom of this approach, whether it was planned or was just stubbornness about giving up power, was evident economically: Prices have been controlled more in Bulgaria than in other Eastern European countries, where inflation increased food costs three and more times. This is not to say that the economic situation in Bulgaria is any better or more stable than in any of the other "blossoming" democracies. Their previous isolation behind the iron curtain, their prior intimacy with Moscow, and their current isolation behind the blockaded Yugoslavia have made economic gains difficult to maintain.

The future of women in Bulgaria has yet to be realized as the country is still busy getting on its feet. Activism is unknown, unheard of, and thought of as impossible. This puts Bulgarian feminism in the same category as Romanian feminism, with the same organizations providing the ground for future endeavors. The Bulgarian Association of University Women is one such group actually daring to call itself feminist. The association is at odds with the university structure but maintains itself on the margins, being shuffled from one empty office to another. The association is responsible for holding feminist conferences largely for an intellectual audience considering issues of language, Sigmund Freud, and other topics condoned by the institution, yet doing so with respect to gender.

Dobrinka Parusheva begins this part with "The Bulgarian Women's Movement," a short history of the beginnings of that movement, and in "My Weakness Is My Strength," Rossica Panova gives a short personal testimony about Bulgaria's treatment of the underprivileged, including women and people with disabilities (categories to which she belongs). Kornelia Merdjanska, in "Forked Tongue," looks at how gender is constructed through language and what the Bulgarian language has to say about men and women.

There are only a few independent Bulgarian scholars carrying the entire load of feminism, and they are doing so outside of their country's borders at Western institutions and international conferences. Given the primarily academic nature of the movement at this point, the influence they bring back with them will do a great deal in bringing Bulgarian feminism into the twenty-first century.

◈ The Bulgarian Women's Movement

A Brief History

DOBRINKA PARUSHEVA

The great changes after the war for liberation from the Ottoman Empire (1877–1878) influenced all spheres of life, the life of Bulgarian women included. Gradually, the Bulgarian woman started moving beyond the confines of the family, struggling to overcome the patriarchal mentality imposed on her for centuries on end. At the end of the nineteenth and the beginning of the twentieth century, an ever-growing number of women directed their attention to the teacher's profession, and consequently, quite soon, women's need for an equal educational qualification with men was obvious. In the beginning, individual women (the most famous of whom was Ekaterina Stoichkova), and later some of the already existing women societies,[1] protested against the law prohibiting the admission of women into universities. The first petition to the National Assembly that insisted Bulgarian women be given the right to higher education was submitted in 1896.[2] It is these first organized protests against imposed limitations on women that can be considered the early manifestations of the women's movement in Bulgaria since they explicitly show the desire for equal rights and opportunities, even if only in one specific area.

At the end of the 1890s, a great number of new women's societies emerged, and in November 1899 the Sofia society Conscience started publishing the newspaper *Women's Voice,* with editors in chief Anna Karima and Julia Malinova. The first issue of the newspaper contained an appeal to all the existing women's societies in the country to unite in one common women's union. After one year of preparation, in July 1901 the constituent congress of the Bulgarian Women's Union was held. The charter that was adopted at that congress aimed at "the intellectual and moral advancement of women and improvement of their situation in all respects."[3] At that stage the major idea of equal rights could be the only common uniting ground for all women's societies; the issue of equal rights was still quite alien and distant to most Bulgarian women. Throughout the following years, the gradual overcoming of the traditional mentality of women brought about certain changes in the wording of the union's aims. In 1907 the phrase "for the establishment of equal rights" was added. In 1921, in a different cultural and political framework, the Bulgarian Women's Union proclaimed the equality of women as its priority.[4]

Feminism has had its roots and major achievement mainly in Western Europe. Coming from a different background, feminist ideas needed time to grow in Bulgarian soil. In addition, there were numerous attempts by various political parties to put the union under their guardianship.[5] On top of all these influences, there were also personal prejudices and struggles for power.[6] For all these reasons, the Bulgarian Women's Union did not manage to reach a large enough section of the female Bulgarian population. As a result, the union remained mainly an urban formation of wives, mothers, and daughters or politically and socially active men.[7] Its activities were limited primarily to education and charity. Only a few of its initiatives were directly related to the struggle for professional, civil, and political equality for women.

Perhaps it is this inability on the part of the Bulgarian Women's Union to follow a truly feminist line that provoked the emergence of another women's union in 1909—the Equality Union, led by Anna Karima. This second union, for example, strongly encouraged and supported women lawyers in their struggles to be admitted to the bar. It also made the first proposals and submitted petitions for women's suffrage.[8] Unfortunately, this union did not last long.

Despite numerous difficulties and crises, the Bulgarian Women's Union existed until the end of World War II.[9] In 1947 the union was simply turned into a government organization—the Women's Union of the Bulgarian People. In this way the intention of the social democrats, since the beginning of the century, to turn the Bulgarian Women's Union into a proletarian organization was accomplished—through power structures.

Notes

1. Even during the renaissance years under Ottoman rule in Bulgaria, there were many women's groups/societies. However, they were the product of specific historical conditions. See Pundeva-Voinikova, *The Bulgarian Woman During the Renaissance* (Sofia: 1940); and V. Paskaleva, *Bulgarian Women in the Renaissance Years* (Sofia: 1964).

2. Anna Karima, *A Women's Movement in Bulgaria* (Sofia: 1910), pp. 5–6.

3. Ibid., pp. 7–99.

4. Ibid., pp. 12–15.

5. In the period 1902–1905 there were debates on whether the Bulgarian Women's Union should have a class or a feminist character. After social democrats failed to turn the union into a proletarian organization, a lot of socialist members left to form their own women's union. See R. Bradinska, *The Emergence and Development of the Socialist Women's Movement in Bulgaria, 1885–1915* (Sofia: 1969).

6. This was quite typical of all social and political formations at the turn of the century in Bulgaria.

7. In 1931 out of eighty-four hundred members, only three hundred lived in rural areas.

8. See Karima, *A Women's Movement*, p. 10.

9. See *Bulgarian Women's Union* (dedicated to its 30th anniversary) 1901–1931 (Sofia: 1931), pp. 15–19.

◼ My Weakness Is My Strength

ROSSICA PANOVA

In this essay I am going to present a personal case that mirrors the whole system. Can a personal case be somehow representative of a certain society? At first glance, this is a difficult question since every individual is characterized by idiosyncratic features and is a microcosm of ideas and feelings. Society, however, is not a mechanical sum of people; it also has its laws and modes of living—it can both support the individual, encouraging his or her happiness and well-being, and easily kill a person. In Bulgaria for the forty-five years of communist rule, people were taught to exclude the individual and adore the group. Therefore, by exploring the relations between the individual and the society, we can define every person/individual case as representative, too.

What is my personal case? Can the relations between me and the rest, between me and the society I am living in, be in any way indicative of the nature of the latter? Can I really change anything in these relations? These are the questions I consider in the following pages.

It is no secret that to determine how humane a system is, we can look at its attitude toward the sick, the old, and the children. I myself belong to the first of those groups: I suffer from multiple sclerosis, and as a result I have difficulty moving around. I am thirty-four years old, married, with a six-year-old child. I am a specialist in medieval history; I have professional ambitions, a book of mine has been published, I have a fair command over several languages, and I am writing a dissertation. The problems I am having can be approached on two levels—personal and professional.

First come my problems within the family. How can I make sense out of my life? How can I be useful to my child? How can I overcome being a prisoner in my own home? This was one of the most grave psychological traumas I had to live through and struggle over. I had to work out a "compensatory mechanism" to neutralize my frustration and my own "inefficiency" complex. As far as my son is concerned, it took a lot of effort since he was growing fonder of his father (who took him for walks and gave him baths, etc.), and I had to fill up the rest of the space around him. I had to overcome my jealousy, clench my teeth, and devote my time to him; play with him, learn poems together by heart, teach him English, listen to classical

154

music, initiate him into the world of art. From time to time it comes to my mind that perhaps in this way I make up for my own inferiority complex or perhaps satisfy my personal desire to listen to classical music, visit art exhibitions—hypocritically presenting it as a wish to educate my son. Perhaps both are true. My greatest achievement is that in certain spheres I am an indisputable authority for my child, and I am sure that when he grows up, he will not suffer from or develop an inferiority complex because his mother is disabled.

But here come the second-level relations: those outside my home-prison. They are much more horrible because our society is still backward, retarded, and uncivilized and run by "the laws of the jungle." We take part in a game without any rules, a game in which the individual has no meaning since our society consists of "masses," not individuals.

What are the advantages of living in a "primitive" society? The first advantage is that it is a patriarchy, and connections by blood and friendship matter a great deal. Therefore, there is a strong mutual aid among people, which sometimes turns out to be crucial in finding the way out of a situation. For example, thanks to my brother-in-law, who works in a pharmaceutical factory, I managed to get myself an essential steroid that was not available in drugstores.

Now, what are the disadvantages of our society? By far the worst is that there are no means to protect and support its socially insecure citizens. Therefore, such citizens live at the whim of bureaucrats' arbitrary decisions. A centralized structure has been established everywhere, from the field of economics to politics and science. Totalitarianism is by nature aggressive, amoral, and oppressive. These features predetermine the dominant male role in society. It is not accidental that almost all dominant positions in enterprises and research institutions are occupied by men. Women can be appreciated as intelligent, hardworking, and promising, but every attempt on their part to make a career meets the silent resistance of the board, consisting exclusively of men.

The controversial relations further worsen in situations in which "physical weakness" is used to derail women's ambition. For example, I couldn't do anything to keep my boss from suspending my application procedure for the DAAD Fellowship in Germany a few years ago. His explanation was that "sick people shouldn't be sent abroad," and there was absolutely no way to send my application documents to Germany since the matter was discussed and solved on the level of the Bulgarian Academy of Sciences. As another example, when I could not manage to hand in my dissertation on time (because of health reasons), my boss and tutor both refused to appoint me and provide me with a job; there is no mechanism to guarantee my human rights. Obviously, my tutor, though being a professor in medieval history, cannot, short of having lived during the Middle Ages, successfully

decide the reality of that era (in which knights defeated thousands of enemies to become heroes but were often extremely generous to weak and
poor people). The attitude of my boss only reinforced my conviction that
independent behavior is the best weapon for self-protection. Thus, my personal weakness is my strength.

This weapon, however, is personal only. The struggle against the system
is really difficult and should be a collaborative exercise. On the surface, the
system was decapitated, but it has been reproducing itself and still functioning without a halt, flawlessly. In similar situations I like quoting the example with the hero who (in the fairy tale) manages to cut off the head of
the dragon, but immediately two new heads emerge to replace it.

But let us get back to our subject: Once becoming an outsider, ostracized
by the system, one remains on the street and cannot go back into society.
Medical service and treatment in Bulgaria are of such a low standard that
one ought never to get ill. Even nowadays hospitals and clinics contain slogans like "The greater number of healthy people, the greater number of
builders of socialism," or "Lenin has said that the greatest asset is health!"
The true meaning behind these words is that we are being treated once
again as "human building material" useful only at work, just the nuts and
bolts necessary for the proper functioning of a system. Only in 1991 did
newspapers reveal for the first time that every day a Sofia citizen enters a
psychiatric ward (*Duma*, April 9, 1991), that a "suicide syndrome" is
rapidly emerging (*Troud*, February 21, 1991), or that infantile paralysis,
scurvy, and abdominal typhus are on the rise (*Troud*, February 21, 1991).

It is more than obvious that the slogans covering the hospital walls are
absurd, that they hide a disastrous situation. We used to paint the facades
of houses along the big boulevards walked by foreign visitors to keep them
from seeing the dirty back streets. In a similar way, sick people and disabled
people have been hidden from society—there are no specially adapted telephone booths, lifts, or wheelchair platforms for them. These people are
forced to become marginal figures of society because the latter doesn't need
their intellect and abilities yet. How long will that go on? This is an extremely unhealthy attitude, pointing out the symptoms of a serious illness—
this time, the illness of society.

There is still another important aspect: Growing into an atheistic society,
doing away with religion and church, we have also done away with human
kindness and compassion. I myself am a pessimist, for economic reasons,
first, and for moral reasons, second. It will take a lot of time to rebuild our
ability to notice people around us, to build up a new sensitivity toward the
surrounding world. The totalitarian system has washed away religion in
people's hearts, replacing it with communist ideology. At the same time,
our nationwide poverty killed our traditions and stole from us the feeling of
being humane. Is it possible that being humane should be a privilege only

for the rich? Yet it turns out that for a single person to be humane, she should possess enough human qualities and intellect, whereas for a society to be humane, it should have traditions and wealth. The road to that goal is sure to be long and painful. Until that time the individual can rely on personal mechanisms of resistance but not on any social protection.

Forked Tongue

On Gender Stereotypes in the Bulgarian Language

KORNELIA MERDJANSKA

Feminist theory and practice from the very beginning have stressed the importance of language as a basic means for structuring and representing the self and society. If one of the goals of feminism is to unveil the workings of the patriarchal value system and to reveal the structures and control of social and cultural "order," then we should start, as Helene Cixous has pointed out, by analyzing the politics of language: "I think that no political reflection can dispense with the reflection on language, with work on language. For as soon as we exist, we are born into language and language speaks [to] us, dictates its law, a law of death: it lays down its familiar model, lays down its conjugal model and even at the moment of uttering a sentence we're already seized by a certain kind of masculine desire, the desire that mobilizes philosophical discourse."[1]

For centuries on end, human consciousness has been defined by men on the basis of male standards and thus has been constructed as a male consciousness. In the patriarchal paradigm the subject of human consciousness (man) hasn't totally ignored or forgotten the woman; we cannot complain that women and women's images are totally missing. On the contrary, the (male) history of human consciousness abounds in women's images and symbols, but only in one role—the negative role of the Other, always defined as the "object" of that consciousness.

In Bulgaria, as in most Christian patriarchal societies, women have been reduced to the grand and grotesque symbol of "Woman." The latter is quite ambivalent and contradictory, expressing everything and anything that men have wanted to put into it simply on the grounds of being different from them. Unfortunately, many women have uncritically internalized that male model, taking it for granted, taking it for generic, the unified male language model included. Only recently has the question of representation come to the attention of social and critical thought in Bulgaria. The rendering of the world is extremely topical when everything exists through representation, through transmission and retransmission. Poststructuralist feminism finds "the tooth of crime" in the very system of representation as an already established patriarchal paradigm.

In what follows I try to analyze the way that a hostile, dualistic, patriarchal consciousness has rendered female nature in the Bulgarian language. Can we speak of two different gender-marked languages within the Bulgarian language—male versus female—or of only one "male," universal, ordered, unified, and antiwomen language?

It would be of extreme interest to trace down the attitude to the two sexes as reflected in the usage and interpretation of language forms, of the grammatical category of gender, of the models for word formation, of pronominal concord, of the usage of the basic generic word *man*. But for the lack of space, I'll concentrate only on a few cases of binary opposition and asymmetry in the Bulgarian language, on phraseological and lexical levels, on the basis of samples from major dictionary entries.

For example, in the entry on the word *woman* in *The Bulgarian Language Dictionary* (Naiden Gerov in 1899),[2] the first meaning of the word refers us to an endless chain of stereotypes and stereotypical expressions related to women's physique, psychology, behavior, and roles. Here is an example: "The woman is weaker than the man"—written in an absolute, categorical mode deprived of any doubt. This example sets not only the mode of expression but also the strategy of definition and illustration. Half of the following expressions in the dictionary entry, mainly borrowed from Bulgarian folklore, define women only through subjugation/relation to men, from the male point of view, and/or in comparison to men. At the same time, the dictionary entry on *men* defines them only on the ground of what they do, what they think, and what their social status is. So here we have an ideal example of misogynist thinking—the male desire to enclose women in rigid male parameters. What is more, the first and foremost principle of defining/categorizing women is dominantly pragmatic: the utility/harmful effect women have in relation to men. Therefore, the binary division is not only external, men versus women, but also internal, within women themselves good versus bad on the ground of the male utilitarian position.

This aspect of the Bulgarian language is evident on the imagery level of all the enlisted expressions and in the common juxtaposition technique applied in them: The generic form of "woman" is quite often opposed to the first-person masculine singular form, equated with the generic. For example: "If anyone should fall ill, let it be me; if anyone should die, let it be my wife." In almost all similar cases the "I" of the first-person singular refers to "he" but never to "she." We cannot ignore the imperative mood in many of the male first-person statements. For example: "Give your wife to me, and you go to sleep in the forest," or "Who listens to a woman is twice a woman."

Out of all the fifty expressions listed under the heading "woman" in the dictionary entry, six are neutral to the semantic category "female," only two offer a positive connotation of the word, and the rest are overtly negative. For the sake of clarity and categorization I have divided the biggest group of expressions where the word "woman" has a negative connotation into three subgroups centered on the image employed: women as animals, women as inanimate objects, and women as items of male possession. Here are three examples of each group:

Group A
1. A bad woman—a ferocious animal.
2. A vicious woman—a furious pig.
3. A woman without a husband is like a horse without reins.

Group B
1. A woman is like a chair without a leg—you can always replace it with another.
2. A house without a woman is a well without a bucket.
3. Wine is for drinking; women, for beating.

Group C
1. I give my wife, but my horse I won't.
2. Who gives his car, he will give his wife, too.
3. A woman is like a willow tree; it will grow anywhere you plant it.

This body of expressions outlines an obvious scale of female values (from the male point of view): First comes work ability; second, female goodness, that is, humbleness; and last, beauty. The analysis also suggests a few basic stereotypes as related to deviations from the male norm—for example, the rough division into the binary oppositions health/sickness, fertility/sterility, stupidity/cleverness. The order in the last binary opposition has not been mistaken. It turns out that the feature "cleverness" is the unmarked, second member of the binary opposition: That is, intelligence and smartness are not evaluated positively by the Bulgarian authoritative male norm. Here is one expression summing it up: "A brooding woman goes unwashed."

The expressions reflecting a deviation from the male patriarchal behavioral norm are quite rough and abusive. For example: "Don't touch an abandoned woman and a pepper bitten into," or "A barren man is a sharp knife, while a barren woman is evil itself," or "A sick woman—a real distress." For whom is the distress?—no need to ask.

If we check out the language prescriptive norm as illustrated in the same dictionary but referring to the lexical item "man," we will come upon a similar symmetry in men—women's correlation as well as the same strategy and direction of definition and self-definition. It is "man" again that is the strongly marked member of the opposition as in most cases this strength and leadership position are grounded in superiority over the "second/weaker" sex. This tendency is so eminent that even when certain negative male features happen to be mentioned, they automatically reflect negatively on women, too. For instance: "A ham-handed man goes with a ham-handed woman." So the direction of identification has been preserved regardless of the male values or lack of values that women have to identify with. The major difference, however, when we compare the two dictionary entries emerges in the overall picture of gender stereotypes they fix and circulate through the language. If the "woman" entry stresses mainly characteristics of weakness, instability, dependence, and deficiencies in women, the "man" entry emphasizes the positive male qualities of strength, power, ability to work hard, courage, and dignity—all those universally acknowledged "human" values.

This situation one hundred years ago is disturbing, but what is even more disturbing is that nowadays, at the end of the twentieth century, the male position in the Bulgarian language, in communication, and in social life has remained unchallenged, unshaken, and unshakable. Leafing through the *Dictionary of Synonyms in the Bulgarian Language,* published by the prestigious Bulgarian Academy of Sciences in 1980,[3] I discovered that the only synonym for the word "woman" was "wife," whereas the synonyms for "man" were (1) "a human being" and (2) "husband." These entries provide evidence of the emergence of an alarming tendency—that the war between the sexes and gender stereotypes are further intensifying. A new feature has come to the surface now: Along with the hostility between the sexes/genders, the demarcation lines between the two have become more rigid, and a new inflexibility is developing. This can be seen in the strongly negative and pejorative connotation behind certain phraseological expressions trying to bring the two sexes together. It has always been recognized that the attribute "woman" or "woman's" in the Bulgarian language has a negative connotation, as in the following expressions: "a woman's logic," "a woman's work," "a woman's faith," "What can you expect of a woman?" But when these supposedly woman's features are attributed to men to mark a deviation from the "correct" male norm, the connotation behind the deviation is not simply negative, it is pronouncedly pejorative. Here are a few examples from *The Bulgarian Language Phraseological Dictionary* (published by the Bulgarian Academy of Sciences in 1974):[4] "a woman's tail," a dialect idiomatic expression meaning a son-in-law living at the house of his wife's parents; "a woman's Holy Virgin," a mocking name for a man who loves talking with women; "woman's Doino/Kaletz/Rajo," meaning an effeminate man who is interested in women's affairs. The list of expressions about men who have deviated from the male stereotypes, codes, and social roles is endless and various. What is persistent in all those expressions is a lack of tolerance of any breaking of the male rules, any signs of closer contacts with the Other. Analogically, whenever the attribute "man's" is attached to women and women's names, we have the same belligerent reaction on the female side. For example, all expressions such as "mannish/manlike Gana/Dragana/Doina/Dana/Raina" signify a woman with rough and arrogant behavior, and here the attribute "man's" again has a pronounced pejorative connotation. What more conspicuous proof do we need of the unwillingness of both sexes to yield to closer contact, to let the Other into their own private territory? Why this growing hostile reaction to the feminization of men and the masculinization of women? Who wants to keep the sex/gender stereotypes, and why?

Social psychology has shown that stereotypes are necessary; we need them because they offer simplified and generalized evaluations of one group of people to another group of people. They serve as a group norm in helping orientation, as a defense mechanism against the foreign/the Other, as a compensatory mechanism, as a mechanism for control over the Other. Yes, indeed, stereotypes are quite comfortable, simple, economical—they save time; they give a sense of pleasure and relief by ridiculing the Other; they are anonymous, and because of that, they are safe and uninvolved; they are parasitic; they do not demand much thinking; they are accessible, creating the feeling of something familiar. A small wonder after being repeated so many times!

And yet I personally hope that just as racial, national, and ethnic stereotypes have exploded, have revolted, have been stripped naked and turned upside down, sexual/gender stereotypes will stop being "innocently" consumed; women and men in Bulgaria would stop internalizing them uncritically. Sooner or later this will happen because of the very contradictory nature of stereotypes: They may simplify human relations, but at the same time they hamper them; they may create a certain feeling of belonging and security within the group, but they create tension outside it. Paradoxically enough, by accepting and using stereotypes, we become more and more a part of the community, of the group. By refusing to accept them, we become more of an individual. I wish we (men and women both) could be more individual in our thinking, communication patterns, and language practice. Let's try to break up the freezing uniformity of the male-created language dogma and speak "more" languages, that is, the various languages of different social, age, sex, national, and ethnic groups. To put it in a nutshell, that would mean building up our own language to be more open, tolerant, and inclusive of the language(s) of the Other.

At this point the discussion goes back to one of the fundamental questions of feminism: Can women have equality, or can we have difference? Or can we have both? Mikhail Bakhtin's dialogical model proposes the latter option: a dialogue in which both identities preserve their entity, in which there is neither integration nor identification; a knowledge-dialogue in which the Other is equal to the I and yet different. Bakhtin poses the question "In what way will the event be enriched if I succeed in fusing with the Other? If instead of two, there is just one?" To my mind, the understanding between the two sexes shouldn't be reduced to identification; the temptation of unity should be resisted. We should strive toward an understanding that ultimately transforms the Other into a self-other. Let me finish with Bakhtin's own argument for such a transformation: "What do I gain by having the other fuse with me? He will know and see but what I know and see, he will but repeat within himself the tragic dimension of my life. Let him rather stay on the outside because from there he can know and see what I cannot see or know from my vantage point, and he can enrich essentially the event of my life. In a mere fusion with someone else's life I only deepen its tragic character, literally double it."[5]

Notes

1. Helene Cixous, *Castration and Decapitation* (1981), p. 45.

2. Naiden Gerov, *The Bulgarian Language Dictionary*, vol. 2 (Sofia: Plovdiv, 1899).

3. *Dictionary of Synonyms in the Bulgarian Language* (Sofia: Bulgarian Academy of Sciences, 1980).

4. *The Bulgarian Language Phraseological Dictionary* (Sofia: Bulgarian Academy of Sciences, 1974).

5. Mikhail Bakhtin, *Author and Character in Aesthetic Activity* (Moscow: Estetika Slovesnogo Tvorchestva, 1979).

Part Six

 # Serbia, Croatia, and Slovenia

Feminism, War, and Peace

I would like to understand how people who speak the same language now speak the language of weapons.

—Feminist activist, Belgrade

Although most active feminists in the former Yugoslavia are occupied with the business of war and all the problems and issues affecting women inherent in it, the feminist movement in the republics of Slovenia, Croatia, and Serbia are the oldest and most solid in the whole of East-Central Europe. The contemporary wave of feminism in Yugoslavia began with an international feminist meeting in Belgrade in 1978 that sparked the formation of independent women's groups in Croatia and Serbia and further established the groundwork for five pan-Yugoslav women's meetings between 1989 and 1992, the location of which rotated among the republics. Yugoslavia's relative openness to the West during the same years, while the rest of Eastern Europe was confined to stimulation from further east, is, in large part, responsible for this early development of independent women's thinking, if not groups, within an alternative movement for social change.

Until the mid- to late 1980s, non-party-affiliated groups were restricted. The loosening of those restrictions, along with the wave of the alternative movement in Slovenia (in the late 1980s), spread across Yugoslavia, and independent groups such as Women's Group Tresnjevka of Zagreb, Women and Society of Belgrade, and Lilit of Ljubljana came into being. As a whole Lilit of Ljubljana became the most comprehensive in forming women's culture through dances, discussions, and consciousness-raising about women's position, rights, and identity.

Partly as a result of this "new" consciousness and looser restrictions, a telephone hotline for women and children victims of violence opened in Zagreb in 1989 and was followed by similar groups in Ljubljana and Belgrade. This common work and the principle of fighting violence against women established the connection among feminist activists throughout Yugoslavia until the onset of the war in 1991. The hotline in Yugoslavia, although preceded by more exclusively intellectual discussions and endeavors, firmly established the grassroots nature of Yugoslav feminism.

With the beginning of war in Slovenia and its spread into Croatia, Yugoslavia crumbled and threatened this link and heretofore common community. Grave difficulties emerged with respect to nationalism—prompted by war and political difficulties—thereby calling into question the strength of sisterhood and common struggle. While some of the women have left their respective hotlines to form other groups, or have branched off into further projects, other feminists—new to the movement and old alike—have maintained contact across various and volatile front lines.

As the republics themselves have become more and more separate and communication has deteriorated, whether because of concrete communication restrictions or public opinion, the movements have become separate and distinct. The fact that Yugoslav feminism was once a shared movement and the fact that its members share a common history and, to some degree, a common goal of antiwar and antiviolence speak clearly to the strengths and weaknesses of sisterhood in times of national and nationalistic crisis.

This part on the former Yugoslavia includes pieces from women in Serbia, Croatia, and Slovenia. Not every women's group or self-proclaimed feminist group is represented here. Instead, I have chosen those most prolific in their work as well as most accessible. It was not my intention to highlight certain groups but rather to represent the situation in general most accurately.

Serbia

The essays included from the republic of Serbia are exclusively concerned with issues of war and nationalism, peace and tolerance. Stasa Zajovic is a well-known peace activist and a founder of Women in Black Against War, Belgrade. In her piece "Nationalism and Serb Women," she talks about how women are used to propagate war and convince the population to support antiwoman arguments for increased birthrate for more soldiers, militarism, and the valuing of death above life. Zajovic tells her personal story of frustration in "Being a Woman." She describes her own sense of homelessness in a country that recognizes women's value only in their willingness to produce sons and then sacrifice them for the good of the nation. She calls for a sisterhood presently threatened in the former Yugoslavia.

Biljana Regodic poetically describes an encounter with a male colleague demanding her allegiance to the state in "Homeland as a Form of Women's Disloyalty." She elucidates her frustration with the nationalist focus on reproducing the nation.

In "Belgrade Feminists," collaborators Vera Litrichin and Lepa Mladjenovic, both feminist activists from the hotline and Women in Black, briefly describe the period leading up to the present in Yugoslav feminism and the feelings and frustrations they have today as members of the Serbian nationality who are feminists and women first. This section concludes with "A Call for Action," a manifesto by the group Women in Black Against Violence.

✦ Nationalism and Serb Women

STASA ZAJOVIC

The militarization of the former Yugoslavia has meant the imposition of military values, symbols, and militaristic language; a cult of necrophilia (expressed in slogans such as "The frontiers of Serbia are where Serbs are buried"); and an acceptance of political and moral totalitarianism. Along with these ideological shifts have come a rigid separation of masculine and feminine roles—in short, woman as mother and man as warrior—and the political marginalization of women.

Throughout the postwar period, concern over women's social condition in Serbia and Yugoslavia has been reduced to an obsession with keeping up the working-class birthrate. As nationalism replaced class struggle as the basis of political discourse in Serbia, this obsession with reproduction was transferred to the nation. With the 1987 "antibureaucratic revolution" (led by Slobodan Milosevic), a strange sort of sisterhood began to show itself in the streets. Huge crowds throughout the country shouted, "We want arms"—in a collective trance, united in hate and desire for vengeance for Serbia's "offended nationhood."

In tandem with the cult of blood and soil, the new Serbian nationalists also summoned to life the symbolic medieval figure of Mother Jugovic—the long-suffering, brave, stoic mother of nine offering her children up to death in defense of the fatherland. Maternity is now to be seen as an obligation, not as a free option for women; women's sexuality is to be controlled and reduced to procreation.

Kosovo: The Democratic Counterrevolution

Serbia's demographic slump has been described as "one of the greatest tragedies of the Serbian people," particularly since the "demographic counterrevolution," a perceived threat posed by the Albanian women of Kosovo province, who have the highest fecundity rate in Europe. Serbian repression in Kosovo has as one of its objectives a reversal of this demographic gap. This reversal has been seen in increasingly militarist (or "national security") terms. The structures of militarized power now insist that the birthrate must grow so that the nation can defend itself in military conflict with other people.

Women are blamed for any shortfall in this sacred mission: "I call upon all Serbian women to give birth to one more son to carry out their national debt," stated one politician. Another, Rada Trajkovic of the Association of Kosovo Serbs, was even more explicit in viewing mothers' sons as cannon fodder: "For each soldier fallen in the war against Slovenia (June 1991) Serbian women must give birth to 100 more sons."

Political Pimps

The manipulation of women by the military establishment began some time ago. The clearest examples, however, are found in the rallies held by the Women's Movement of Yugoslavia, which is linked to the promilitary parties and formed in 1990. In February 1991 the women of this movement publicly lent their support to the Jugoslav Narodni Armi, saying they considered it the only force capable of saving the country. The women have been used; the military hierarchy carries out the function of "political pimp," putting women on the street to give their approval to ends that are contrary to women's own interests.

Before the massive wave of mobilization for civil war, there were warnings in some parts of the country—such as Montenegro, known for its martial traditions—that men should be prepared to give up their lives for the fatherland and that anything less would be a blow to their masculine dignity. Men were expected to follow national tradition, whereby "in war not one Montenegrin man can be protected by a woman." One parliamentarian stated, "We in Montenegro believe that a man who is fighting at the front and allows himself to be hauled back by a woman should commit suicide at once." This perception that women are preventing men from fulfilling their national duty was reinforced in radio broadcasts from the Dubrovnik front, in which a high percentage of Montenegrins were involved. Soldiers would send greetings to their fathers, brothers, and male friends but not to their wives or girlfriends.

Rejecting Manipulation

Happily, the number of men who wish to free themselves from this macho war culture is growing, and more are not ashamed of being protected by their mothers, wives, and sisters. A committee of women was formed in Montenegro in October 1991: "We raise the voice of protest against the private war which those in charge are making from their offices. They have sent their sons out of the country and onto the tennis courts, while our sons carry on being carried by force to the front and to their graves. We demand that these demented leaders, politicians and members of the military resign immediately in order to save this country."

Women as Soldiers

An increase in the number of women in the army is no indicator of sexual equality, least of all where there has been no corresponding democratization of society. There are women in all the militias and national armies now active in the former Yugoslavia, and these women are appropriating the most brutal patriarchal values.

Women members of the Serbian military in Croatia do not occupy important positions in the military hierarchy. The front line is for the men; the *knidze*, or "female militia," in the words of one member, "occupy the administrative jobs, communication services, health, stores. We are simply replacing the boys who have gone into combat. But we, too, have passed the military entrance exam, and we can help the boys at any moment."

A small number of Croatian and Serbian women fighters have gone to the front and have been rapidly converted into mythical figures. This confirms what patriarchal history teaches us: that women enter history only when they have taken on masculine roles. The media celebrate these women as heroines when they kill the enemy; but when women fighters from the other side are captured, they are denounced as "monstrous women."

The first female battalion of the war was established in Glina (a Serb-majority town in Croatia annexed to the Serbian autonomous region in December 1991). Members took the oath "We will fight against all of Serbia's enemies under the protection of God" and heard male officers declare sentiments like "If our mothers would not have been heroines, they would not have given birth to such valiant children." Patriotic women also fight on the "home front," of course. In Belgrade, women knit socks and gather winter clothing to keep the boys at the front warm. The progovernment media fawn on every evidence of maternal mobilization, at the same time ridiculing the work of women in the antiwar communities and centers.

Clearly, the majority of women are on the side of peace. They are convinced that they can offer the historical female alternative: nonviolence in place of violence, life in place of death, vitality in place of destruction. Stana Pavic, an elderly refugee from a Serbian village in Croatia, told me that "we women . . . should have united like them [the military]—we could have made a peace accord in no time at all."

The Mothers' Movement

With the end of the war in Slovenia in early July 1991, human rights—above all, the right to life—lay in ruins all over Yugoslavia. In such a situation, women burst onto the political scene demanding the right to live. On July 2 a parliamentary session in Belgrade was interrupted by several hundred parents, mostly conscripts' mothers. This was the first civil society initiative against the war in the federal capitol and the first protest against the abuse of women's reproductive work by the state, nation, army, and party. "Men are the controllers of the war and of our sons. We do not give them permission to push our sons forward to kill one another."

As a result, the very role that marginalizes women in their private lives— reproduction—has had the effect of converting them into active participants in the political life of the nation. So the patriarchal divide between the personal and the political weakens; the personal has become the political in this war. The mothers' movement has contained all the ingredients for a militarist's nightmare. Nevertheless, the mother's movement has been subject to different types of manipulation by political structures. A part of the mother's movement has been used—both in Serbia and Croatia—for patriotic propaganda. It is easy to exploit the sentiments of mothers whose sons' lives are in danger. The soldiers' mothers at times feel confused, internalizing the struggle between the "patriotic" sentiment that underlies official propaganda and the desire to save their own sons.

Yugoslav women have been linked in a feminist network since 1987; they have managed to maintain solidarity and plan joint activities ever since, rejecting the conditions that support policies of divide and rule. As the war continues, normal communication is impossible with the cutting of telephone lines, post, and transport between the republics. In spite of such practicable obstacles, feminists—Serbs, Albanians, Croats, Slovenes, Hungarians, and Montenegrins—are united in organizing against the war. Joint and simultaneous protests, such as the weekly Women in Black Against War demonstrations, are a product of this unity of purpose.

◈ Being a Woman

STASA ZAJOVIC

Being a woman I have no homeland.
> —**Virginia Woolf**

Women have entered history only when playing male roles, most often as warriors, sometimes as martyrs: like the mother of Jugovic, the sister of Batric, Joan of Arc, Marija Bursac. Not long ago, one of the groups of Kosovo's Serbs sent a message to Slobodan Milosevic that he must not resign not only for the sake of "all the Obilichs, brothers Jugovic but also for the sake of all Mothers of Jugovic."

Have women ever had their own country? What is our homeland? Can it be our body if the "first territory that was and still is colonized is our body, the body of a woman"? Has the body of a woman ever belonged to herself? They say that a woman belongs to the family, to the nation, to the homeland. A woman transfers her body to children (through birth), but which body is it: the one that commits violence or the one that suffers violence? Violence has its gender.

In my native country people still say that having daughters is the same as not having children at all, that daughters are "other people's dinner." A woman bearing sons brings to the world "pride," "happiness," "treasure." If a woman cannot have children, such households are still called "empty houses" or "deserted." Biological reasons for barrenness used to, and still are, searched for in women, never in men. I left my native country a long time ago, but whenever I come back, I hear the same thing again: "He chased his wife away from his house; she can't bear children for him." No wonder that many internationally recognized ethnologists claim that Montenegrins deny the existence of blood relation between the mother and her male children. "This is my son, and those are your daughters"—that's what they say. Men would even want to take over the power of childbearing, especially over certain fruits: children of male sex. Unable to create themselves, they pride themselves for heroism and make wars: "war as a symmetric addition to motherhood." And women, often in order to survive, speak male, warriors' language. The movement of women from Niksic warned men in this war again to "follow the tribal, popular, and national tradition": to go to war. The women will be there to duly cry and mourn after them, after they have been "sacrificed on the altar of the homeland."

A mother gives birth to, mourns after, buries the dead; she visits the graves of dead soldiers, of warriors. A philosopher from Montenegro, V. Vujacic, gave the following explanation of this necrophiliac social role of women (mourning, wailing): "Female qualities are especially evident in a mournful song. A mourning song renders evident not only the emotionality of a woman but also her 'natural' right to judge the events and people. She appears in several roles through a mourning song—as a guardian and a builder of morality." Everything is in perfect accord with a necrophiliac culture: woman as a mother, guardian of morality, guardian of death.

My childhood memories are filled with pictures of women in black clothes, be they cousins or strangers. Women in black, women who wear largely black and sometimes black and white or dark colors. Black as the impossibility of choice, ultimate picture of life without colors, without nuances. Maybe they also wanted to express their protest by the black, but would they dare? The sister of Batric is torn by pain after her brother's death, but nevertheless she encourages men to fight against their foes. While I am standing every Wednesday in black and silence "in order to think about ourselves and the others," pictures of women from my childhood would appear in my mind. Unlike their black clothes, mine were here to mourn not only loved ones but also, after all the victims of this war, those who have died in all wars. The wearing of black does not represent surrender to mourning, to sorrow; it is resistance against the killing of towns and of people, against the violence in everyday life.

Women in my native country still do not talk about their own oppression. I know that their very silence is a sign of a very powerful oppression. The fact that they do not speak does not mean that men are supposed to talk for them. Women in my native country sometimes interrupt the silence about themselves; they make their suffering visible by committing suicide.

I left my native country a long time ago, but when I come back I hear the same as before: "She slipped away" (she hung herself). The rate of women suicides related to the total number of inhabitants is the highest in the world. Women who commit suicide are commonly over fifty years of age. Body for the others, life for the others, they finally take control over their own bodies, but only after they have taken care of other people's needs. Is this part of the history of traditional Montenegrin heroism? That kind of history never allowed women to enter it. What is patriarchal history but the slaughter of the Other? It does not recognize Others, Different Ones, an Other Sex. Even women have never shown interest in that kind of history.

Men's and women's worlds are segregated in my native country. Women are separated among themselves (by their families, by their husbands, by their sons), but nevertheless they are often together as friends. I have never heard, not in my childhood and not now, that during their meetings they talk about the "glorious battles for the fatherland." They always talk about other things, about "their own history," about the things that they have created, built, freshened, healed, mended, comforted, made strong, reconciled. Neither history nor the fatherland has ever shown any interest in these qualities and values. However, this does not mean that women from my native country and elsewhere are "outside of history." They and all of us with them want to build another history, not the one of fatherland, "land of fathers," as a sequence of killings and deaths. We want to construct a homeland as a "country of life and feelings," or, to use the words of a dear friend, "There are as many homelands as there are life forms, as there are alliances and contracts on cooperation, as many as the possibilities for each of us to create love, friendship, respect."

Homeland as a Form of Women's Disloyalty

BILJANA REGODIC

My body is my biggest trap. I'm not getting caught in a country, not just any country and anyway, not easily. When I think about my country, when I search for it, I find it in the boundaries of my body. My country spreads along my body, reaches the boundaries of my senses, searching for colors, for sights, for smells and sounds.

Inside my body I carry the coast of Istria, with the grass rushing into the sea, the politeness of the local people; the walls of the ancient town of Motovun woven into the rocky hills behind the coast; the trees of Slovenia on the road to Porec; the sounds of Bascarsija on a sunny morning; the face of an Albanian who, in Sarajevo, talks lovingly about Belgrade the very moment that the war begins; the heated cobblestones of Stradun; the sounds of different languages in a summer camp in Makarska; Slavonian villages like swans in blue-green waters; the vineyards on the slopes of Macedonia; the silence in Ravanica; the liveliness of impoverished Kosovo, swarming with children; huge snowflakes about the fir trees of Zlatibor and the closeness of starlit waterfalls in the night; the sand of Sutumore; skies, skies across Vojvodina, the endless rich soil, crows, rains, frosts, and wheat. . . .

Peace is the possibility to realize one's country. To make it grow. To discover new colors. To find out that countless forms of existence are within it. War kills with its lack of imagination. It imposes life in limited forms. Whatever happens in a war has happened thousands of times already. In the novel *Cassandra*, Christa Wolf has drawn with a hand of a woman the line that embodies all wars—from the war of Troy to our days, through the sameness of their contents and the forms in which they appear. Here are several stereotypes evoked by Christa Wolf:

- Helena, in fact, does not exist—the war is waged because of a phantom. The reason for the war is only a myth.
- "It's our gold they are after" (the excuse used by Priam to avoid turning a lie into the truth; pronounced aloud, it would bear no value).

- "Negotiate, give them loads of gold, all the treasures that you have, just make them go away, let Troy stay intact!" (implored Cassandra). "Nobody negotiates about the rights and unquestionable properties!" (replies Priam).
- "The king is scowling and people are less afraid of killing and bloodshed than of the angry eyebrows of their king."
- Women, go away, this is man's business! Women were "equally afraid of their maddened husbands as of the enemies." Push away that woman lest her wailing weaken the morale of heroes.
- "I would rather have Troy perish than have my beautiful son killed." He does not even know his son. It's not the son that he is saving but the very idea of maleness. So let everything perish for that idea to be maintained.
- Everybody has to think about the homeland in the same way: "Whoever is not with us is our potential murderer." (It seems to me that from this moment onward the name *fatherland* would fit better than *homeland*.)

Many women have been stopped by such sentences. Even more men have done the same. An enormous strength is needed by both men and women to avoid this trap, to avoid becoming the prey of a male impoverished concept of existence in which only the repetitive talk of parrots is heard and we can fly only as target pigeons. It is a long way to an understanding that Father, too, can be a sinner, that Greeks and Trojans are alike. In the end one becomes indifferent to the "family honor." When Cassandra reached the end, she said, "One can tell when a war begins, but when does a pre-war start?"

If there were any rules about war, we would be obliged to tell them to the others, and on and on. To write them in clay, to carve them in stone. What would be written there? Among the rest would be the following words: "Don't let yourself be deceived by your own people." It's been a long time to be deceived by one's own people, even before the war crushed Yugoslavia. Only recently was I able to recognize open offenses against the territory of my country. My cousins, acquaintances, colleagues, passersby, all of them keep shouting, just as a colleague did: "Can't you see that we are getting ruined? And you want to know why? Because our women are ruined. Ruined, because they are more engaged in politics than in bearing children. It's the law of nature! You must obey it. That's what happiness is all about. I know. You should be bearing children instead of. . . ."

He also thinks that the leader is right. Well, whom can you trust if you can't trust the government? They are in power because they are capable. This is all the fault of Europe, of the whole world. What is Milosevic supposed to do? The war was unavoidable. You could not just leave the Serbs to the mercy of other people. At the same time, my colleague avoided the draft. He was not really ready to fight in the war. Well, it's because of his work, you know; he had no time for fighting.

But I am supposed to give birth to children, to save the fatherland from complete ruin. Well, I had enough of this bully being at my throat—shaking colors, sights, and sounds out of my head; pushing me into a cage; turning me into an incubator. I screamed, defending myself from this monkeylike compatriot of mine, miserable bearded thing, intelligent as a worm, who dares to insult the border of my country. "You miserable idiot, kissing the feet of the tyrant, pushing others into the war while being careful about your own work. You let steam out by assigning capital punishment to women. To reproduce the country of death and senselessness at the very moment when there are no medicines, no sterilizers, no surgeons' thread to sew up the wounds, no food for children, no diapers. What does that mean? Will women die in childbirth just because men do not know what to do with themselves? Because men won't give up the myth of themselves? It is already too much to force us to live without the smells, without the colors, sights—but this? To die for them or to be unable to have children if you want to, as nonethnically acceptable women would not."

My colleague was astonished, but I managed to silence him. He won't talk with me about politics anymore. He realized that I will not take part in the reproduction of male impoverishment. Nothing will force me to have anything in common with this insane genetics. Such miserable idiots do not deserve progeny.

Let the light perish completely in the fatherland so that the criminals will not be able to act anymore, so that we, who think it humiliating to talk about our eagerness for life in front of them, will be able to start thinking about it more easily.

I do not need Croats, Serbs, or Muslims to blame for grabbing away the homeland. Mere men are quite enough. The closer they get to me, the more dangerous they become.

Belgrade Feminists

Separation, Guilt, and Identity Crisis

VERA LITRICHIN
LEPA MLADJENOVIC

Writing this essay about feminist activities and our lives during the past couple of years, the three of us are here in the kitchen thinking about the most horrible fact of our lives: the war. Two million people have already been moved from their homes, many are injured, and many others are dead. A couple of million more have no food, heat, or much hope to hold onto. We are aware that citizens around us do not want to know that winter will kill thousands of more people, that soldiers and other men will rape thousands of more women, that rape is not a national but a gender issue. One of us is nervous on and off; the other cannot even hear Srb (the spelling of Serb in Serbo-Croat) in one place without being angry. The time has come for women to get out on the streets and scream.

For forty years, the ideology of the equality of the genders, so well known to the entire Eastern bloc, masked the reality of everyday life for women. Nevertheless, a semiautonomous women's association, the Anti-Fascist Front of Women, was formed during World War II (1942), and many of our mothers were active there. In 1953 the front evolved into the Union of Women's Association, which included approximately two thousand small women's units all over Yugoslavia. In 1961 these women's organizations were abolished, and the party formed the Conference for the Social Activities of Women, which was hierarchically organized and governmentally divided.

The history of Yugoslav postwar feminism started with an international feminist meeting in Belgrade in 1978, which was the turning point for the rise of women's groups. Since 1980 two Women and Society groups have been formed, first in Zagreb and then in Belgrade. The Belgrade group provided an open forum for discussing women's issues. But in 1986 women decided to call the group "feminist," create "women-only space," and start with activities and meeting on a regular basis. At this time the Conference for the Social Activities of Women was accusing the group of being an "enemy of the state," "procapitalists," and a "pro-Western element."

Activities of the group included action surveys on the streets of Belgrade concerning violence, solidarity, and housework; and workshops and public discussions on topics such as mothers and daughters, guilt, violence, abortion, sexuality, working rights for women, psychiatry, the medical system, and cinema. From the beginning the group was without any institutional, financial, or other state support, working completely independently.

At that time there was a great deal of cooperation among feminists in Ljubljana, Zagreb, and Belgrade, the result of which was the first feminist meeting of Yugoslav feminists in Ljubljana in 1987, where the Network of Yugoslav Feminists was formed. Three similar meetings were held following this: in Zagreb and Belgrade, the last being in Ljubljana in May 1991.

In summer 1991 Yugoslavia disintegrated. In April 1992 the so-called Third Yugoslavia was formed with a new constitution that, among other things, eliminated Article 191 (included in the constitution of 1974), which concerned "free parenthood." This article protected "the human right to decide about the birth of one's own children." And now its absence introduces the possibility of reduced access to abortion and reproductive rights.

In 1990 the feminist group Women and Society disbanded and multiplied into several other women's groups. The first of them was a telephone hotline for women and children victims of violence, established March 8, 1990, and the second, a women's lobby. That summer, in response to the first "free" elections, women from different nonnationalist parties formed the Women's Lobby in order to put pressure on political parties running for election. Then in autumn of the same year, the Women's Party—ZEST—was born with the aim of improving the quality of women's lives in every respect. It was formed with the intention of utilizing political campaigns for promoting consciousness about women's issues.

On March 8, 1991, a women's parliament was formed in response to the mere 1.6 percent presence of women in the Serbian parliament (the lowest percentage in Europe). The purpose of the Women's Parliament was to observe and respond to all new laws that discriminated against women. On October 9, 1991, Women in Black Against War appeared on the streets of Belgrade in protest against the war in Croatia (later in Bosnia) and was afterward joined by women in Pancevo. On March 8, 1992, after a year of preparation, a women's studies group was formed with the intention of presenting and discussing feminist knowledge. Subjects included women's perspectives on patriarchy, philosophy, lesbianism, family, socialism, literature. The course is still outside the university, free and open to all women. A lesbian and gay lobby, Arkadia, was founded in winter 1990 with the intention of working on the social visibility of lesbians and homosexuals. The group organized public discussions, some activists wrote articles, but student and youth institutions refused to offer a space for group meetings and a few times denied the proposal for a public discussion.

One of the first actions of the Women's Lobby was a "minimal program of women's demands" addressed to parties and movements. The demands concerned the fields of work and unemployment, sexist education, reproductive rights, violence against women, health care, and the change in certain laws concerning women. The final demands were for a ministry of women, a refuge for women and children victims of violence, an inclusion of a certain percentage of women in parliament and the parties themselves, a decriminalization of prostitution, a recognition of rape in marriage as a crime, and mandatory child support for all children of divorce.

In September 1990 the lobby issued an open letter to the public in reaction to one of the leaders of the oppositional nationalist party, the Serbian Movement of Renovation, who urged Serbian women to "reproduce the greater Serbian nation." Among other things, the letter said, "One supposes that young Serbian fetuses will be immediately baptized, conditioned to hate and to lead the war against the many Enemies of the Serbian nation." Just before the elections, on December 5, 1990, the Women's Lobby issued an appeal to the public that read as follows: "Don't vote for the Socialist Party of Serbia. . . . Don't vote for their leader Slobodan Milosevic. . . . Don't vote for nationalist, Serbo-chauvinistic parties (SRS, SPO, SNO . . .). . . . Vote for the candidates of the civil democratic parties."

At the beginning of 1991, a joint demand for the creation of a ministry of women was handed to the Serb parliament and signed by the Women's Lobby, the Women's Parliament, and the feminist group Women and Society. Other protests/actions included:

- A petition regarding the Resolution of Population Politics in Serbia and a law concerning family planning (June 1990).
- A protest against the representation of women in the 1990 census (in which women were instructed to give their husband's or father's name) (August 1990).
- An appeal for the demilitarization of Yugoslavia (August 1990).
- Support for the Mothers' Peace Initiatives in Serbia and Croatia (August 1990).
- A protest against new textbooks based on nationalist, patriarchal, and sexist values (December 1990).
- A protest against discrimination against lesbians and gay men in derogatory political discourse (August 1991).
- Protests against the sexist behavior of the members of the Serb parliament (1991–1992).
- A protest against the document "Warning," issued by the Serbian Academy of Science and approved by the leading party program. Eight men who signed it condemned the high birthrate of Albanians,

Muslims, and Gypsies as being "deviant from rational human reproduction" (1992).

- Critiques of the sexist language used in the independent media
  (1992).

Appeals made together with Women in Black made clear that feminist
groups of Belgrade believed that the Serbian regime was responsible for violence, war, and an absence of civil democracy and civil society.

Women in Black consists of a small number of women who have been
coming out into the streets since 1991. Even though their number is small,
their vigil is important in maintaining the pressure and presence of women
against the war in the streets of Belgrade. They symbolize women's condition in war: as refugees, as those who care for refugees, as mothers and sisters of the dead, as those raped and forced into prostitution. In their appeals they point to the patriarchal and sexist essence of nationalism and
war. Women in Black has become part of international women's peace initiatives in Italy, Germany, Belgium, Israel, France, Switzerland, and Great
Britain. In international meetings in Venice and Novi Sad, the group created space for specific themes such as women and the fatherland, nationalism and gender identity, and women and the embargo and provided an opportunity for women in the former Yugoslavia to experience the globality
of sisterhood.

The telephone hotline for victims of violence is run by about 30 women;
in 1990–1992 more than 150 women volunteered, responding to more
than 3,500 calls. Women who called testified that 80 percent of the perpe-
trators were either husbands, ex-husbands, sons, brothers, or fathers. They
also stated that in 30 percent of the cases they suffered severe injuries and
that in 60 percent of the cases the violence had lasted more than ten years.
The work of the hotline has substantiated well-known facts about male violence against women, but in 1992 new types of war-related violence appeared:

- Death threats increased from 30 to 55 percent of all calls.
- The percentage of guns present in assaults against women doubled.
- Veterans of the war turned violent against their wives and mothers
  for the first time. There was an increased incidence of machine guns
  (often kept under the pillow), rape of wives, constant mental abuse,
  and severe injuries.
- Violence in interethnic marriage increased.
- The post–TV news violence syndrome appeared. Men were violent
  against their wives after being exposed to nationalist propaganda.
  The wives in these cases were of every nationality.

As a general conclusion, the hotline proves that the war has led to an increase in all types of male violence against women and that within the family men are using nationalist hatred as an instrument of violence against women.

Issues Facing Us Since the Beginning of the War

Separation

When the war started, nationalist hatred increased drastically, and the Serbian government began to produce propaganda and the notion of the enemy. Suddenly Slovenians became an enemy, then Croats, then Muslims, then Americans, then Albanians, and so on. Deep conflicts emerged in families and in workplaces, and women began to separate on that basis. Completely new questions appeared in women's groups. Can a feminist be a nationalist chauvinist? Can a pacifist be a nationalist? Is a weapon an instrument of defense? Should the groups take clear attitudes toward nationalist questions and in that way lose some women? Should the groups avoid the issue of nationalism altogether? Should women merely sit down and confront their beliefs about it and see what happens?

In any case, apart from Women in Black and the Women's Lobby, where the nonnationalist statement is clear, all the other groups had problems. The most difficult situation, and the most often avoided, was a confrontation. Every time the nationalist question came up, there was no way to overcome the fact that a lot of women were being hurt. Women suffered but usually did not change their attitudes. There was a great deal of silence and crisis. For example, the Women's Party was eventually not able to continue. The conflicts over nationalism were far too strong in dividing women, and there was no way to go on. The party decided to "freeze" its activities until the war was over and then see. The hotline had many problems as well. Despite the fact that the group had had a deliberately nonnationalist policy from the beginning, some volunteers were unable to keep their nationalist feelings out of their hotline work. Several attempts were made to reconcile the opposing viewpoints; after that some of the women left, and some of them stayed and remained silent.

Nationalism made some women split within themselves. It caused painful wounds in Zagreb-Belgrade feminist relationships. Nationalism brought new discriminative population policies. The reduction of available abortion, already true for Croatia, is on the way in Serbia. Here we find ourselves in the unfamiliar situation of witnessing the legitimation of hatred against women, and it is increasing daily. These new nation-states dominate women's bodies. These states need their national body and women to reproduce it. They are fed with hate and on the separation of women from one another. They are based on violence against Others, but everyone is a potential Other; neither the "sacred nationality" nor "the sacred gender" is a guarantee anymore. Nationalist policy brought in the war, the death, the war rapes, the refugees, then the punishment of ordinary people through an economic embargo.

Guilt

Not all feminists in Belgrade feel guilt about the ongoing war. They do not feel guilt either because they have anarchist orientations or because they have separatist tendencies. Some of the women do feel guilt, and it's a guilt for what a government they didn't voted for has done in their names. Others feel guilt for the fact that innocent women die and are being raped and they can do little or nothing about it. We came to a conclusion that some of this guilt can be stimulating, giving energy and the drive to work, but too much of it can overwhelm us and make us feel helpless. Moreover, the absence of guilt does not mean the absence of responsibility.

How can I speak to a friend in Sarajevo? Just because I have electricity and food and she has not makes the gap sometimes unbearable to overcome, and what am I to do? Can peace activities lessen my feelings of guilt? Does my presence at opposition (chauvinist and male-oriented) demonstrations against Milosevic reduce my feelings of helplessness? If I tell her that I care and that I think of her and that my dreams are full of fear, will that help her? If I tell her that we stand here in black on the corner every week and people spit on us, saying that we are "the bloody traitors of the Serbian nation" and "idle whores of Tudjman and Izetbegovic"—if I tell her all this, will she say I am a fool, that she risks her life every moment? If I publish an essay in which I express hatred of the war massacrers and rapists of all sides, and in which her suffering becomes the essay's pulse and a value beyond telling, will that help at all? And if I say we've been in Italy, Germany, and France and women are sending their love and support from all around the world, will she even blink? If her windows are broken, if a liter of water costs DM 20, if her hair has turned white and her cheeks are sunken . . . ? Seven months later she is speechless, awaiting the winter that could wipe them all out.

Identity

Many women in Belgrade have no ethnic identity problems; they have always felt Serbian. Others are able to feel "positively Serbian" as pacifists and feminists. Some of us, though a small group, cannot identify with the "Serbian nation." Before this we were "Yugoslavs" and therefore never really identified with Serbs at all. At this point when we are forced to take a Serbian nationality as our own, we see that there is nothing, but nothing, at all that can cause feminists to accept it as their own national identity. The "Serbian Nation," as the present government creates it, certainly has nothing in common with "Women's Nation." Our Yugoslav post–World War II feminist movement has never done anything in the name of this/their Serbian nation.

In addition, some of us believed in some of the socialist ideas legitimated by former communist governments: relative social equality, free education, free health care and access to abortion, inexpensive housing, and cultural events. But we are facing the fact that the realization of our beliefs has come to an end. So for those of us who are not Serbs, yet who are not Yugoslavs anymore and feel the loss of women's rights with the fall of communism, there is a lot of identity work to be done. Women-identified women have a strong basis of identity for beginning that work.

We know that to overthrow the present government, we have to vote for another one that will be against us, and we must take that responsibility. We know that if we are to manifest our disobedience toward the war and be noticed, we have to stand in the opposition's street crowds and feel awful among sexist, royalist speeches and songs. We know that if we stand on the streets as small women's groups against war, and are not noticed, we expose ourselves to insults, but we do that and feel brave. We know that if we are to deny the concept of national identity, there is nothing else they'll allow us to stand for in exchange. We know that while men are urged to die courageously for their nation, raped, murdered women will never be considered brave, except by us. We know that if we are to say aloud who we are and what we want, there will be no historically accepted political patterns for our experience or our language. And yet here we are.

❋ A Call for Action

WOMEN IN BLACK AGAINST WAR

They have been ceaselessly killing, torturing, and raping for two and a half years already. They have banished more than 3 million lives. They manipulate women. They blackmail men. They spread hate, destruction, and death. We are left without words to express our horror and anger.

They haven't stopped yet.

Fascist leaders of Serbian politics threaten us with war in Kosovo, Macedonia, and Serbia. Meanwhile, they have stopped all electricity, water, and telephone systems in Bosnia and Herzegovina. People die by the minute. No matter which names they have, they die of the cold, illness, and hunger. And it is only November.

Fascist leaders of Serbian politics continue to destroy all positive interethnic communications. They have separated streets, classrooms, families, and cities. They are drawing lines on mountains and corridors through the countryside.

Since 9 October Women in Black Against War has come out every Wednesday on the streets to express its absolute disapproval of all nationalist politics. Above all, Women in Black accuses the fascist Serbian regime of being responsible for the death and destruction. According to their ideology, not a single life has value, not a thousand lives, not 1 million, not 3 million and counting. In the end it doesn't matter if they are Serbian or not.

Since their bullets and the cold will wipe out another one hundred thousand people in Bosnia and Herzegovina, since men will rape thousands of women of every nationality, since war is possible in Belgrade and anywhere—Women in Black calls all women for all types of civil disobedience.

The misery in which we live should not frighten us but incite us to resistance. It is strange that we have not yet started to scream. Our friends from Sarajevo, Bihac, Mostar, sit every day in darkness and cold without any hope. If we ever see them again, they will be difficult to recognize: Their hair has gone white, they are thinner, and they have aged in this short time. Refusing to know how they live and refusing to confront the government that tortures people are crimes.

Croatia

The section on Croatia begins with an interview with Neva Tolle, "For Women, About Women, by Women," in which she speaks of her awakening to feminism and women's projects through her own life experience. Her words speak for so many women in their experience with violence and women's solidarity, through which so many feminist activists come to know and work in women's projects around the world.

Martina Belic continues, in "The Center for Women War Survivors," by speaking about the center and its effect on her life, the life of the activists involved, and the lives of the women refugees they are reaching out to daily.

In "Confessions of a 'Yugo-Nostalgic' Witch," Vesna Kesic pokes fun at the media's reaction to feminism in Croatia by telling us her story as a feminist journalist approaching feminism. She also describes the media's treatment of feminists and the difficulties in growing up as a "witch" in Yugoslavia.

Aida Bagic, Mica Desnica, and Durda Knezevic introduce Women's Infoteka (a women's information and documentation center) and its publication *Bread and Roses* in two essays, "Bread and Roses," and "Something Unexpected." They talk about the access to information and women's right to know as a new principle whose "time has come."

In "The Lesbian Question," Andrea Spehar tracks the recent history of women's progressive movements in Yugoslavia and how they have influenced lesbian organizing in Croatia. She describes the difficulties of organizing, the marginal existence to which lesbians are consigned, the discrimination to which they are subjected, and the efforts of the first organization of lesbians and gay men in Croatia to reverse all these.

◈ For Women, About Women, by Women

An Interview with Neva Tolle

TANYA RENNE

I came to feminism through my own life experience. In my life there was a phase when I decided to divorce my husband, and I experienced abuse and violence on many levels. It was just too much, so I called one feminist women's house for help; I called them for information, legal advice, and support. And they gave it to me. I settled my problems and myself with their help. After two years of stabilizing myself, I became an external volunteer in this organization. After a few years of this work, I went back to Zagreb and found myself missing the work a lot. I was in a panic to find such an initiative or group here; that's when I saw an advertisement for Women's Group Tresnjevka. I started to work with this women's group every Wednesday, discussing various women's problems and issues. Out of those discussions came an initiative to found a telephone hotline, and I worked there three or four years on the telephone; we realized, after only a few years, that it was not enough: We needed a shelter. We started to write requests for space for the shelter, but we had no results, so we squatted the apartment we are in now. It was a great pleasure for me because I realized the strength of women together fighting for change. Since then the shelter has been living and working that way for three years. And now we are fighting again for legal status and looking for a new, bigger space.

When the war started, with it came problems in our women's group. Women split on emotional and rational bases. Some of them thought that work around feminism had to stop for a while because our country was at war and we had to do humanitarian and volunteer work. Another part of the group thought it was time for more intensive work than before because violence against women was increasing during the war. We split into two groups; the Autonomous Women's House Zagreb was a separate organization. We completely split with the telephone hotline. The reason was completely different approaches in work.

In autumn 1992 a big media campaign started about rape in war. We knew that all three parties of the war could manipulate people, opinion, and reality for their use and political aims. Then we decided to form an informal group for political pressure: Zagreb Women's Lobby. There was a lot of money around for the purpose of helping raped women, so we thought that it would be completely wrong for groups supporting their governments to use that money. There are a lot of groups now that are so-called nongovernmental, but we wanted real nongovernmental and autonomous women's groups to get the money to help the women, all women. We were not completely prepared, we were not ready because there were a lot of things that we were already doing, but we founded a new center—the Center for Women War Victims.

So my aims and opinions are very clear now about what I want to do—only in women's projects, for women, with women. Through all these groups and all our work, I realized that my affinity was with women, for women, around women's needs, issues, and projects.

My definition of feminism is to work with women in a way as to raise their consciousness and self-esteem. If you do that, raise their consciousness and awareness, they will be able to take control of their lives, their bodies, and their emotions. When they take control of their lives, their level of tolerance for violence will be much lower. Because in that moment a woman becomes truly independent. The beginning of this autonomy is her consciousness. It is very clear in women who come to the shelter. If the woman comes the first time and goes back, when she comes back, she says, "Now he slaps me only three times, but I didn't wait for more violence to leave." When she comes the third time, she says, "He didn't even hit me; he only raised his hand and I left." She changed her consciousness with going and coming back, and through the consciousness she gained from the groups she works with at the shelter, she is not willing to tolerate violence at all. When they come for the first time, they say, "What you are saying is impossible; you don't know my husband, my partner." Other women in the shelter say, "I did succeed. We thought the same thing. She succeeded and she succeeded and so did she; three hundred women who were here before did, and so will you." So they are together, and they are raising each other.

The Center for Women War Survivors

An Interview with Martina Belic

TANYA RENNE

I don't have a clear definition of feminism because I always think that clear definitions fuck things up somehow, but feminism has a lot to do with empowering women and has a lot to do with the way you live your life and the way you think, and that has to mean something to personal change, and after that personal change you should try to change a few people around you, and then, after three hundred years, our grand-grand-grand-grand children will have a pretty nice place to live—I know it is pretty idealistic.

I came to work in the feminist movement first with the telephone hotline five or six years ago. I joined the line, and I had some vague idea that it should be feminist, but I didn't join it for that reason. Rather, I joined it for very personal reasons, and those were that I had a friend, not a very close one, who was living in a marriage, not a very good one, but so-so, bearable, and one day she came without her front teeth, and after that I joined the telephone hotline, and I was happy to find women who thought like I did. I thought that I was the only one who had experienced it, and it is very empowering to meet more women who think like you do to stop it all. After the split I worked in the shelter. I preferred it there, not only because of the political problems in the group, but because you can communicate with women more directly—the telephone is too remote for me. In the shelter you work with women face to face, and it's much more personal.

One Saturday night Nela called me and asked me if I would work part-time as a coordinator of something that didn't exist yet—something like a center for women raped in war. That was a time of massive hysteria about raped women in Bosnia and Herzegovina. So seven or ten of us started the center in the office of the antiwar campaign. We knew before that we had to do something about it, but in a way we were too scared; we didn't want to begin with that because it was such a big problem. We (the women in shelter) were not quite sure what it would mean, and we were quite conscious that we didn't have time and energy and all that. Then some more women joined us, so we started the center. It was completely crazy in that time. We produced a project in three days or something like that and started to do the fund-raising and training for field workers all at the same time. Before we started, we thought it should be like that, for women raped in war, but that changed at the very beginning. It changed because rape is a horrible thing, but it isn't the only thing that is bothering these women. The crazy situation was that the rape was not the most important thing for them and their experience regarding rape because they had all kinds of different problems—for instance, safety and what to do if you have nothing at all. When we first visited the camps, we realized you can't work only with raped women, and you can't isolate them. That's one thing, and the other thing is what can you do for them—because more or less they try to suppress that experience. Now and then also it wasn't the time to deal with it because the basic thing is not secure, and that's safety. So we decided we would work with all women refugees, and that's how the concept changed; we decided that even in our first project. Of course, we would help raped women on an individual basis—if they chose to ask and wanted to talk to us about it; we just didn't want to force them to speak about it. That issue of raped women also shows how raped women were used because it emerged at a time when military intervention was a possibility, and in a way these women were used by journalists and Western politicians to manipulate the people in their countries to approve of military action. But then when that idea of military action failed and the politicians decided they didn't want to do that, all that hysteria also died down—which just goes to show you that the women were used somehow.

The way it was used was horrible because there were hundreds of journalists and fact-finding missions going to the camps and interviewing women. The effects were the women started to resent everyone. I remember first going to Karlovac, where there was a huge transit camp for refugees. When I arrived, the woman who runs the place said, "Okay, so you are looking for raped women." And I said, "No, I just want to talk to women, refugees, and we are not planning to work only with raped women," and she was relieved. Women started to resent and be suspicious of everyone coming to the camps; they would go there and get the stories, and the women would be left alone with no one to support them after they had told their story. Some of them tried to commit suicide—they were really victimized. At first they gave their testimonies very willingly because they thought something would come out of it, but nothing came. You just can't do that in that way. When we started working in the camps, the biggest problem was to build trust because whether the women were raped or no, their real problem is the trust issue. They don't trust anybody. To build up trust, it takes a lot of effort, and now, after nine months of working in the camps, they believe us, not completely, but they were checking us out. And now that they are sure we will come every week and we will be there for them and that we will try to help them to help themselves and do little things for them and share information with them, they start to believe us.

Until the end of November we were in twelve camps with twenty-one field workers working in pairs. We also have two self-help groups in the center for women living outside of the camps. It's about three hundred women now in all. We go in and establish self-help groups that meet once or twice a week. The number of women ranges from five to twenty. It is really going amazingly well. What we expected was that there would be a big dropout rate, but actually women only leave when they are relocated to third countries or to other places. We have very little dropout because a woman doesn't want to go anymore to the group. To establish self-help groups can be a problem because sometimes they don't even know the time—so if they don't show up, it doesn't mean they don't want to come; it's only that they don't know it's Tuesday, for instance.

To establish a group it takes two to three months in a camp. In the camp they live together all the time—twenty-four hours a day—and the organizer goes in as a foreigner at first. They know each other already, but they don't know you. The dynamics of the group are very different, too, especially in the beginning, because they don't trust you and they don't trust each other, and it takes more time for them to open up because they are afraid to say something and then somebody will use it against them. It isn't a question of neighborhood—it's much closer than that. Usually there are two groups in a camp, sometimes three or four. We are not dealing only with information now—they are talking about their feelings and fears; it's getting harder. The problems now are not how to deliver humanitarian aid or what to do about toilets, but you have to deal with the feelings, and it's really hard. I am very happy now because they don't talk to me anymore; they talk to each other, and there is less and less individual counseling because they talk to each other or in the group. We ask them what they want to change, if they want to quit, and these things, and they absolutely refuse any suggestion to stop it. Because they say they need a group and they are in ongoing crisis, they need that support.

The principles are every woman has the right to speak and everyone has the right to remain silent, and in fact every woman has a right to have a place to be herself. We try to do some empowerment work, and that means we strongly believe that if you have ten women in one group working together, they can solve their own problems more easily, and that is what we are trying to do: to empower them to solve their problems.

For the women in the camps, they learn very slowly that they can trust each other, and it's important for them to know they can do something about things, and it gives them some sense of stability because they know that at least once a week the group will be there. It becomes the point around which they can organize their lives. In the beginning we thought they came to our group because of the financial support and the humanitarian aid we gave. But it's not true—they don't even ask anymore; it's not relevant anymore. Their problems before the war, their problems during the war, their problems in flight, and their lives in the camp now—because it's very difficult to live in a refugee camp. Lack of privacy is the hardest thing; it's just not allowed. You can't even close yourself in the toilet because someone is queuing for it. And boredom—they have nothing to do. Women living in the camp are usually less educated and from the rural areas of Bosnia Herzegovina, so they are used to working physically, and they are not used to sitting around all day doing nothing in very small rooms.

The activists are trained as feminists. They've had workshops on feminism, but don't think that it's only the training that is important—their work here is also important. With working they become more and more empowered themselves. When they become more empowered, it's something that they can take with them to their groups and do the same with their groups in the camps.

The activists have really changed since the beginning. They have become more independent: They want to have a part in decisionmaking, and they are able to fight for it, and some activists in their personal lives are very changed. The best example is probably Goga, who went back to Sarajevo. She said that in the beginning she heard of a new group and someone said to her, "Oh, my dear, go see about it, but don't stay there because they are a bunch of crazy feminists and lesbians." When she came, she was a little bit scared, but after more than six months of working, she became a feminist herself. I would say this feeling is very common with the activists; at first their feelings about feminism were bad, but now lots of them declare themselves openly as feminists—which isn't an easy thing to do here. There is a lot of ignorance about feminism in our society, and usually the image of a feminist is a frustrated, ugly, divorcee who doesn't have anything to do with her life, so she becomes a feminist. Or the other possibility is that she is mentally ill—ugly, overweight, can't get a man, and all that. Something like walking monsters in the streets. So when you start to talk about a project as feminist, it can be very problematic. But problematic wasn't enough to scare people away because at one point or another forty-five women were part of our training and twenty-three or twenty-four remained.

Where will it go from here? I think that now the most important thing is to continue working at the same level or even better. The best thing the activists are getting is a lot of knowledge, and there is a lot of space for clearing personal things, and really they are obtaining skills here that they never dreamed in their lives they would obtain—counseling skills, organizational skills. It is very important that half of them are from Bosnia Herzegovina, so if this war ever stops, they can go back home, and they would be a very strong root of feminism there. They learned that they can start something from the basic level and make it work, and they also get the feeling of support from other women. I think for some of them they had strong relationships with women before, but some of them not, and now they all do, and that is very important.

Working in the center and with the refugees hasn't really changed me because I worked on the telephone hotline and in the shelter before—I was probably already changed because of that. It has strengthened the beliefs I had before. Because personally I come from a family of women—I had my grandmother, her sister, my mother, her sister, and me—we were a kind of unit. The way of thinking in my family, although they wouldn't call it feminist, is feminist. I sometimes feel like I have had enough and I would just like to quit—I feel this way at least once a week. But the tremendous need keeps me going and going and going. When something has to be done, then somebody has to do it, so why not me? It's not just the need; there is tremendous gratification in this work—it is incredibly empowering.

Confessions of a "Yugo-Nostalgic" Witch

VESNA KESIC

Almost forty-five and finally a witch! Thinking back, I wonder if I have ever wanted anything else. But because young witches are never completely emancipated, in my early childhood such fantasies appeared in some other, socially acceptable form. One of my first answers to the question "What are you going to do when you grow up?" (as far as I remember) was "A stewardess." In my mind I had traveled to great unknown worlds, cities like New York, Berlin, London, exotic countries, encounters with interesting people. Some male "shrink" would probably discover, in this young girl's longing to fly, "a lack of the fear of sex," as well as a hidden wish to abandon her family and tribe.

I also remember a secret wish to become a sailor. If possible, a captain of a transatlantic ship. This time I had to face the disapproval of the family, as well as one other, even bigger, obstacle: At that time girls were not admitted to the nautical schools. Later, when the doors to that bit of male empire were finally opened to us as well, it was clearly stated that women would not be allowed to sail. They would work in shipping companies and ports, do the bills, see off and welcome sailors and their ships. Exactly the same as our grandmothers had done. How boring! Times hadn't changed that much. After all, "a woman on board brings misfortune," says one ancient maritime refrain.

I finally gave up my romantic dreams of flying and sailing. I decided to become a physician. That was probably the consequence of the known "innate woman-need": If you cannot fly on the wings of fantasy, then at least be useful, help people, cure their bodies and souls. Healing of everything and everyone is the oldest women's profession. In the end, I studied psychology at the University of Zagreb. By then I had thoroughly experienced the fact that I was different: a witch (although I did not dare confess that fact—neither to myself, nor my closest friends). But why the hell psychology? Sounds like a reasonable question from the point of view of present knowledge. Then I believed I would learn something about human souls, their differences and likenesses. Yes, as a real witch I already wanted nothing less than human soul.

The famous Zagreb School of Psychology was a peculiar mixture of nineteenth-century psycho-physiology and American experimental, functional psychology. They taught me a lot of statistical and psychometric techniques for determining all kinds of different "parameters." For example, how valid data are obtained in the difference between the male and female intelligence or the scientifically proven "fact" that the male intelligence is, on the average, higher, and the female is concentrated on the extreme values (more often the lower extremes). They also taught me how to measure the "limes" of the tongue receptors for different intensities of saltiness (incidentally, never sweetness). With pleasure I successfully forgot all this knowledge immediately after graduation.

Consequently, purely by accident, I became a journalist. Successful, they say; known for skillful and lucid interviews. But within the ascetic socialist public sphere there were no precise parameters for measuring "success." It was especially unclear if one did not belong to the Communist Party machinery, which moved people very precisely on the hierarchical scale of success. Where success was called "promotion." But apart from that, once one was deprived of the ambition for promotion, it was easy to be "successful": One had to have only a little bit of civil courage and independent thinking, had not to be so damned banal and obedient, and, finally, had to start liking being a witch; maybe they do not love you too much, but they respect you and even slightly fear you.

In spite of everything, Yugoslav "totalitarianism" did not resemble, even to a slight degree, the Bulgarian, Romanian, or even Czechoslovakian or Hungarian type. A regime capable of imprisoning national poets and philosophers—which Yugoslav communists did—or of silencing oppositional journalists is, of course, repressive and stupid. In the manner of Voltaire, I will always defend the right of those who think differently to speak. But at that time, equally as today, I could not share the paranoid passion of national intellectuals, especially not their cultural racism expressed in phrases such as "We Croats are one of the oldest cultured nations in Europe, and 'they' are Byzantine savages"; "they did not even use a fork when the Viennese waltz was danced here." At that time the silent majority had squeezed out nationalists as well as leftists from their lines. They did it under the same collective agreement under which they now recognize the coryphaei of their newly freed political sentiments among nationalists.

Whatever the economic, social, and ideological background of socialism might have been, it had been a system psychologically based on mass conformism and never-ending hypocrisy. The church, being marginalized under socialism, had been successfully substituted by the Communist Party and its rituals. The party had been the highest criteria for good and bad, justice and injustice, as well as the creator of public morale. The party had been the inexhaustible source of patriarchal male power, as well as sexist and ideological domination over women. To be different, to be a witch, an existential outsider, had its advantages. One was freed of obligations to internal discipline and the fear of excommunication.

It also had its price. Sometime in the late 1970s, when the modern feminist movement in Yugoslavia had only just started to constitute and articulate, the political and cultural establishment reacted somewhat nervously. The first generation of feminists was accused of the "import of decadent Western bourgeois ideology." Leading Croatian party ideologists wrote authoritative sociopolitical essays criticizing feminism from the class position. One arrogant leftist pseudodissident proclaimed feminism to be an—watch it now—unstructured mass (read "rightist") movement that fell below the epoch-making level of history. A professor of education, at that time a leading writer of socialist ethics manuals, proclaimed feminists to be hotbeds of obscenity and victims of uncontrolled and unnatural sexual instincts. Today that professor is a Christian democrat who preaches national and religious spiritual renewal and abortion ban. An ambitious young journalist in the very popular "alternative" youth newspaper *Polet* did not hesitate: "Feminists should be kicked in *picka*," wrote the guy in a newspaper that allegedly challenged party discipline. (I don't know if it is possible to translate and publish *picka*—a vulgar popular term for women's genitalia—in "respectable" languages such as English or German. I don't ever remember, before or after, seeing it published in written form in a public paper here, although in spoken language it is completely common. Women here are often colloquially called *picke*. It was so during totalitarian communism, and it is so today in democratic nationalism.)

In the late 1980s, two cultural and political tendencies coexisted in Yugoslavia. On the one hand, there was liberalization—the embryo of political pluralism, general vividness, and increased criticism in media. Popular mass culture exploded slowly, but certainly repressing traditional cultural forms and values. On the other hand, in Serbia the nationalist mythologies as well as the populist "antibureaucratic revolution" expanded. Conflicts were increasing among the political parties and within the party hierarchies. Maybe that was the moment when one could still choose: peace or war, chaotic disintegration of the country and national etatisms or hard but peaceful and respectful transformation by means of the market, democracy, enlightenment, and a tolerant political culture.

At that time, even the *Encyclopedia of Yugoslavia* noted an unusual breakthrough of women in Croatian authorial journalism. Five names were mentioned, among them three actual witches (Lovric, Drakulic, Kesic). The fourth, Maja Miles, introduced competent and uncorrupted writing about

lawfulness, the judiciary, law, and other terms of the state to Yugoslav journalism for the first time since the war (the previous one). She courageously
unmasked all sorts of crime, including economic and political ones. At the
apex of her career, she committed suicide. It was one of those stories of a
woman putting her head in the oven because of an unbearable mixture of
intimate drama and public, party-political pressures. Her case was described by Slavenka Drakulic in the book *How We Survived Communism
and Kept Laughing*. It is obvious that we did not laugh all the time.

Besides all the classical explanations for maneuvering women into a profession—flow of men into more profitable ones, decrease of public respect,
increase of education among women, etc.—something else was in the game
here. The language. I am convinced that women introduced "I" to Yugoslav media. Women, with personal engagement and energy, opposed the
collective male, mystic, powerful, and cowardly "we," backed by the
power of the whole party. For years I had an editor in chief who never said,
"I" when political judgments and decisions were to be made. After the
changes, he, as well as many others, exchanged a "we the party" identity
for "we the nation."

Women journalists exchanged the poor, bureaucratized, and ideologized
language of agencies and communications that dominated socialist journalism for concrete speech. In their articles they brought the taste and color of
everyday life. Their discourse demolished the very root of totalitarian re-
ductions. Then, as well as today, it appeared subversive. Of course, not
only women did that, but successful women journalists did it almost without exception.

Haven't witches always absorbed part of their power through speech
that confused or enchanted the others? Not even this time witches could
prevent catastrophe, although they predicted it. I think that subsequent political analysis of the articles of proscribed women journalists and writers
will show a high degree of anticipation and dramatic warnings about the
tragic chaos Yugoslavia would end in. We were Cassandra.

In Croatia, of course, there are many excellent women writers, or at least
"successful" women journalists. Some of them, as the "five witches" themselves, have been the target of sexist and political attacks. Some have nevertheless established their identity through attacks on other women. They do
it with surprising hatred. The conclusion is clear: Not all women are
witches, nor are all witches the same, even if they are women.

Let's have a quick look at the short histories of five "Witches from Rio."
Who are they, and could they be put under the same label of feminism, alias
witchcraft, just like that? They are, of course, women. But besides their sex
and generation, they do not necessarily have in common what most male
groups do: points of view and professional orientation. First, not all of
them are feminists. Jelena Lovric (forty-four) in former Yugoslavia, as well

as in independent Croatia, is one of the most influential political columnists. Her terrain is "high politics"; she is a critic of the government institutions of power, party and interparty power games, and the public ethics of those segments of society. Some time ago, she belonged to the progressive, reformist Yugoslav Communist Party, and she never dealt with women's issues. She always categorically refused the word *feminism* because here it still sounds insulting and undervaluing. A woman who wants to deal with high politics will not easily incline to feminism.

Rada Ivekovic (forty-five), Slavenka Drakulic (forty-three), and I belong to the first generation of Yugoslav feminists, those who were cited for "decadent bourgeois deviation" at that time and today are "Marxist feminists." Rada Ivekovic, philosopher and Indologist (teaches temporarily at a university in Paris), has approached women questions from the point of view of French poststructuralism and women's writing, as a "speech of the other." Slavenka Drakulic has enjoyed success in recent years with her autobiographical novels and stories describing the destiny of women in communism and postcommunism. These stories have not been published in Croatia, and the public learns of her success only through attacks on her. In these transition years I dealt primarily with the critique of popular culture and art, especially with analysis of the ideology of the media and their influence on prewar and war reality.

Dubravka Ugresic (forty-three) had, until recently, been recognized and celebrated as the most talented woman writer in the nation. Her novels and stories have become real best-sellers, making publishers fight over them. Her novels have been translated into many foreign languages, filmed, and staged. Ugresic is a Russian literature specialist and has translated many important volumes of avant-garde and contemporary Russian prose. She creatively combines her knowledge of literature with her exuberant, hearty, ironic imagination. Describing everyday life and using common stereotypes of male and female "mentality," she artfully plays with literature, genres, and styles. With such a hand, she is the most important representative of women's writing in Croatian literature. But as a disciplined literature theoretician, she absolutely refuses this qualification, not accepting the division of literature based on "male" and "female."

These women are not necessarily feminists after all. But they have something else in common: In Croatian and foreign magazines and newspapers they have written critically about the war and nationalism. They oppose the Serbian and Croatian war-mongering machinery, media manipulation, corruption, and autocratic government tendencies. They write; they speak publicly; they are fairly brave; they dare to be eccentric; they are curious, pushy, and independent. Since their existence has been noticed in the public, they have been disputed, but publicly respected and influential as well. And finally they have been proclaimed what they are: "Witches," screams the crowd and the executioners among them, invoking the historical, those few centuries when 9 million of our sisters were burned in Europe and America.

Fortunately, we live in the era of television. Today everything unfolds more rapidly. The hunt will probably not last for centuries, and literal burning will probably not be necessary. The substitutes in media are enough.

If you ask me how I feel about being called a witch, "Very well indeed, thank you!" I have been expelled from my tribe, I fly above the ground from country to country a great deal, I meet interesting people, and I don't feel like a victim of any other obscure forces save my own character and temperament. Naturally, I am scared. Of course, I'm appalled and sad about what is happening to people and the countries of my former home-land. I became a witch there, and early traumas are never forgotten. Some would call that "Yugo-nostalgia."

▦ Bread and Roses

AIDA BAGIC

Bread and Roses is an information magazine of Women's Infoteka in Zagreb. We chose the name *Bread and Roses* because we wanted to express our connection with the history of the international women's movement and because we wanted both bread and roses to become our reality. Since the war in former Yugoslavia started, we have been experiencing international women's solidarity in many different ways. We have, however, often lacked the time and space to deal with our own issues in our own language. *Bread and Roses* provides a space for women to raise their voices to address the domestic public. Women write about their own experiences, as survivors, activists, writers, artists, in a way that changes the order of priorities usually set by a male-dominated media. *Bread and Roses* looks into the future; without this opportunity to develop women's vision, we may lose our place in that future.

◫ Something Unexpected

MICA DESNICA
DURDA KNEZEVIC

While the streets of Clara Zetkin and the squares of Rosa Luxembourg have been swept away by national kings and traditional heroes, something unexpected has appeared in Zagreb—Women's Infoteka, a women's information and documentation center. Women's Infoteka was founded and registered in December 1992, with regular activities beginning in March 1993. In the interim funds were raised and office space was located and equipped.

The reasons for establishing such a women's center are of a dual nature. On the one hand, the need for a women's information and documentation center to collect data and documentation on women's activities and initiatives and to disseminate information has existed for a long time. The feminist/women's movement in the former Yugoslavia was one of the most developed within Eastern European countries. In the mid-1970s in Zagreb, the first (neo)feminist group, Woman and Society, held lectures, discussions, and workshops that opened a new approach to women's issues; in this way a generation of women was educated. Several women's groups were created as a result, and they tackled and exposed to the public the many layers of women's reality that were previously invisible. The original Women's Group Tresnjevka (active in the 1980s) started the SOS Telephone for Women and Children Victims of Violence and was the first to speak out in public about domestic violence—sanctioned male violence against women. In 1989 the SOS telephone branched out to form Women's Aid Now, which established—by squatting in a city-owned apartment—the first refuge for abused women in this region. Today the refuge is run by a separate group of women—Autonomous Women's House. Women's groups in Croatia, including the Lila Initiative, the feminist group and magazine *Kareta,* the Independent Alliance of Women, the female part of the Lesbian and Gay Men's Association (LIGMA), Zagreb Women's Lobby, and the Center for Women War Victims, have created, and continue to create, herstory in this part of the world.

On the other hand, since the beginning of war in Croatia in 1991, feminism has undergone a fundamental crisis of identity due partially to the war but also to difficulties inherent in feminism. In the current moment, a time of neither war nor peace, some of the rights achieved by women are jeopardized. The lack of democratic principles in the construction of the state and society is most radically manifested through a restriction of independent media, increased conservatism, and a revival of patriarchal values (numerous attempts to restrict the right to abortion being the most obvious examples), with the war situation often used as justification.

Repercussions on the economic and social status of women are enormous. We are the first to be affected by rising unemployment, and we are forced out of the public labor sphere by a policy that is reinforced by ideological pressures demanding women to increase the national birthrate. The effects are clearly seen in the dwindling number of women in the Croatian parliament; currently there are ten, the lowest level in recent history. The race toward a free-market economy has been applied through sex discrimination, and the effects of this race, which have been escalated by the war, have fallen most heavily on women: Women have fewer job retraining opportunities than men, we feel the effects of the drastic reduction in affordable day care services, and the current economic crisis pushes many women to the very edge of existence. In such a social context attempts are made to restrict women to their three famous functions—kitchen, kids, church.

In light of the antiwoman trends that are threatening to erase our knowledge, presence, and herstory, the setting up of a women's information and documentation center imposed itself as necessary for reversing the deconstruction process we are witnessing today and for opening up new possibilities for and approaches to the women's movement in Croatia. The basic function of Women's Infoteka is to make women visible and present.

Women's Infoteka collects data and documentation on the development of the women's movement, on women's groups and organizations that are active today, and on women's/feminist research in various fields. Our goal is to make the official figures that are usually called "gray" (women are invisible) "bright red." These include statistical data on the social status and needs of women, on women's health care (health education, contraception, abortion), and on violence against women (physical and psychological violence in/out of family, rape in/out of family, prostitution). Databases will be constructed according to international women's information standards.

The women's library at Infoteka is growing, and there is a reading room with current feminist publications and periodicals. This space is also used for group discussions and meetings. The archives, library, and databases are available to all users—women's/feminist groups and individuals—for research and other activities. We initiate and support women's projects, provide women's groups and activists with information and assistance in organizing public demonstrations and campaigns, and sponsor and support research on women by women. We also have plans to translate feminist books and to publish works of domestic authors on women's issues. We hope that Women's Infoteka will become a place for women gathering and coming closer to each other, a place to exchange experience and knowledge. We also hope Women's Infoteka will not be alone—let it be just one among many public spaces created by women. The time has come!

▓ The Lesbian Question

ANDREA SPEHAR

A Critical Review of the Lesbian Question in Socialism

Some forty years ago, Yugoslavia made a great step compared to other communist countries by abandoning the Soviet political regime and undertaking many reforms. Beginning with the student movement in the late 1960s and early 1970s, there was a sign of gradual liberalization of the communist system in Croatia. The main political issues among the students of that time were social diversity and the student union's desire to escape from the Communist Party's grip. The activists in youth organizations were the only pioneers of that time who were gathering points for further progress in politics. At that time there were some liberal programs trying to confront the dogmatic, militaristic, and centralist power of the Yugoslav government, which put obstacles in the way of any form of democracy, cultural, economic, or political, in Croatian society.

Those liberalization movements provided a new approach to the problems of women in Croatian society. Some groups of Croatian women from a liberal provenance began reconsidering dogmatic, Marxist attitudes toward women and tried to resolve them by using Western traditions and terminology, making new assumptions for a modern feminist movement under the conditions of collapsing communism. The women who were occupied with the "woman question" timidly emphasized the "lesbian question," too, but that work was not organized. The question of lesbians in Croatia was taboo among feminists themselves. Feminists would put the question of lesbians aside as a matter of private orientation for each individual. Public opinion about the movement was extremely negative and falsely colored.

In the constitution of Croatia and Slovenia a clause prohibiting homosexual relationships was abolished in 1977, while in the other republics and provinces the same paragraph was still enforced. There were no public lesbian gatherings, so lesbians lived, and still do, in isolation. Lesbian culture did not exist. Lectures on lesbianism were organized, but not by lesbians themselves, which says something about the lesbian population's fear of being revealed.

Some of the liberalization that occurred in the 1970s did not touch the private lives of women. Progress was made primarily in journalism, where feminists greatly influenced the making of images of women in the media. Of course, these journalists did not write exclusively about women's problems, but, with their attitudes toward life, they appealed for more liberal thinking and ushered in a broader understanding of various human relations.

The Wave of the 1980s

The nonexistence of an organized lesbian movement in the 1970s can be explained by the fact that in Yugoslavia there was no specific youth movement or alternative youth culture. The society was extremely passive; most resistance to the repressive system of the state occurred at home, behind closed doors. Such acts nevertheless required a great deal of civil courage. And there were some groups and individuals who tried to realize alternative ideas on their own.

The central point in the development of new social movements in Yugoslavia was the punk movement from 1979 to 1982. Provocative slogans appeared for the first time with punk: "Down with communism!" "Communism is terror!" This was especially expressed in Slovenia, where the alternative scene was the predecessor of civil society (which implies justice, more democracy and freedom, market relations, and free enterprise).

The neighboring Republic of Slovenia is obviously a great influence on political happenings in Croatia, as well as on Croatia's desire for independence. For example, the Assembly of Slovenia was the first to announce its right to secede from Yugoslavia in 1989, and Slovenes were the first to demand the breaking of the restraints of socialist self-management, totalitarianism, and so on. This spirit of independence notwithstanding, the late 1970s and early 1980s saw state repression manifested through slander campaigns against progressives, mass media and other kinds of attacks on them, and disinformation by the government about the alternative scene (which was monitored by the police). The police obtained information about the participants of the movement and in the process infringed upon the privacy and intimacy of the individual (e.g., asking whether one is a homosexual or not, who is involved in sexual affairs and with whom). The mass media were difficult to approach or completely closed to the alternative scene.

In the mid-1980s, after the punk era, the youth subculture was differentiated into categories such as pacifist, environmentalist, homosexual, and feminist. At that time the first independent feminist associations were organized (independent from the woman's union). In 1987 the first all-Yugoslav feminist meeting was organized in Ljubljana. The first gay organization,

Magnus, was founded in Ljubljana in 1984. In 1987 the first lesbian group was founded in Ljubljana, some of whose members started their activity in the feminist group Lilit, which became independent in January 1988. The activity of Lilit itself was directly responsible for inspiring the initiative to form a similar organization in Zagreb.

The late 1980s brought drastic changes to international politics. Reforms that started in the USSR gradually transformed the whole family of communist countries. Activities in Poland, Hungary, Czechoslovakia, and Romania in 1989 dramatically altered the social, political, and ideological structure of these countries. The symbolic and spectacular dismantling of the Berlin Wall crowned these events in importance. This act was a clear confirmation of the fact that changes were inevitable and that the communist regimes belonged to history.

Immediately before the first democratic elections were held in Croatia and even before the constitution of the independent republic of Croatia was drafted, the Lila Initiative was implemented in Zagreb, the first lesbian organization in (Croatia), within the feminist group Tresnjevka. The very idea of such an organization was due, in part, to an anonymous survey of public opinion done in December 1988 during the second feminist meeting held in Zagreb. A significant number of women suggested that the issues of lesbians should be treated more openly. As a result of publicity, a large number of women became members. During the period of one year, seventy women, of varied ages and backgrounds, were in the group.

In spite of being taboo in our society, the Lila Initiative set high goals for itself: for instance, to gain equal rights for lesbians and bisexuals, to eliminate homophobia, to popularize all aspects of female culture (literature, movies, expositions). For a year and a half of work the Lila Initiative was very strong. The greatest aspect of the initiative was that it gave women a place to be together and relax. It helped lesbians overcome feelings of isolation, panic, and loneliness. In this space they were able to talk without prejudices and to receive positive information about the life of lesbians all around the world. The importance of the Lila Initiative is described best by one of the members: "When I ended a relationship with my lover, I was desperate and really alone. It was not possible to talk about it to friends or with my mother. When I came to the group, for the first time I felt that this problem of mine is also a problem of these women and that it is not a problem, at least not here."

After the elections in May 1990 and the victory of the Croatian Democratic Union, as well as that of Franjo Tudjman, the Lila Initiative lost the physical space in which it was organized and was dissolved. The reasons for this were not only the loss of space but also a lack of funding and motivated women to help manage and run the group.

The New Constitution of the Republic of Croatia

On December 22, 1990, a new constitution of the Republic of Croatia was approved by all three chambers of the Republic of Croatia. When a new government as well as new values were established in the year in which both women and lesbians for the first time in the history of Croatia had the opportunity to take a part in the creation of democracy, there were no organized women's parties, no means to influence other parties to adopt women's platforms and proposals for rights and roles in present-day Croatian society.

Forty-five years of socialism has had its influence on the self-confidence of women. The result has been an absence of women in government (in 1990 only 4 percent of the members of parliament were women); their influence on political events in the country is nil. Furthermore, politicians, legislators, and priests continue with their practice of not caring about the interests of women.

The new system (which was supposed to create a society of equality, free of conflicts, in which all differences were accepted and embraced) started with enthusiasm and hope for pluralism, a legal state, human rights, and other virtues, all of which are characteristic of a modern and democratic society. But as a result of different political statements and errors by politicians of all parties (actions contrary to any definition of democracy), the new system could only be a kind of liberalism not agreeable to all. So the president of the Republic of Croatia, Franjo Tudjman, during the first pre-electoral campaign in 1990 said that in Croatia homosexuality should be recognized and allowed to be as invisible as possible.

While the British series *Oranges Are Not the Only Fruit* was airing on Croatian TV, the program was interrupted because of "technical problems" just after a sexual encounter between Jess and Melany. The response to this on Radio 101 was great. One whole program was dedicated to this event. People at the television station who were responsible for the movie program stated that during the program they had received several phone calls from church leaders asking that they stop such "immoral drama." Since the church has such a significant influence on life in Croatia, the television station complied. According to church leaders, one lesbian relationship is a danger to accepted relationships, to all values, to the roles of men and women in society.

The special point, of course, is population policy in this time of war and the attitudes that support this policy. To practice sex that does not result in the conception of children is, according to the views of the warmakers, to destroy all hopes of a strong nation-state. Croatia can be only heterosexual. If homosexuals are allowed to take free and equal part in Croatian life, relations between men and women will be damaged, and in these relations, according to the Croatian government, women exist only as a basis for the reproduction of the nation. If homosexuals are free in Croatia, Croatia will cease to exist as a nation-state.

There are campaigns against women and lesbians who fight to secure their rights. According to public opinion, we are the ones trying to destroy Croatia, destroy Christianity. We are supposed to be reeducated according to spiritual values. We are accused of being against independent Croatia and having no love for Croatia. In a referendum on May 19, 1991, we voted for the independence of Croatia (as did 94 percent of Croatian citizens), but we did not mean a state in which, instead of democracy, we have a dictatorship and instead of pluralism, we have nationalist frenzy.

Lesbians are forced to live in a total isolation. We are not only isolated from society, but we are also isolated from one another. In Croatia there is not a single public place (except for LIGMA) where lesbians can talk without prejudice, socialize, and share their experiences. A lesbian cannot read a book about her ideas and lifestyle. The only thing that she hears about herself is that she is a whore, ill, unnatural, or that she does not exist at all and in a direct, political sense is an obstruction to the state and its moral values.

One of the main problems is a conservative, patriarchal culture responsible for many of the problems that women in our society encounter. According to the constitution, women and men are equal. According to the new Croatian penal law, being a lesbian is not punishable. But in practice this is not so. Most of the families in Croatia are patriarchally structured; looking after children and doing housework are strictly female duties. Lesbians are pressured to continue this tradition, which denies them independence and the development of their own identity. Most lesbians wind up marrying men. Those who successfully refuse to marry and become involved with other women often assume the stereotypical roles of heterosexual couples, with one partner playing the "husband" and the other the "wife."

The reason for our marginal position is not only public pressure but also the passivity of Croatian lesbians who do not want to get involved politically and unknowingly help those who deny our existence. If one wants to work on transforming the way people look at things, including the social life in Croatia, one is alone in doing so because people in this country are used to being led by someone and accepting certain rules about living according to cultural traditions and current politics. For most lesbians, that means it is impossible to go public or tell their friends and families about their sexual orientation, not to mention their rights; they see the only possible solution in hiding from and escaping the problem. Doing so causes great psychological problems and loneliness. Nevertheless, they consider a "loss of jobs" a greater misfortune, as well as a loss of friends, family, and reputation. There are plenty of women who are accustomed to comfort and have no idea that things ought to be changed. Those who are aware of it soon adjust to the present social situation. We must have a clear idea about the importance and development of one's own identity; otherwise we, as marginal groups, have no chance of surviving.

Lesbians who live in smaller Croatian towns see their only chance in moving to Zagreb, where they can be freer, far from their families and intolerant surroundings. But in Zagreb there is no lesbian culture either; the only way to live more freely is to get close with an already closed circle of lesbians who socialize strictly among themselves. Because of the unequal status of women in Croatian society, lesbians have lagged behind gay men in developing a sense of identity and community.

In such conditions LIGMA was formed in June 1992, the first such organization in Croatia (with Transnational Radical Party). LIGMA is our only hope for organizing. A few lesbians have decided to unite with gay men in a mutual struggle because to act separately means we could not work at all.

LIGMA operates only in Zagreb, although it has members and sympathizers in other Croatian towns. It has a membership of about twenty-five and many more sympathizers, who fear the consequences of being affiliated with our group more openly. We are trying hard to attract people who can help us. Our minimal success is due to the fact that people are worried about securing food in these harsh economic conditions and haven't the time or energy to struggle for rights.

A provisional list of our goals includes struggle against all discrimination, protection of lesbians and gays in Croatia, AIDS education, an end to homophobia, presentation of all aspects of lesbian and gay culture, and contacts with groups from abroad. We are ready to invest a lot of effort as well as work to support the growth of a greater movement through which homosexuality will be truly legalized and accepted in everyday life.

Slovenia

Women's concerns in Slovenia are more audible than anywhere else in East-Central Europe. This progressiveness can be attributed to both the beginnings of reform in the mid-1980s and the relative wealth and stability of the citizens. They are willing and able to consider more abstract issues, such as women in government, than their eastern neighbors are.

In "It's a Shame!" Vlasta Jalusic gives an account of the campaign to get the right to abortion written into the new constitution when Slovenia became independent. This campaign represents a kind of best-case scenario in terms of organization, street demonstrations, and the end result of a fight for reproductive rights.

Metka Mencin, in "Women and Politics," contributes her introduction to the publication *Report on the Position of Women in Slovenia*, written originally for the Commission for Women's Politics. Mirjana Ule and Tanja Rener consider "Nationalism and Gender in Postsocialist Societies" and their embrace of nationalism in reprivatization reforms.

Erika Repovz closes the section with a personal essay about her experience "undercover" in a refugee center in Ljubljana. As a journalist she knew the stories of the refugee centers as they were presented to the public. But what she found shocked and dismayed her. In this account, "Women Without Identity," she expresses her feelings at being on the "inside."

It's a Shame!

The Campaign for Constitutional Reproductive Rights in Slovenia

VLASTA JALUSIC

During the disintegration of the Yugoslav federal state in the 1980s (not in the 1990s because the overall disintegration and war were only a consequence of earlier ongoing processes), a certain ideological shift occurred within the official attitude toward the so-called woman question under self-managed socialism. This shift was marked by a discussion that arose among demographers in the mid-1980s about the Yugoslav birthrate. The main issue was the "problem of the high Albanian birthrate" in Kosovo (a formerly autonomous province with a majority ethnic Albanian, non-Slavic population) and the low birthrate in Slovenia, Serbia, and Croatia. This issue gave rise to discussion about abortion and reproductive rights. All of this happened before the so-called change from socialism to political pluralism and the market system, still within the one-party system. The need for a population policy was one of the few points of agreement among such dramatically different orientations as the Slovenian Communist Party, the Slovenian National Opposition (self-proclaimed dissidents), and the Serbian Communist Party, among others.

In Slovenia demographers started with catastrophic projections of national failure if the birthrate didn't increase. They spoke of the "death of the Slovenian nation," and there were headlines in the newspapers such as "Two Children Are Not Enough," and "Fewer and Fewer Slovenians." This was in 1987. The antiabortion campaign from the Catholic corner started in 1987 with the showing of the U.S. antiabortion film *The Silent Scream*. These were foundations of the later, much larger, antiabortion campaign at the beginning of the 1990s, which coincided with the self-determination referendum in 1990, the first multiparty elections in 1991, and the discussion about the constitution of the new Slovenian state.

Socialist Solution

A unique solution in the area of reproductive rights existed within socialist Yugoslavia. Since 1974 there had been a paragraph in the federal constitution guaranteeing reproductive rights. It was defined as a "human right to decide over the birth of one's own children," which included abortion rights and the duties of the state to provide the facilities (the opportunities) to make this right possible. In the Republic of Slovenia, for example, this right included abortion (on demand until the tenth week of pregnancy and paid for by health insurance), accessible (free) contraception, facilities to enable women to give birth to desired children, a whole network of women's health centers, and health care for mothers and their children.

I was born at the end of the 1950s, and I have experienced times of liberal attitudes toward contraception and abortion, when reproductive rights weren't questioned by the state or politicians. To be able to make decisions about one's own body was "natural." But this was only one side of the coin. Since the old socialist legislation came first "from above," there also existed among many women a feeling that they did not have to fight for these rights. So when the antiabortion campaign started, nobody really believed that these long-lasting rights could be taken away. Because democratization carried with it many promises of freedom and happiness for everyone, no one thought that newborn democrats would call reproductive rights seriously into question.

Antiabortion Campaign

After the first multiparty elections in 1990, very few women were in parliament (11 percent). In spite of an early reformist approach, the Slovenian Communist Party (in the 1980s the most socialist-oriented party) lost its influence and power. Christian Democrats were the leading party among the winning party coalition, Demos (with 53 percent). The emancipation of women ceased to be part of the system's agenda. With this change in the social agenda came a legitimization of special social politics, which assumed that the role women had had under socialism would prove "useless" in the transition to a market economy. Furthermore, all changes were very closely connected to the growing nationalism in the whole of Yugoslavia, which showed how fragile women's rights and formal equality could be if there was no longer a tradition of a women's movement, independent women's political forums, and a public, political consciousness among women about the meaning of these rights.

The first new feminist groups in Slovenia came into existence during the mid-1980s. They emerged within several so-called new social movement groups, being more or less self-sufficient already, within the one-party system. Later, before the first multiparty elections in 1990, when the antiabortion campaign was started by members of some parties (Christian Democrats, Greens, People's Party), some new initiatives emerged. Both independent and party groups became the main protagonists in the campaign for constitutional abortion rights.

The boiling point in the discussion about the new Slovenian constitution was reached over the paragraph on reproductive rights. Since it was the only nonconsensual point in the constitutional proposal, there was a threat that Slovenia would remain without a new constitution and thus without the means to initiate multiparty elections. Therefore, there was a danger that the paragraph would simply be left out so that the "whole constitution" could be accepted. If this happened, the foundations of all existing legal solutions would be dismantled, and the possibility that abortion on demand might be abolished would remain. Since parliament had to decide about this question with two-thirds majority and only 11 percent of the representatives in parliament were women, the chances that the paragraph would be retained appeared rather small.

In spite of differences of opinion, ideology, and structure among existing women's groups (especially whether they were feminist and what allegiance they had to different parties), they decided to start a common action before parliamentary decisionmaking on the paragraph led to its disappearance. After the group Women for Politics published a book on the whole (anti)abortion discussion, several round tables were organized in autumn 1991. Because it quickly became clear that such actions were not enough, the decision by activist women to hold a big demonstration was natural in spite of hesitation on women's part to organize in a mass-response action. Once the decision was made, great support emerged among different organized and individual women. Thousands of signatures were collected to support the action called "the right to choose." Thousands of leaflets were distributed. I can still remember one elderly woman's comment when I gave her a leaflet: "Isn't it a shame that they even dare to mention the possibility of changing this right, that they discuss it in the public?" "They" meant the newborn democrats, politicians. Her rhetorical question showed her belief that the right to choose was a woman's most natural right. The abortion rights campaign was one occasion in which the relatively small size of the Slovenian state was an advantage: Nobody was left untouched by the discussion; everybody expressed an opinion.

Demonstration

The demonstration took place on December 11, 1991. All the women on the organizational board feared that only a few women would come. This fear was the result of inexperience in "going to the street" and of almost forty years of no independent women's organizations. It was the first time since World War II that women had their own demonstration. In spite of these odds, approximately three thousand people, most of them women, came to join the protest. The parliamentary session was interrupted. Many representatives joined the women on the street. Twenty-four of the twenty-five female representatives in parliament stated that they would not support the omission of reproduction rights from the constitution. Women on the street held placards and shouted slogans: "Women in parliament!" "We want a women's ministry!" "Abortion without compromise!" Since women protested with imagination and without prejudices, the prime minister (a Christian Democrat) declared them "nasty" and "tasteless." But one daily newspaper rightly called this action the "first civil demonstration after the 1990 elections."

It was obvious that neither the government nor parliament had expected such strong opposition to the omission or reduction of the paragraph concerning reproductive rights. The demonstration was a success for independent and party women's groups. Although later a slight compromise was made in the very conservative constitutional commission (the word *right* was changed to *freedom*), the foundations for the existing legislation were left unchanged. Abortion on demand remained a legal constitutional solution.

Opposing Arguments

It is very interesting to look at the arguments presented to the public for retaining or abolishing the right to abortion. One of the most trivial arguments advanced by antiabortionists was that "no other European constitution contains such a right" and that "Europe" would "really laugh at us" if "we were quarreling over such a marginal problem." Those for choice argued that Slovenia had very good experience with existing legal solutions and that throwing the paragraph out of the constitution would mean the law could be changed by a simple majority in parliament. In other words, democratic decisionmaking would produce a situation in which certain rights could be "democratically" abolished. No wonder many women took a "natural rights" position to argue for the intimate right to choose.

The discussion took place as a discourse about "care": for women, nation, health. The abortion issue also covered all other problems connected to the political and social position of women (in the transition from a self-managed economy to a market system and from a one-party system to a multiparty parliament). In part it was in the interest of different parties to open this question in order to arouse public interest in the election campaign and mobilize apatriotic voters. Besides this, Catholic foes of abortion really did believe that most women under socialism had been subjected to "forced emancipation through work" and that now they couldn't wait to "return to the household." These Catholics claimed that all socialist legislation, including constitutional reproductive rights, was some kind of "totalitarian holdover."

Within the public debate, there was (except in women's circles) no real interest in discussing the introduction of women's politics on the government level. On the contrary, the intent behind the antiabortion campaign was to produce a "really big problem" behind which all other problems, such as social policy, employment, the impact of the market, and political representation, could hide. Simultaneously, there was a common Eastern European "transitional" situation that enabled antiabortion campaigns.

Troubles with Legitimization

If we analyze the position of women and take a backward look at European social structure before the fall of the Berlin Wall, we see one main ideological difference between socialism and democracy: The emancipation of women has always been the legitimizing principle of socialist societies/Eastern European states. (This was less the case in those countries, such as Poland, Hungary, and the northwestern republics of Yugoslavia in the early 1980s, in which movement toward a reformation of society started earlier.) Here I am not trying to address whether women in socialist countries were really emancipated or whether they were forced into emancipation through economic necessity. I am only trying to underline the connection between socialism and women's emancipation, which shouldn't be underestimated in our understanding of present processes.

If socialism as a system of governing had in women's emancipation a powerful legitimizing principle from the beginning, there was no similar case with democracy (in the sense that nobody except feminists tried to legitimize democracy with women's rights or women's emancipation). The very concept of democracy until lately was exclusive and excluded women (at least partially, if not completely) from the public realm. Women's rights, equality, and so on were never a fundamental principle of any democratic system, although there was always a struggle to put some institutions and achievements, including those concerning women, on the list of "democratic achievements."

Therefore, when postsocialist societies started to reconcile themselves with their inner "democracy," they understood democracy as majority rule within parliament (with some corrections, such as quotas for national minorities). Women's rights and their participation in politics were of no consequence. Indeed, because women's rights were one of the legitimizing principles of the old system, the main tendency in postsocialism was to declare all such efforts illegitimate. Every good or bad heritage from the old, socialist system was declared suspicious, including abortion rights. And thus an up-to-date revolutionary legitimation of the antiabortion campaign was very successful against everything, including women's rights, gained in socialism.

Why, in spite of all this, were reproductive rights in Slovenia retained? First, the transition in Slovenia was a slow process, which began in the 1980s when the first "new social movement groups" appeared. Since the reform process started within the Communist Party, a strong anticommunism, as developed in some other Eastern European states, did not develop here. Although demands for a complete overturn of the old system were present, they were not the majority. Second, separate feminist groups were an important part of civil society long before the fall of the Berlin Wall; therefore they were a part of the forces of democratization. After the first elections, the Parliamentary Commission for Women's Politics was founded; the Office for Women's Politics was established later. And third, female party members already had some consciousness about acting in solidarity if such basic rights were endangered. In addition, women's groups decided to go to the public in the greatest sense—by demonstrating in the streets—and through this powerful means to silence the fear among women of showing public solidarity.

Bibliography

Jalusic, Vlasta. "Letter from Yugoslavia." In Paula Snyder, *The European Women's Almanac* (London: Scarlett Press), 1992.

_____. "The So-Called Transition, Democracy, and Women's Rights in the East European States." In *Colloquium Papers: Conference on Women's Daily Life and Equal Opportunity Policies.* Florence: 1993.

_____. "Troubles with Democracy: Women and Slovene Independence." 1994.

_____. "Zuruck in den 'Naturzustand'? Desintegration Jugoslawiens und ihre Folgen für die Frauen" (Back to the "natural stand"? Disintegration of Yugoslavia and its consequences for women). *Feministische Studien* 2, no. 9 (1992).

Melodic, Marija. "The Reappearance of Civil Society." *Intruder,* no. 3 (1991).

Molyneux, Maxine. "Women in Socialist Societies Old and New: Progress Towards Women's Emancipation?" *Feminist Review* 8, no. 1 (1994).

Office for Women's Politics. *Preliminary Report from the Republic of Slovenia on Measures Taken for the Abolishment of All Forms of Discrimination Against Women.* Ljubljana: Office for Women's Politics, 1993.

_____. *Report on the Position of Women in Slovenia.* Ljubljana: Office for Women's Politics, 1992.

Women and Politics

A Note of Introduction

METKA MENCIN

Reactions to the discussion of female politics reflect the ratio of political power in Slovenia, which, following the 1990 elections, defines the borders among the important, less important, and unimportant as far as the responsibilities of the state to individuals (male and female) and vice versa are concerned. Discussions on politics aimed at doing away with the subordination of conditions linked to gender mainly come up against belittlement and laughter in government institutions. Even rare expressions of sympathy are usually given in relation to proposals presumed to have no hope of success.

When the Commission for Women's Politics was founded in the parliament of the Republic of Slovenia in July 1990, the great majority of government institutions behaved as though this were the first time they had heard of the juxtaposition of the words *women's* and *politics,* although it was frequently written about in the mass media thanks to the efforts of the Autonomous Women's Initiative. Thus, we had to reveal something to the institutions of government that had been articulated in civil society long ago: that the issue of "equality without regard to sex" is politically relevant. Not only this—we even have to fight for discussions on equality to be acknowledged.

Here we can find the reasons for the fact that the Commission for Women's Politics has limited its goals—to defend the level of women's rights already attained (not an easy task, especially in connection with the right to abortion) and to focus the government agenda on that end. The latter was concerned not only with an explicit demand for an independent interdepartmental government body (which was obtained with a change of government), but also with a milder (at first impression) demand for a comprehensive analysis of the situation of women.

This analysis, which we called the *Report on the Position of Women in Slovenia,* was the result of the work of women who met for two years in the commission. In accordance with the distribution of work between the government and parliament and, above all, in accordance with the possibilities and conditions of work, the preparation of such a report was the task of the government.

But instead of an integral analysis, we have only a short report, but we hope that the information, despite its deficiencies, will aid, at least a little, those who work in the field of women's politics or in adjacent fields. The deficiencies of the report also point to the vacuum in research on the position of women (in the proposal for measures to be taken we call attention to some of these deficiencies). But above all, we hope that the government and parliament (present and future) will use the proposal, which is our most important supplement to the government text, as a guideline for policies in individual fields. We hope that they will implement those that belong within their jurisdiction. Here we are primarily thinking of legislation, which will have to establish that the possibilities for employment in all fields would no longer depend on sex. We hope that as far as the government has power to it will enforce customs that prevent discrimination against women and their marginalization. With the proposal of measures that go beyond the activities of the present and former governments, the commission overstepped its unofficial limits, placed on it by the political climate or by itself in response to this climate.

Nationalism and Gender in Postsocialist Societies

Is Nationalism Female?

MIRJANA ULE
TANJA RENER

The Constitutive Role of the Postmodern Trinity: The Nation, the Family, Women in the Process of Industrial Modernization

Of the three great dispositions of modernity/modernization—the nation-state, industrialization, and the urban way of life—one element, the nation-state, is dangerous and potentially antimodern. Despite its constitutive nature, the nation-state is modern only when it is tightly bound into the mechanisms of the other two elements, which prevent it from realizing the principles upon which it is founded. Distinct from industrialization and urbanization, which are founded upon modern principles of individualism and rationalism, nationalism as the substance of every nation-state feeds itself from entirely different sources: the community and sentiment. Here it is difficult to overlook the similarities with one of the presuppositions that may be of a central and constitutive nature within modernization—the social construction of (the female) gender.

The thesis that we are bringing forth is not new. One of the essential contributions of the new social history of the family lies in the realization that the small nuclear family based upon sentiment is not a consequence of the processes of modernization but was, on the contrary, a condition and basis for modernization. But for the family to play its own modern productive role, it had to remain anachronistic, that is, premodern. This condition was already being lamented by John Stuart Mill in the middle of the last century (Mill 1980). The construction and maintenance of the premodern elements of the family became the social domain of the female gender. Family privacy together with its spatial dimension became the symbolic, the imaginary, and the real place of women. Women's "good-bye" to individuality and rationality in favor of a community based on sentiment was in fact a precondition for a politically public and bourgeois civil society.

Modern interpolations of women into mothers and wives take place together with the shaping of modern nation-states. The similarity of these parallel processes is therefore double: The "national" and "woman" are foreign to modernity even though they are indispensable and constitutive. Their social function is analogous: With the help of sentiment, they construct the community or at least the image of the community.

For this reason, we think that the generalizations of nationalist discourse should be taken extremely seriously. These articulate themselves in forms such as "The nation is one big family" or the concept of "the motherland." Even though those who utter these generalizations do not seem to take them seriously, we must take them word for word to understand their ideological productivity. We take these hypotheses as the cue for our analysis of the outbreak of nationalist passion and conflict in former socialist states.

Nationalism and Women in Postsocialist Societies

All postsocialist countries have in common certain problems, as well as slogans that they wish to use ideologically to contain and articulate these problems. The basic common problems are the establishment of a market economy of goods, work, and capital; unarranged ownership relationships; an underdeveloped rule of law; national and social conflicts; and political instability. The fundamental ideological-political answers to these problems are reprivatization, the ideal of the nation-state, entry into Europe, and the rehabilitation of traditional values.[1]

Postsocialist societies have reclaimed the status of the privileged subject that was once held by certain social groups and classes (for instance, the working-class, youth, the party) and given this status to new groups and classes (entrepreneurs, new political parties, churches). Some social groups witnessed the "redelegation" of their social status (social subjectivity). "Women," who in socialism were supposed to have achieved their social and personal emancipation and equality with men and who were one of the preferred "social subjects" within the ideology of socialist societies, became in postsocialism once again the target of a special ideological interpolation, even though this interpolation is now of a radically different nature.

In the ideology of socialist societies, women were one of the social subjects of emancipation and revolutionary change. In postsocialist societies they became the targets of redelegation into "mothers who should ensure the biological survival and moral progress of the nation," "the guardians of the home," and the "guardians of privacy." Thus, instead of the former (mostly economically enforced) "proletarianization" and (politically enforced) "emancipation of women," we are now dealing with the "domestication" of women, which is also economically and politically enforced.[2] The foremost tendency of the domestication of women does not lie in the desire for women to give up their jobs and "come back to the family" but rather in the internalization of the classification of "public men" and "private women."[3]

The redelegation of social status into the field of privacy is accompanied by the mass social pacification of women. This is particularly evident if we compare the current weak political activity of women in postsocialist countries with the mass participation of women in various demonstrations and movements for the implementation of democracy, civil society, and the rule of law at the end of the 1980s. It is true that political and economic conditions differ in various postsocialist societies (from relatively hopeful conditions in Hungary and Czechoslovakia, to extreme misery in Albania, Romania, and the countries of the Commonwealth of Independent States, to war in Croatia, Serbia, Bosnia, Armenia, and Azerbaijan), but as far as women go, their political passivity and nonexistence in public life are very evident.

What is most important here is the long-term connection between the ideological domestication of women and traditional and conservative views related to the social role of gender, the relationship between the private and the public, politics in general and in the nation-state. We see this connection in the idea of a society that has pledged itself to some kind of organic whole (this whole being represented by the "nation") that overcomes all internal conflict by homogenizing society. In this light, differences and conflicts within society are interpreted as opposition to the whole, as different kinds of "conspiracies" (for instance, the conspiracy of the supporters of former socialist governments), or as "acts of hostility" of foreign elements (for instance, acts of hostility carried out by "foreign minorities" or by neighboring countries), but not as preconditions for social progress. This exterior projection of social conflicts, the helplessness or refusal to see them as the result of the inner dynamics of society and its problems, can temporarily ease situations of conflict in the imagination and within the processes of ideological projection but also makes them unsolvable and traumatic in the long run.

From where does this premodern view of society originate? We think that it is a necessary result of the contradictions within the fundamental ideological options of postsocialist societies: reprivatization, the establishment of nation-states, the way into Europe, and the return of traditional values. The concepts and ideas about nationally homogeneous social entities that the nationalist political programs offer succeed in bridging the gaps among these options.

The project of reprivatization, accompanied by a trust in "Europe," helps reaffirm in people a paradoxical mixture of expectations. These expectations anticipate that the process of reprivatization will be quick and that it will represent a jump to the better, as well as maintaining the preconceived unity of the social community and "reconciling it with itself."

The idea of strengthening the nation-state and the return of traditional values help form and reinforce these expectations. The idea of an autonomous nation-state serves as the political and historical secessionist superstructure of the organic understanding of recapitalization—that is, the conversion from a (post)socialist into a modern market society. Meanwhile, the return to traditional values (home, nation, God) ensures that individuals within their microcosms (in private and within the family) can cope with the perils of this process.

The trinity of the ideas of home, nation, and God is ideally suited to the organic (self-)understanding of society. The "home" signifies the illusion of a guarded and organic nonconflictual community, the "nation" signifies a big family to which all individual action must be subservient, and "God" signifies the transcendental self-conception of one's own life as unforeseeable fate. Thus, all the fundamental ideological conceptions (and premises) of social reform in postsocialist societies coincide with one another. They represent a mechanism of defense against the challenges of the present and the future instead of just being temporarily rational and productive.

The ideological views of real socialism and new national collectivism are both opposed to individual ways of life that are not subservient to the collective "vision" and "self-image." Both views stand against those differences between individuals that cannot be reduced to some social type (class, gender, religion, nationality, etc.). Within these ideologies, the individual is understood to be "free" only if his or her individual action belongs to the superstructure of supraindividuality, as is the case in a nationally defined role.

The Redelegation of Privacy

The ideological options being promoted in postsocialist societies are not so distant from their socialist predecessors, even though they have the image of "modernity." Socialism represented a constant defense against the Western world, as well as a defense against the necessity of the market, competition, conflicts within society, economic and political pluralism, and antagonism. "Real existing socialisms" were a mixture of premodern and industrial societies founded upon concepts of organic, nonconflictual, or, at least, industrial societies.

In socialist societies the slogans of the equality between the sexes and the liberation of women quickly changed into their own contradiction. The employment of women led to a new dependency and burdened women instead of offering economic emancipation. The political activation of women resulted in the formalistic and ritualistic participation of women in the lower

strata of the political power structure, whereas toward the top of the political pyramid of power their participation was drastically minimized
(Frauenoffensive 1980; Lovenduski 1986). In addition, women did not
have any special reason to participate in such empty and ritualized political
activities, which only ate up the already tight spare time of women.

The critics of real socialism find that, despite this turn of emancipation
into its own contradiction, the fundamental lack in the political structure of
socialist societies that prevented the political emancipation and participation of women lies elsewhere—that is, in the lack of an economic and political civil society (Arato 1981; Vajda 1981; Pierson 1984). Because of this
lack, a "normal" functional distribution of social spheres—especially the
public and the private spheres—as known by Western societies could not
develop. This was the fatal consequence of "half modernization."[4] The
public and the private spheres did not achieve an actual functional autonomy. The result of real socialism was thus a "dictatorship over needs"
(Feher, Heller, and Markus 1983) that neutralized all attempts at emancipation and democracy.

The private sphere did not constitute itself as the legitimate element of
civil society. Rather, it became a particular sphere that was exposed to constant pressure and control because of the suspicion that within it "bourgeois" consciousness was being regenerated. Privacy reduced to such a level
could not grant autonomy and the liberalization of relationships either to
individuals or to families. The average family of postsocialist societies was
a haven against the repression of those in power. The family was the necessary mechanism of survival, although it was still an authoritarian community of parents and their children.

The lack of civil society also rendered impossible the development of a
mediating social sphere between the public and the private spheres—that is,
the sphere of "social dominion" (the social sphere). This sphere in well-
advanced Western democracies combines the field of private initiative and
public affairs (Arendt 1964). The social sphere regulates, socializes, and
commercializes the production and distribution of goods and services, and
together with family privacy and public opinion, it also forms an opposition to political power.

Despite the manipulative interventions of economic and political monopolies into the social sphere and privacy in Western societies,[5] the social
sphere still allowed women participation in public in such a way that it me-
diated the patterns of action and the mutual relationships of the private
sphere. Without a well-developed social sphere, the constitution of modern
civil society would not be possible today, and without it the constitution of
relatively autonomous private and public spheres would also be impossible.

As a result of the long-term lack of civil society and of modern, relatively
autonomous private and public spheres in socialist societies, we cannot ex-

pect that in the few years since socialism started collapsing a modern civil society would develop and within it a corresponding private sphere that would be the social base for the formation of the individuality of women and men. This is why in postsocialist societies there is no intermediate social sphere that would make public action possible for women without them being forced to give up their family roles. This lack of a developed social sphere also signifies that families are left to themselves and atomized. As a consequence, women are faced with the unrealizable task of replacing the social tissue of civil society with family activity. The lack of the social sphere can be replaced neither by the assistance of friends and relatives nor by the participation/involvement of women in the gray economy. The privacy into which women are placed by economic conditions and by postsocialist nationalist ideologies is therefore not a privacy corresponding to the development of the identity of the individual's ego. Rather, this privacy is an asylum for protecting the individual from "society"—it is a privatized sphere of particular interests.

That is why advocacy of "the return of women to the family" is closely related to national-ideological rhetoric since according to such conceptions, only women who have dedicated themselves exclusively to their families are capable of preserving traditional values and the national consciousness of new generations. Such "engagement in disciplining" new generations at the same time disciplines women themselves and subjects them to the authorities and the institutions of society. Neither former socialist nor present national-oriented policies allow women to express their individuality and their potential disagreement with the aggression of such ideologies and policies.

Such a position of women is not a historical novelty as such since it is present in most traditional societies. What is new is that the postsocialist societies following national ideologies (despite their urge to "catch up with" developed Europe) cannot notice the historical shift in the position and perception of women that has taken place in developed European societies. Namely, in modern postindustrial societies there is an increasing tendency toward the individualization of strategies of life, patterns, needs, views, and opinions, followed by a decrease in the significance of social identifiers (class, gender, profession, nationality) considered up to now to be more or less lifelong (Beck 1986). For a woman, this means that she connects her life, work, and needs less and less to her gender identity and especially to her family role.

The attempts to return women to the family in postsocialist societies are contrary to this principal tendency toward the individualization of the way of life and of the formation of identity. These attempts thus put women into *premodern* social conditions instead of putting them into *postmodern* ones. Pressures experienced by women under such present or future conditions are necessarily transferred to the rest of the population—if not in any other way, then at least in the division of roles within the family. Should a woman, for example, because of unemployment, actually "return to the family"? This would definitely mean a loss of social identity and of individuality. Inside the family this loss will then reflect itself in the form of tense interpersonal relations, suppressed fears, hopeless attempts at emotional replacements, and so forth. The withdrawal of women into domestic privacy will not, however, be complete because of economic crisis and low incomes. Women will still (in the way they have always been) be forced to supplement the family budget by working outside their homes.

The result of social pressures will therefore not be the mass return of women to their families planned by the architects of national projects. A strongly frustrating, "parafamily" type of existence of women will occur instead. Women will be, just like unemployed men, looking for work and jobs; they will thus encourage competition on the labor market, which will reduce the value of their work. This reduction of the (already low) value of work might become one of the main sources of profit for private and state enterprises. Undoubtedly, the pressures on women will have a negative feedback as far as the development of democracy is concerned because an eventual social agreement will be reached under conditions of a repressive disciplining and domestication of a large part of the population.

The tendencies toward the domestication of women and the glorification of the family (as the primary bond in the society) are therefore an expression of a regressive social process in postsocialist countries. However, we believe that an irrational regression is not the case we are dealing with. Rather, we believe that we are dealing with a "return" to the irrational fundamentals of modernization that is intended to get postsocialist countries back in touch with the processes of modernization in developed Europe. At this point such tendencies in postsocialist countries intertwine with nationalist delirium.

Nationalism and the Community

Whenever a social phenomenon strikes in such a powerful way as have the "Yugoslav nationalisms" in the last few years, our astonishment is often expressed in the form of (naive) questions. First, how have acute, destructive, and therefore deeply antisocial forms of nationalism manifested themselves on the fringes of a Europe that is in the middle of a transition to a postindustrial and postmodern phase? And second, why is nationalism successfully "dropping its anchor" in the less aggressive half of the population—that is, why is it becoming a "real power" among women?

These two questions are, of course, naive because they are put the wrong way. Modern Yugoslav nationalisms are not a residual element of the nineteenth century. They are not a retrograde and regressive expression of societies undergoing modernization. Rather, they are a materialization of the dark side of the same Europe that professes amazement at the aggressive eccentricity of the Balkan tribes.

Nationalism is not antisocial. On the contrary, it is an extremely social response to the so-called crisis of industrial modernity. In a world where the permanent restructuralization and differentiation of society represent a condition for growth and expansion, the nondifferential and totalizing "we" plays the role of an asylum or a therapeutic environment of protection and mutual solidarity. Not so long ago it seemed that such a social role would be played by the family. But the social struggle of women (above all, feminism), which laid claim to a consequential modernization (a possibility of autonomous individualization for women), has been a cause of destabilization. That is why the "Yugoslav" search for surrogate communities through nationalism is such a vulgar and unfortunate, yet vanguard, consequence of the problem of community that is unsolved by modern societies.

The three rules that condition communities are a tendency toward egalitarianism, a sharing of ideas and sentiments, and a severe selectivity when dealing with the Other (the latter being a constitutive, rather than a marginal and disturbing, element). It is only with identification and with the excommunication of the Other that one can recognize unity and the community. It is only by differing from the others and by rejecting them that we become We.

Systems of real socialism, seemingly suppressing the national element intensely, have actually followed the same thought pattern: While promising communalism, they have demanded, first and above all, faith. That is why "socialist" life habits, which remain our daily *forma mentis* despite the breakdown of socialism, remain an extreme basis for nationalist sentiments. The (national) community as a transfunctional, transnational, and transindividual entity is regaining its social value precisely in boundary situations. By not being directly dependent on the modern social structure, the community is a social form that under conditions of rapid change can become predominant.

Nationalist experience as a collective experience has the following basic attributes:

1. On the level of thinking, there exists a common and unique truth.
2. On the level of sentiments, there exists something that is good on its own behalf, something that represents an absolute object for Eros, with pleasure and duty thus becoming one.
3. On the level of interpersonal social relationships, there exist a promise of community and a tendency toward breaking up the existing social barriers in the name of common truth and common (authentic) sentiment.

When elements of the community's national experience are institutional-
ized, a deadlock occurs; barbaric totalitarianism then becomes the only
possible outcome. Since national unity does not and cannot exist but is at
the same time a premise for the national experience of the community, it is
achieved by means of repression and moral stigmatization of the Other
and/or of those in opposition to this national experience.

Nationalism, Sentiment, and Eros

In communities faith comes first—it is more important than action. The
will to "be together" is what counts; outcomes, failures/successes, and
losses/profits are a secondary issue compared to the genuineness of this sentiment of faith.

What we are interested in here are not the political uses and abuses of nationalism but rather the secret of nationalism's attraction. We wonder what
it is that makes individuals not only recognize themselves as members of
some national community but also willingly give up their everyday life and
contingency for the sake of the national community.

It seems that women in the former Yugoslavia have an ambivalent attitude toward nationalism. But in any case they have no trouble finding
themselves in its social matrix, regardless of whether they reject nationalism or accept it. Recognizing the social matrix of nationalism is certainly
not difficult for women. This is so, either because they accept their own elements of the community and sentiment as a traditionally female milieu and
thus see in this the affirmation and legitimization of that which every "normal society" frowns upon and undervalues, or they reject the nationalist
matrix as being nearly identical to the one that women have been able to
escape from through employment, their own social struggle, "a change of
consciousness," or otherwise. That is why we can safely claim that in the
former Yugoslavia nationalism is extremely unattractive to feminists.

By asserting that nationalism relates particularly to women (that it is a
sexualized experience), we do not mean that it suits women. Quite the contrary, our claim regards men. Nationalistic metaphors of the family are stories that speak of men as sons and the fathers (of the nation) and as lovers
(of the homeland). Nationalism always deals with historical regressions in
the form of the return to national myths and legends. The "homeland/na-
tion as the mother" expresses the infantile regression of the return to the
mother's breast—it is the affirmation of the dual relationship between the
mother and the (lost) son. In the conditions of postsocialist societies, such
regression has an extra meaning—the stress is on the return of the lost son,
who under the socialist "brotherhood and unity of the nations" lost his real
mother and was adopted instead by the "socialist community," which

turned out to be a cheating stepmother instead of a caring adoptive mother. This is also why the return is so sincere and so violent. How could we otherwise understand the unintelligible and unimaginable heroic acts of personal sacrifice taking place in the struggle for Us (for our nation) if it wasn't for this ecstatic, erotic investment?

Such a strong experience of national sentiment, which gets stronger according to the degree of the suffering/bleeding of the mother, is at the same time as enthusiastic as it is extremely dramatic. It is similar to an exceptional and fantastic sexual act. It is the promise of the realization of an extreme desire. It is love as death. Of course, it is also attractive to those who do not live through such an experience. If it is true, as Julia Kristeva states, that (apart from wars and the stock exchange) Europe is bored to death, then surely Europe's gaze toward the Balkans offers voyeuristic pleasure.

The imaginary of "Yugoslav nationalisms" is intertwined with sexual phantasmagorias. Here we also note that stories of women actually talk of men. In the case of Yugoslavia, the sexual phantasmagorias showed themselves as the main agent of national sentiment. This imaginary started with the stories of alleged (nationalistic) rapes in Kosovo. The actual concrete situation and context of the transgression were unimportant. What was important was the national identity of the raping phallus. Castration stories had a similar mobilization effect in the escalation of the Serbian-Croatian conflict. They were reported more or less on a daily basis by media on both sides of the conflict. The horror of deformed bodies is always the horror of castration, regardless of whether the act is the putting out of eyes, the cutting of ears and tongues, or (if castration was explicit) the slashing of the sexual organs. The morbid fury thus showed its real face: This was not a simple extermination of the enemy but much more—an act to prevent the enemy from having any sexual relationship and to preserve the relationship between the homeland and its sons.

The Opposition to the Ban on Abortion as a Symbol of Opposition to the Domestication of Women and to Nationalist Policy

Socialist systems that lasted for over fifty years undoubtedly left profound traces in the people who lived in these systems, regardless of whether they rebelled and regardless of the degree of their rebellion. We who live in postsocialist societies are probably not aware of how deep inside us lies the atavistic inclination to leave the resolution of our own economic and social problems to somebody else. We are also not aware of our willingness to gladly put ourselves in the custody of authorities, "powerful" people, or influential institutions and how much we tend to minimize the shock of change by using as buffers organic concepts of society, the state, the nation, enterprise, and the family. The shift from socialist society to a genuine market-based functional society will therefore be more difficult than most people imagine and shall cause quite a few frustrations, as well as opposition.

Hence, it is plausible that expectations and presumptions about the future of people in postsocialist societies remain within the circle of relations concerned with the "shock of the new" and "future shock."[6] It is also no surprise that even intellectually advanced political and economic programs carry those shocks inside them. At this point traditional values, on one side, and the mythology of the national state, on the other, become more than handy. The domestication of women is easily included in the defense mechanisms of society since it is a natural reaction to the former underestimation of (and threats toward) privacy, the family, religion, and nationality and represents a seeming reaffirmation of "real womanliness."

It cannot be denied that such a perspective has up to now appeared promising to many women in postsocialist societies. This is the only way to explain the considerable quantity of votes cast by women in favor of conservative or religiously oriented parties in the first free democratic elections held in postsocialist countries between 1989 and 1991. However, this enthusiasm declined shortly after the first negative measures had been taken against rights of women that had been formally established in former socialist systems. This was particularly the case for abortion, duration of maternity leave, assurance of a work post for the period of children's illnesses, and so on. That was where the limits to the process of "domestication" came to light. It seems that the point beyond which women could no longer remain indulgent and politically anemic was the ban on abortion. They considered this right to be an obligatory component of civilization and were not prepared to give it away. The data, obtained from public opinion researches in Slovenia from the last two decades, clearly showed a permanent increase in number of those (women and men) in favor of the right to abortion (Ule 1990).

Wherever an attempt has been made in former socialist countries to ban abortion, a spontaneous politicization of women (or rather the majority of the population) has taken place. It is characteristic of many postsocialist countries that the opponents of abortion cite the "threat to the nation" being posed by the decreasing birthrate. The use of nation-defending arguments has not had a great success in public, however, because women do not agree with giving birth to their children for the sake of the "survival of the nation." They want to give birth to their children for their own sake and for the sake of the children themselves.

In Slovenia we witnessed angry debates and conflicts in parliament, as well as in public, over the right to abortion. The pressure of public opinion, especially of various movements and women's organizations, against attempts to abandon the right to abortion were so strong that an article was included in the Slovenian constitution providing women and men with the liberty to decide over the birth of their children (*Abortus* 1991). All of the women who stood up in public against the threat to the right to abortion were aware that our basic human rights were being jeopardized. We knew that the pressure would not stop at the right to abortion but would continue until we became obedient subjects of the new rulers. That is why opposition to the ban on abortion was not just a particular, "women's" protest. It was also a general protest that succeeded in delegitimizing the political forces aimed at limiting the basic human rights of women (Ule 1991). We presume that such considerations can be applied to similar protests of women throughout the postsocialist world (for example, in Poland, Hungary, and the former German Democratic Republic).

The political protests of women against the cancellation of their basic rights are an efficient remedy for the pseudo-organic concept of national unity and for the tendencies toward the domestication of women. The more the leaders of "national policies" count on the assumption that women will allow their own depolarization and domestication without offering significant resistance, the larger are the cracks (which are caused by women's protests) in the imaginary tissue of the national unity. The same goes for men who protest against the same pressures that would turn them into an obedient and faithful labor force (the slogan "Work and pray!" was publicly presented by some Slovenian ministers), or, which is even worse, into "cannon fodder." The protests of men also serve to prevent attempts to silence and depoliticize the public, and these protests open cracks in the construction of national unity. Minor, yet important steps have been taken toward disassembling organic ideologies and related socioeconomic projects.

Notes

1. In "Women's Rights in East-Central Europe: Back to Cinderella?" (1990), Barbara Einhorn stated that we are dealing with the triumvirate of rational values: the home, the homeland (nationalism), and God; these illustrate the search for new spiritual and ethical values in postsocialist societies. In fact, we are dealing with the rebirth of the values that the old regime violently repressed and that were in themselves legitimate. However, what is dangerous is that they are being used to manipulate—that is, the revived values serve as the ideological backbone for the reduction of the already achieved and well-settled economic, social, health, and political rights of women.

2. The essential characteristic of nationalist ideologies and sociopolitical strategies of the domestication of women is that they do not accept women as individuals with their own ways of life and needs but rather as the bearers of roles defined in advance. It is true that in nationally defined collectives women are put on a pedestal

of motherhood as saintly guardians of the home and family, but at the same time they are—through this position—tightly controlled and contained.

3. Here we are dealing with the equalization of three different categories: public-private, political-apolitical, and man-woman. This equalization is quite common in sociology and serves to justify the real or just the "surface" apoliticalness of women. In "The Politics of Public Man and Private Woman," J. Siltanen and M. Stanworth (1984) criticized this theoretical domestication of women. They believed that women's disinclination for political activity is the result of quiet resistance to the kind of confrontational politics that has been appropriated by men as their own domain. Women's skepticism toward politics can therefore also be the sign of a realistic analysis of current political conditions and a rejection of instrumental calculation within politics and trade union activity. A lot of facts point toward political processes being anchored within privacy as well as toward the differences between the public sphere and political awareness. Also, the activity of men within the public sphere has its own private origins, just as women's privacy has its political meaning and expression ("the personal is political!") (Ule, Ferligoj, and Rener 1990).

4. Maybe we could say "quarter modernization." We take into account the beliefs of the critics of industrial modernization in the West—that it was a "halfway" modernization because it still had a lot of unresolved premodern components (the organic concept of the family, the class nature of family and social roles, the submission of individuals to defined hierarchies and authorities, professional and gender roles set for life) (Beck 1986).

5. The theme of the return of the contestation of the relative autonomy of individual social spheres and in particular the sphere of social dominion is discussed by Jurgen Habermas (1972). According to Habermas, the political state, monopolies, and the mass media are taking the control of the social sphere away from the public. With this they are also hiding from critical insight the penetration of the state into privacy as well as the manipulation of public opinion.

6. The stronger the tendency toward individualization is, the more important is the individual contribution of people to the products of their work, especially in terms of knowledge and capability for communication and control. With the passing of industrialism, the difference is increasing between new individuality, which is developed through an individual's activities, and privatism, which comprehends individuality as possession manifesting itself predominantly in the private sphere. This difference between the two kinds of individualism is typically manifested in comprehension of gender roles and relations between the genders. Whereas privatistic individualism observes the differences between the genders and their roles only through their typified and uniform image, the new individualism recognizes individuality and also roles of gender.

References

Abortus (Abortion). Ljubljana: Skupina Neodvisnih Zensk, 1991.

Arato, A. "Civil Society Against the State: Poland, 1980–1981." *Telos,* no. 47 (1981).

Arendt, Hannah. *Vita activa* (Active life). Milan: Bompiani, 1964.

Beck, U. *Risikogesellschaft* (Society of risks). Frankfurt: Suhrkamp, 1986.

Einhorn, Barbara. "Women's Rights in East-Central Europe: Back to Cinderella?" Glasgow: University Department, 1990, seminar paper.

Feher, F., A. Heller, and G. Markus. *Dictatorship over Needs.* Oxford: Blackwell, 1983.

Frauenoffensive. *Die Frau und Russland* (Woman and Russia). Munich: Frauenoffensive, 1980.

Habermas, Jurgen. *Prassi politica e teoria critica della societa* (Political praxis and social critical theory). Milan: Bompiani, 1972.

Lovenduski, J. *Women and European Politics.* Brighton, England: Wheatsheat Books, 1986.

Mill, John Stuart. *The Subjection of Women.* London: Virago, 1980.

Pierson, C. "New Theories on State and Civil Society." *Sociology,* no. 4 (1984).

Siltanen, J., and M. Stanworth. "The Politics of Public Man and Private Woman." In *Women and the Public Sphere: A Critique of Sociology and Politics.* London: Hutchinson, 1984.

Ule, Mirjana. *Individualizacija kot dejavnik in izraz poindustrijske modernizacije.* (Individualization as a factor and an expression of postindustrial modernization). Ljubljana: FDV, 1990.

_____. "Javno mnenje o splavu" (Public opinion on abortion). In *Abortus.* Ljubljana: Skupina Neodvisnih Zensk, 1991.

Ule, Mirjana, A. Ferligoj, and Tanja Rener. *Zenska, zasebno, politicno* (Women, private, political). Ljubljana: ZPS, 1990.

Vajda, M. *The State and Socialism: Political Essays.* London: Allison and Busby, 1981.

Women Without Identity

The Life of a Refugee Woman in Slovenia

ERIKA REPOVZ

The idea started to look promising only when I obtained a name and wrapped it in a likely story of a refugee from Zenica. As a reporter I had been following the Bosnia and Herzegovina refugee saga in Slovenia for two years. I had attended press conferences one after the other, visited an immense number of humanitarian organizations, talked with a great deal of people who were professionally or voluntarily dealing with the refugee situation, but all this had meant nothing. It was only when I stepped over the threshold of a refugee center as a refugee that I realized I had been writing about something I knew nothing about.

Press conferences are manipulated ceremonies designed to throw sand in the eyes of the public; the dull statistics acquire their true meaning only through proper interpretation. The category "refugee" applies to thirty thousand registered individuals plus an estimated equal number of unregistered men, women, and children who are searching for hope on the edge of an economically impossible existence. Regarding the problem, the Slovene media behave as medieval scientists to whom empiricism was strongly forbidden, and the Slovene public resembles a cowardly ostrich that has dug its head in the sand. An average Slovene has never had a personal encounter with someone expelled from her homeland because of war, who lives in a ghetto population discretely hidden behind the walls of an old army barracks.

The Balkan nomad who is occupying the Slovene army barracks is rarely given a chance to address the Slovene public. Instead, a few public relations employees of the Office for Immigration and Refugees or of some other similar department, center, or institution speak for the nomads. Those "inside" hardly ever learn what is said and written about them, and those "outside" self-confidently explain things they have never experienced. After witnessing two years of war and the constant arrival of new refugees, I find no meaning in actions by outsiders.

It was Monday. I was standing in a long queue formed outside the door of the Office for Immigration and Refugees. My name was Esma Halilovic, I was twenty-eight years old, and I was going through my made-up story in my mind. Would I be believed? I was restless. The oppression of those waiting with me was spreading along the narrow hallway like a virus. We were explaining our problems to one another and waiting for confirmation that our requests would be resolved positively. I cannot remember when I ever felt as helpless as when I was standing in front of the official. She was explaining in a strict way that without documents I was illegally in the country and could not be helped. "Nothing can be done. You should go to a detention camp. Of course, I understand, I am very sorry, but I don't write the laws." I heard this sentence a million times that week. I became discouraged, and I realized that for a refugee there is no point in beseeching the Slovene authorities. That day at least a dozen similar cases had the door shut in their faces. These cases were, unfortunately, not fictitious like mine.

I decided to change my story and try somewhere else. I managed to convince the administrator of one center and in so doing acquired a bed, three refugee meals a day, a schedule for cleaning, and experience as a woman who lost not only the warmth of her home but also her true identity.

The life of women in refugee camps passes by in queues. Every day begins with forming a line for two pieces of bread and a cup of tea. People with cups in one hand and food coupons in the other crowd in front of the dining hall. The breakfast line is the fastest of them all. Feet in knitted or plastic slippers move toward the counter, behind which two sleepy refugees are handing out the food. While drinking tea, the children drowsily watch the monotonous sight before them and then rush across the yard to school. I used to observe them through the window every morning. They could pass for normal children attending a normal school. They have their schoolbags on their shoulders, plastic bags in their hands, and they shove and insult one another or even get involved in fights. In the meantime their mothers form a line in front of the bathroom. Dirty dishes left over from supper the day before and toothbrushes in their hands. Afterward they start washing the hallways, toilets, and sinks. Each day anew everything is dirty, clogged, and stinking. Some are bothered by this; others don't care. They are forced to live with each other even though they are different. Before the war Salena wished for her children to attend university, whereas Fikreta has so many children that she hardly notices if one of them disappears now and then. She does not know how to read or write, and dates are of no importance in her life. She does not remember if her daughter Fatima was born five, six, or seven years ago.

Every day I stand in a line of women of various ages and professions. Their former status is of no importance on the inside. The only important fact is who is first and who is last in line. They used to be able to decide and to choose, but now this is done for them. Somebody else decides how many tampons per month can be used, how many times the women are supposed to wash the hallways or clean the yard. Somebody else decides if their children are too old to wear diapers and if they are clever enough to receive a scholarship.

While I am surrounded by these women, young, old, intellectuals, peasants, or workers, mothers, widows, or happily married wives, the question that arises in my mind is, Which one of them finds it easiest to bear all of this? Each of them is shifting from one leg to another in the cold in front of the laundry. Beside them lies a huge pile of clothing that needs to be washed, and they have only a tiny amount of detergent, with which they must be economical. If one is used to a washing machine, washing a pile of dirty clothes in ice cold water in the middle of winter can be thrilling if one is on holiday. But every holiday has its end, whereas these refugees cannot see the end of their saga. They could be stuck here for months, years, decades. . . . They are special kinds of tourists who move from one deserted army barracks to another. This could go on forever.

Zorica, who is at the Roska refugee camp with her husband and three kids, tells me she has become apathetic. At the age of forty she has given up and doesn't expect anything from life anymore. All that is left is fear for her children. Because of them, she is waiting for visas to Canada. The children are looking forward to their new life, while the only feeling she has left is fear. At night when she cannot fall asleep, she cries. Time and time again I hear her lose her temper and scream at the children. The next day when we meet in the flooded bathroom in a never-ending line for a cold shower, she apologizes. Why? She knows I can hear every detail of her family life through the paper-thin wall that separates our living quarters. It must be terrible to argue, make love, and raise your children knowing that every breath you take is heard.

A day comes when I feel better, and I wish I could take a look in a mirror. Can it be noticed that I am living among refugees? Can the lifestyle of a refugee be noticed in the eyes, in untidy hair, in a melancholic or hardened look on the face? Have I a right to be a woman who is aware of her body, a woman who falls in love and makes herself look nice for a beloved? Have I got a right to visit a hair salon? Is this appropriate for a refugee? I cannot find a mirror. On our floor only one family owns one. It is cracked and black around the edges. A woman tells me reproachfully that she does not remember when she last looked in a mirror. I realize this is not in order for a refugee. I am not sorry for myself. In a week's time I will be able to observe myself in the mirror for as long as I wish. Anyway, I never think about these things when I am at home. Sometimes a day goes by when I hardly bother to comb my hair. But while I am on the inside, this seems terribly important to me. When I go into town, I have a feeling that anyone can see from a hundred miles that I come from a refugee camp. Nobody likes to be eliminated at first glance. I feel sorry for all of the young girls I have met. During puberty looks can mean everything. At the age of fifteen one wants to be pretty, pretty, and, once more, pretty. So many things depend on proper clothing, the right shade of lipstick, French perfume, carefully hidden spots on the face. . . . On the inside youth is deprived of all this junk. Young girls become old women overnight. Age is measured not by beauty but by experience. This is the only luxury they have in overwhelming amounts.

Appendix: A Postscript to Laura Busheikin

ANN SNITOW

As an admirer of Laura Busheikin's political work and of her wonderful piece "Is Sisterhood Really Global?" I never felt much like pointing out a factual error or two. But now this piece is being republished and will no doubt become a classic for its observant, subtle, and respectful description of East-West feminist relationships. So I would like to set the record straight by telling the bits I know about the founding of the Prague Gender Center.

In the spring of 1990, Slavenka Drakulic asked a small group of U.S. feminists "to help eastern and central European feminists get in touch with each other." This interesting request led to the founding meeting of the Network of East-West Women (NEWW) in Dubrovnik in June 1991. After the conference, I went to Prague—my first time there—to meet, among others, the well-known political activist, Jirina Siklova. I had heard much about her from friends, who described her courage as a dissident, her shrewd observations about Czech political culture, and her advocacy for all sorts of groups—her social work students, the elderly, and also women, whose special postcommunist problems she was early to recognize.

The revision I want to make to Laura's piece revolves around this generous, complex, and protean figure. For whatever combination of reasons, when I arrived at Jirina Siklova's flat in June of 1991, the gender center was already there in embryo. There were the books, mostly sent by Western women Jirina had met at all kinds of conferences from Germany to the United States. And there was the concept. She wanted a place, she told me, where her students and others could come to look at these books about gender, where they could meet to discuss them, and where, perhaps, they could develop active groups of various kinds. I looked through the piles, some still in their original boxes, and got excited. Here was a library.

I asked what prevented the center from opening. Jirina said, only a place and a librarian. But like so many Eastern European dissidents, she knew how to do politics with no resources at all. She took me to see a smallish room the university had promised (they never came through with it, or with any resources) but told me at the same time that no failure of outside support could really stop this idea of a gender center. She would simply make it a part of her flat, rather than let the idea die.

No fancy rhetoric, you understand, no theoretical statement of the need; just a simple declaration of will. But what about the salary for someone to keep the center open, to catalogue and maintain its resources? I assumed this would be the real sticking point, a lot of money, certainly more than the fledgling Network of East-West Women had. But I thought I'd just ask, for the record, how much Jirina thought she would need to start up. To my amazement, she said a few hundred dollars would keep the center open for several months. Back then, relatively low prices and the exchange rate made such miracles possible. I had about $500 in cash with me, left over from the conference budget. Would that help?

We went straight to the bank, where the lines were incredible, the chaos of the transitional banking system grotesque. Jirina threaded her way through all this and found someone tucked away upstairs who was happy to receive U.S. dollars in a joint account. Later we learned the bank was confused about who we were to each other (an echo of Laura Busheikin's observations about pervasive inequalities), for when Jirina first tried to draw money out, the bank demanded my permission. Though we dealt with this by a permanent letter of access, it was less obvious how to deal with the suspicions the bank tellers had about Jirina. What is a "gender center"? Perhaps a brothel?

So, in June of 1991, we opened a bank account, and Jirina, who had already lined up her librarian, hired Jana Hradilkova at once. Jana began to keep the flat/center open for scholars and meetings several days a week. Perhaps Laura Busheikin's attribution of the idea for the center to me and Sonia Jaffe Robbins (Communications Director of NEWW) comes from the scrupulous care the center has always taken to acknowledge this start-up money and the books and very small funds NEWW has subsequently donated. The network has always been grateful for the warm way the Prague Gender Center places us at the beginning whenever it recalls its history. Nonetheless, what I have described here was our entire role in starting the center. Whatever East-West discussions, exchanges, visits, and debates we have had since, our role in conceptualizing what the center does, whom it serves, what resources it seeks, has been nil.

To know more about the origins of this well-established Prague institution, now with its own address (Prague Gender Center, Namestri 14, rijna 16, 150 00 Prague 5), a large collection of books and other materials, and a history of support from many foundations that, unlike NEWW, can offer real, sustaining funds, one would have to explore where Jirina Siklova learned of feminism, of women's centers, of what such places might be able to do. Did other women help her conceive of the center? Did she also get ideas from her long-term connections with Western political culture before 1989, or from her post-1989 flood of visits back and forth? How are Jirina's own doubts about the relevance of the category "gender" for Czech politics connected to the center's history and goals? (She has written several pieces exploring these doubts, one in the collection where Laura's piece originally appeared, *Bodies of Bread and Butter*). What has been the mixture of East and West at the Gender Center since Jirina started it, with what political results for Czech women's movements?

Some of this history already exists in the excellent bulletin and other documents produced by the center. But, as Laura says in her piece, the exchange of ideas and models between East and West is a complex business; every origin story is, inevitably, partial. Perhaps even the small story of origins I have told here hides the more difficult question of the multiple sources that fed Jirina's vision and helped give it form. What were those founding ideas and how have they been passed along, interpreted, and changed?

When I departed for New York, I couldn't have told you the answer to any of these questions. Hats off to Jana, Laura, and all the women who have worked so hard to make the center alive and real. They are the best first source for knowledge about how their center evolved and what they wish it to become.

About the Book and Editor

Facing negative public opinion and nearly impossible conditions in their home-lands, east European women are struggling to establish their human rights and to solidify the shaky social gains that were made under state-sponsored socialism. This unique collection gives unmediated voice to women throughout the region, from ac-tivists and scholars to high-school students. In a variety of genres, including schol-arly essays, interviews, and autobiography, they address issues such as abortion, forced unemployment, rape and domestic violence, lesbianism, motherhood, ethnic-ity, war, media, and religion.

This grassroots anthology is an invaluable primary source for Western feminists and scholars of women's studies, east European studies, human rights, and post-communist transitions as well as for general readers seeking insight into women's experiences and perspectives in a region undergoing dramatic social change.

Tanya Renne worked with feminist peace organizations in Serbia and Croatia while she collected the essays for this anthology. She also taught at the University of Ljubljana while on a Fulbright grant and speaks Serbo-Croatian, Slovenian, Hun-garian, and Italian. She is currently an independent activist and artist living in Washington, D.C.